NAAGA

NAAGA

Discovering *the* Extraordinary
World *of* Serpent Worship

K. HARI KUMAR

HARPER
NON-FICTION

An Imprint of HarperCollins *Publishers*

First published in India by Harper Non-fiction 2025
An imprint of HarperCollins *Publishers*
HarperCollins *Publishers* India, Cyber City,
Building 10-A, Gurugram, Haryana – 122002, India
www.harpercollins.co.in

2 4 6 8 10 9 7 5 3 1

Copyright © K. Hari Kumar 2025

P-ISBN: 978-93-6989-265-5
E-ISBN: 978-93-6989-322-5

Typeset in 10.5 pt/13.7 Adobe Garamond Pro
by HarperCollins *Publishers* India Pvt. Ltd

Printed and bound at
Replika Press Pvt. Ltd.

HarperCollins *Publishers*, Macken House, 39/40 Mayor Street Upper,
Dublin 1, D01 C9W8, Ireland

To the Naagadevatas of my ancestral serpent grove

Ophiolatry (noun): the worship of serpents

How the Journey Began

It was the evening of 21 February 2023—a night marked by a gentle breeze sweeping through the coastal town of Padubidri in Karnataka. I had arrived for my cousin's wedding, set for the following morning, but beneath the festive atmosphere, I carried a heavy burden. It had been exactly one year since I lost my baby, and grief clung to me with an intensity I could barely contain. This was also my first long journey after two months of complete bedrest. Amidst this turbulence, however, there was a faint glimmer of hope—I had recently signed the contract for *Daiva* with HarperCollins. This trip marked the beginning of my journey, both as a writer and as someone seeking for something far more profound.

That evening, after a brief prayer at the ancient Janaardhana temple, I was preparing to retire when I heard about the Dakkebali ritual at the nearby Khadgeshwari Brahmasthaana. I had missed many previous opportunities to attend this unique serpent worship ceremony, which takes place every alternate year. It felt like a chance to reconnect with something sacred—something buried deep in my blood.

Compelled by an unshakable urge, I set off with my wife towards the Brahmasthaana. As we approached the shrine around 8 p.m., we were met by throngs of devotees gathered under the open sky. There were no seating arrangements—everyone sat on the earth, the sandy ground beneath them. Padubidri, with its proximity to the sea, felt alive with the scent of saltwater mingling with incense and the warmth of the assembled crowd. Not long ago, the beach had been awarded the prestigious Blue Flag for environmental cleanliness—a small point of pride reflecting the region's dedication to environmental best practices.

While offering prayers at the shrine, an elderly priest approached us. He recognized my wife—he had once worked with her father in Mangalore and had even attended our wedding. After a few warm exchanges, he turned to me and asked, 'Where is your ancestral serpent grove?'

His question struck me with unexpected force. For years, I had been searching for the sacred place where my ancestors once worshipped our family's Naaga deity. His question felt almost like a sign.

'That is my quest,' I replied. 'Our family left Tulunadu over 125 years ago. I believe the place is near Kateel, but I cannot say for certain. I'm still looking for it.'

'And your children?' he asked gently.

'We don't have children yet,' I answered.

'It has been quite long since your marriage,' he said, not unkindly, with a softness that held no judgment.

I paused, feeling my throat tighten. 'Actually, we lost one last year. On February twenty-first.'

He rested a hand on my shoulder and, with quiet assurance, said, 'Do not worry. Pray with all your heart tonight to the Naagadevatas and Khadgeshwari. Before you return here again, you will be blessed.'

With his words echoing within, we found a place beside a large stone worn smooth by time—perhaps a remnant of some forgotten age. The night unfolded like a vision from centuries past; no loudspeakers, no flashes of camera phones, only the rhythmic beat of the dakke drum, the flickering lamps, and the ancient possession dance of the naagapaatri and naagakanyaka. For a moment, it felt as though my forefathers were there beside me, watching through the firelight, their memories etched into the sand.

As the hours passed, I was entranced—barely aware of the hard ground beneath me or the lower back pain that had plagued me for months. It was as if something powerful—a protective force—was watching over me.

I spent the next two months travelling across different parts of south Karnataka, searching for my ancestral serpent grove (naagabana) and the stories of the Daivas. Whispers spoke of a moola naagabana where my ancestors may have once prayed before the Naagadevatas. The whispers danced on the wind, woven from ancient tales and prayers, drawing me like a snake charmer's flute.

It was in April that the mists lifted, and I finally stood before my ancestral naagabana. Five generations had passed since their prayers echoed through its emerald embrace. Though doubts lingered— was this truly the original serpent grove, or merely a phantom of someone's memory?

The journey had only just begun.

The Daivas of Tulunadu remained with me, even after I returned. Writing *Daiva* became an act of healing, a way to transcend the grief that had consumed me. I submitted the manuscript and found myself once again searching. I was restless, awaiting the whisper of a new story. Then one night, I dreamed of a serpent deity—a Naaga. My closest friends and readers know that dreams often stir the beginnings of my books and films, and this one was no different. In this particular dream, Naagas—beautiful, dangerous, ancient— moved through the darkness trying to find the path towards light. I started getting an idea for a fantasy fiction trilogy. Since, I had already written *Dakini,* this new novel, I decided, would be called *Naaga.*

I approached my editor, ready to share the seed of this story.

'I have an idea,' I began. 'Something inspired by my travels through Tulunadu and Kerala. It's fiction—rooted in ancient lore but built as a modern tale.'

Before I could go further, she smiled and said, almost as if she'd been waiting, 'Actually, I wanted to ask if you'd consider writing non-fiction.'

I blinked. 'Non-fiction?'

'Yes. A book about the Naagas—a deep dive into the serpent deities, the mythology, the culture. The truth behind the folklore.'

Her voice carried the weight of something fated. Goosebumps prickled my skin. The Naagas I had dreamed of mirrored the very vision she was laying before me. Could this be coincidence? Or was it another sign—another whisper from the deities I had been chasing?

My wife, ever grounded in the ways of her land, didn't hesitate. 'This is a message from the Naagadevatas,' she said, her smile wide. 'They want you to explore the truth.'

In the world of serpent worship, every rustle of leaves, every ripple of wind, every shaft of light between trees carries an omen. My life, like the serpent deities I now sought, had curved upon itself, forming a loop of memory, myth and meaning.

Dear reader, you walked with me through the realm of the spirit deities of Tulunadu in *Daiva*. Now, prepare to descend deeper—into the coils of time, into stories that have survived in stone and breath. Into the heart of the Naaga.

And perhaps I should tell you—on the very day I shared this idea with my editor, a quiet miracle occurred. From the brittle stem of a long-forgotten dried-up money plant on my writing desk, two tender leaves emerged, curling gently towards the light, like the raised hoods of a Naaga and his consort entwined in an eternal dance. It was as if the serpent deities themselves had whispered back, affirming the path I was about to take.

With that, we begin.

How to Read this Book

In this book, I aim to explore ophiolatry—the worship of serpent deities—in the Indian context to the best of my knowledge, based on stories from the *Puraanas*, folktales and living customs that have survived in our culture, with a special focus on Tulunadu and Kerala, regions that hold deep ancestral connections for me.

You won't find miraculous cures or mantras for wealth here. This is not a manual for the mystical, but a celebration and preservation of a cultural tradition often misunderstood and overlooked. My intent is to present serpent worship to readers of all backgrounds, free from monocular bias, and grounded in reverence, storytelling, and lived experience.

I also hope to dispel the myths and misconceptions that surround this tradition, especially those formed through a Western lens. Serpent worship, as it exists in India, is layered—rich with symbolic, ecological, and even scientific significance. As I have iterated before, I am no practicing expert or an erudite scholar, but just a seeker looking for answers. This book is just a humble introduction for those who wish to learn more about the *Naagas*—not only as mythic beings but as enduring symbols in our folklore and collective psyche.

The book is organised into four parts, each exploring a distinct aspect of the tradition.

Think of it as walking through a temple—first the outer gates, then the inner sanctum, and finally—the stories that coil like serpents around your heart.

Part 1: Naagaloka

This first part introduces ophiolatry in India and offers foundational insights; Who are the Naaga deities? What is the spiritual and ecological significance of the anthill, and how does it connect to the subterranean realm of *Naagaloka*? Most importantly, does *Naagaloka* exist—as described in the *Puraanas*?

Part 2: Naagaraadhana

The second part explores the diverse expressions of serpent worship across India—from Alexander's encounter with serpent worshipping cults in Punjab to the awe-inspiring rituals of *Dakkebali* in Karnataka. Here, I discuss possession dances, regional practices, and the sacred serpent groves of south India, known as *kaavus* or *naagabanas*. Why must we preserve some of these traditions before they vanish into the margins of memory?

Parts 3 and 4: Naagapuraanam and Sarpakatha

The final two parts are devoted to the mythologies and folktales of serpents. You'll find stories from the Hindu *Puraanas*, Buddhist cosmology, and local legends that have evolved across regions and generations. If you prefer to start with the stories, feel free to begin with *Naagapuraanam* or *Sarpakatha*. However, reading the first two parts will offer valuable context, especially in understanding the depth and symbolism that underpin these traditions.

This work draws from a range of sources—ancient texts, contemporary research, oral histories, personal encounters, and memories gathered over years of travel. You may have heard some of these stories with some minor differences here and there. Variations in stories reflect the beauty of India's living traditions, where myths breathe and evolve. Whether you approach this book as a reference or a quiet journey into one of India's most enigmatic traditions, I hope it serves as a bridge—between past and present, myth and meaning, story and spirit.

PART 1

*Naagaloka—A Quest for
the Netherworlds*

I

The Serpent in World Mythology

In the labyrinthine alleys of the ancient world's cultural and religious corridors, serpents hold a special place. These remarkable reptiles captured the imagination of ancient peoples, who wove them into their most important myths and legends. Their ability to disappear into the earth, shed their skin as if reborn, and deliver a venomous bite made them seem connected to hidden powers and the cycles of nature. As symbols, they came to represent some of life's biggest concepts—creation itself, ongoing fertility, secret knowledge, and the very idea of eternity.

But this brings up interesting questions—why was this animal, often feared in real life, held in such high regard, even worshipped, in so many ancient traditions? What made people see divinity and profound meaning in a creature that could also represent danger? The practice of serpent worship, known as ophiolatry, spread far and wide, showing how deeply these creatures impressed the human mind.

We see powerful serpent symbols repeated across cultures— consider the Ouroboros, the image of a serpent eating its tail, in a way representing the endless cycle of time, or think of the familiar image of two serpents coiled around a staff, often linked to healing, balance, and hidden knowledge. What can these varied myths and symbols tell us about how ancient people saw the world and the powerful forces within it? This chapter explores these fascinating serpent stories from different parts of the globe to understand their significance.

Jörmungandr: Serpent of the North

In Norse mythology, the serpent is far from a heroic figure. Jörmungandr (pronounced yorr-mun-ganthr), the world serpent, plays a crucial role in the mythological landscape, embodying chaos and destruction. Born of the mischievous god Loki and the giantess Angrboda, Jörmungandr was one of three monstrous children destined to bring turmoil to the world. Loki hid the serpent in a cave alongside its siblings—Fenrir, the wolf, and Hel, the ruler of the dead.

However, Jörmungandr's rapid growth soon became impossible to conceal, as its tail began to extend beyond the confines of the cave. When this monstrous creature was discovered, Jörmungandr was banished to the sea, where it continued to grow until it encircled the entire earth, its tail clenched between its jaws. From its watery prison, the serpent's writhing was said to stir up the most fearsome tempests, embodying the chaotic forces of nature.

Jörmungandr is portrayed as a key villain in Norse mythology, particularly as the arch-nemesis of Thor, the god of thunder. Their enmity is one of the most iconic in Norse legend, culminating in their epic battle during Ragnarök, the end of the world.

The encounter between Thor and Jörmungandr is not just a physical confrontation but a clash of cosmic forces—order versus chaos, the divine versus the monstrous. So, while Marvel's Thor is battling aliens and saving the universe, his original Norse counterpart had his hands full with a giant, grumpy sea serpent.

Thunder Gods and Chaos Serpents

Parallels can be drawn between the battle of Jörmungandr and Thor with other ancient narratives, such as the Vedic tale of Vritra and Indra. Vritra, like Jörmungandr, is an enormous serpent embodying chaos and drought, while Indra, the god of thunder, must slay this serpent to restore balance. Interestingly, Typhon, a monstrous giant with serpentine features, was a significant figure in Greek mythology. His battle with Zeus (the thunder god) represented a struggle between the forces of chaos and order. These recurring themes highlight an ancient symbolic pattern—thunder gods battling serpents of chaos to restore cosmic balance.

Egyptian Serpents and Solar Cycles

The sacredness of serpents in ancient Egyptian religion reflected their role in the cycle of life, death and rebirth, emphasizing their importance in both the material and spiritual realms.

The serpent Bai was specifically depicted as the guardian of the doorways of Egyptian tombs, which were seen as the gateways to the afterlife. Bai's role underscored the serpent's association with immortality and protection in the journey to the afterlife. This role extended to all Egyptian temples, where sacred serpents were often housed, symbolizing eternal life and divine protection.

The Sun and the Snake demon

'Ra' was the sun-god of ancient Egyptian religion who embodied the daily cycle of life (day), death (night) and rebirth (sunrise). His journey from east to west, symbolizing the sun's movement across the sky, and his daily rebirth at dawn were metaphors for the perpetual cycles of existence. During this journey, Ra faced

Apophis, a formidable serpent representing chaos, who sought to obstruct his progress.

This narrative parallels the Hindu myth of Surya and Rahu. Surya, the sun god in Hinduism, mirrors Ra in his role as the source of life and the regulator of day and night. Rahu, a half-serpent asura, periodically obscures Surya (and the moon) during eclipses. According to the puraanas, Rahu was a serpent who drank the elixir of immortality (amrita) but was beheaded by Vishnu. His head, a celestial entity, chases the sun and moon across the sky, causing eclipses when he catches them.

The Cosmic Egg

In the dusty annals of Egyptian myth, we encounter another serpentine deity, Kneph. Revered as the divine architect of the universe, Kneph is often depicted clutching an egg in its jaws. This imagery, rich with symbolism, entwines the serpent—symbolic of the mysteries of creation—with the egg, representing the primordial elements from which life springs.

Similarly, Apophis, the enemy of the Egyptian sun god, Ra, was believed to have emerged from the primordial waters of Nu, the cosmic ocean of chaos. This primordial chaos concept aligns with the idea of the cosmic egg in other creation myths, where the universe emerges from a state of primordial disorder or nothingness.

The cosmic egg, or mundane egg, is a timeless symbol threaded through the myths of countless cultures, from the Proto-Indo-Europeans to the ancient Egyptians. This primordial concept often centres around an egg from which the universe is either born directly or through a primordial being who subsequently shapes existence. The egg may rest upon the primordial waters of the Earth, signifying the fertile chaos from which all things spring. According to Witzel, in many traditions, the upper half of the egg becomes the firmament or heaven, while the lower half forms the Earth—an evocative image of celestial and terrestrial realms emerging from a unified whole.

In Orphic mythology, which is a later development within Greek religious thought, the concept of a cosmic egg is present. According to Orphic texts, the universe began from a cosmic egg, from which Phanes (the primordial deity of creation) emerged. Phanes is often depicted with serpentine features or accompanied by serpents. The egg, in this myth, represents the origin of the cosmos, and the serpent symbolizes the life-giving and transformative powers associated with creation.

In the ancient Hermopolitan tradition of Middle Egypt, this motif takes on a rich and detailed form. Here, the primordial landscape is dominated by the Ogdoad, a group of eight deities—four male gods with frog heads and four female deities with serpent heads—residing in the chaotic waters that predate the world. These gods, in their serpentine ways, bring forth a cosmic egg, the source of creation. The egg's hatching heralds the emergence of the sun god, signified by the bloom of a lotus flower, and marks the formation of the primeval mound, the first land to rise from the waters.

The Egg, the Phallus and the Serpent

The idea of creation, spurred by the mere existence of things, marks the dawn of human reasoning. Early humans, observing the natural world, began to wonder how life began. One of the most striking phenomena was the hatching of a snake from an egg—a miracle that seemed to capture the essence of creation itself.

Naturally, the egg emerged as a primordial symbol—a quiet container of potential, suspended between life and death. In early cosmogonies, the egg often represented a dormant, unshaped universe—formless and floating—until life burst forth.

Alongside the egg, the phallus became a powerful emblem of creation, embodying reproductive energy and the active force of genesis. In ancient iconography, the phallus and serpent often appeared together—or were symbolically interchangeable. Both evoked fertility, continuity and the mysterious forces that pulse through all living things.

The entwining of the serpent and the egg reveals a doctrine of reciprocal principles found across early mythologies. The egg represents the latent, passive potential of the universe; the serpent, with its kinetic motion and regenerative power, symbolizes activation and renewal. Together, they embody the rhythmic interplay of opposites—life and death, chaos and order, the seen and the unseen. This symbolic pairing lies at the heart of many ancient cosmologies, reflecting the dynamic balance that sustains the cosmos.

Why were the ancients so mesmerized by serpents?

The ancients regarded serpents as possessing divine qualities. They admired the serpent for its unique, fiery nature and its ability to move swiftly and fluidly without limbs. Its capacity to change forms, such as moving in a spiral and darting forward with great speed, added to its mystique.

Serpents were also noted for their longevity and ability to rejuvenate by shedding their old skin, symbolizing renewal and the cyclical nature of life. This regenerative quality made them central in sacred rites and mysteries. Its association with eternal succession and the constant cycle of life and death connected it to ancient beliefs about the cyclical nature of existence.

Yet, their complex symbolism cannot be fully understood through a single cultural lens. While many ancient traditions revered serpents as guardians of sacred knowledge, protectors of the underworld and keepers of cosmic secrets, later some Western interpretations may have skewed their image—casting them as evil, deceptive and cursed.

The entwining of Solar, Phallic and Serpent worship across ancient traditions reminds us that the serpent once stood for something far more potent and purer—an active, renewing force of the natural world, a symbol of vitality, duality and the timeless dance of transformation. Yet, this reverence was not universal, nor did it remain unchallenged. As cultural and religious landscapes shifted, particularly in the West, the serpent's image underwent a dramatic change, often cast in a far more sinister light.

II

Fall of the Serpent

A few months back, I shared the first draft of my book, *Dakini*, with a filmmaker friend for some honest feedback. After reading it, he asked me whether the serpent hinted at in the story was the antagonist of the literary universe I was building. I could barely reply—the answer would be revealed in the next book—but what surprised me was how quickly he associated the character with the serpent tattoo with evil or conspiracy when I had not mentioned anything else about him or his intentions. Not a word!

In Western literature and cinema, serpents are often linked to the darker side or 'the other'. Is it fear of their slithering motion? Or a visceral reaction to their scaly, cold-blooded form?

The Serpent of Eden

In the Western tradition, the serpent of Eden emerges as a figure of profound betrayal, its sinuous form forever entwined with the notion of treachery. This symbolism became a foundational element in the narrative of humanity's fall from grace. In the Biblical account found in the Book of Genesis, Adam and Eve, the first man and woman created by the biblical God, live in the Garden of Eden—a paradise filled with lush vegetation and abundant life.

The biblical God places them in the garden with the freedom to eat from any tree except one—the Tree of Knowledge of Good and Evil.

The serpent, described as more cunning than any other creature, approaches Eve with a deceitful question—'Did God really say you must not eat from any tree in the garden?'

When Eve clarifies that they may eat from all but one tree, the serpent contradicts her, saying that eating the fruit from the Tree of Knowledge of Good and Evil will not lead to death as the biblical God warned. Instead, it promises that the fruit will open their eyes, making them like the biblical God, knowing good and evil. Intrigued by the serpent's words and the fruit's appearance, Eve eats it and then shares it with Adam. This act of disobedience brings immediate awareness and shame, marking their fall from innocence.

God's response is swift and severe—Eve is condemned to experience pain in childbirth and subordination, and Adam is sentenced to toil for his sustenance. Their expulsion from Eden signifies the beginning of human suffering and a life outside paradise, symbolizing the consequences of their transgression.

The serpent is cursed to crawl on its belly and eat dust all the days of its life. This imagery signifies a fall from a previously more exalted or upright status, representing the serpent's degradation. The serpent's role in this story has cast a long shadow, with its association with Satan further cemented by later Christian interpretation. *Revelation 12:9* refers to Satan as 'that ancient serpent', linking the serpent of Eden to the devil and reinforcing its aura of evil that persists to this day.

This biblical fall may also metaphorically reflect the cultural decline of serpent worship with the rise of monotheism. In Ireland, for instance, legends claim that St. Patrick drove the snakes from the island—a story that may be interpreted as a metaphor for the eradication of pagan serpent cults.

Treacherous Serpents in Literature and Pop Culture

Serpent symbolism slithers far beyond sacred texts into English literature and pop culture. In J.K. Rowling's *Harry Potter* series, Voldemort—whose very name evokes dread—is intimately tied to serpents. His companion, Nagini, and his ability to speak Parseltongue reinforce the ancient fear and suspicion surrounding snake symbolism. Slytherin House, with its emblematic serpent, embodies ambition, secrecy and cunning—all traits historically ascribed to the serpent archetype.

Even Severus Snape's name hints at serpentine associations. As a child, I often found myself rooting for Slytherin during Quidditch matches—perhaps a subconscious nod to my south Indian upbringing, where serpents have long been revered.

Another childhood favourite of mine was *The Jungle Book*, which featured Kaa, the hypnotic python. Kaa may not be overtly evil, but its cunning and manipulative nature certainly aligns with the serpent's traditional role as a deceiver—much like the serpent in Eden.

In C.S. Lewis's *The Silver Chair*, the Lady of the Green Kirtle, who can transform into a serpent, serves as the antagonist.

In modern conspiracy theory, David Icke's Reptilian agenda claims that a race of serpent-like beings controls global politics. These 'reptilians' supposedly originate from the Draco constellation, a name rooted in the Latin draco (dragon/serpent), itself derived from the Greek drakon meaning 'sharp-sighted one.'

The iconic villain Dracula also carries this serpentine legacy. The name Dracula means 'son of Dracul,' and in Romanian, dracul signifies the devil—a term that evolved from draco.

The ancient draco once described great serpents before becoming synonymous with dragons and, later, demonic forces— a lineage coiling even into modern fiction, from Dracula to Harry Potter's rival, Draco Malfoy.

Serpents in Indian Culture

In contrast to the demonization seen in Western literature, Indian sacred narratives present serpents as layered and often divine. While serpents in India can be both protectors (Vasuki, Ananta Shesha) and harbingers of doom (Vritra, Rahu and Ketu), they are revered as sacred beings with connections to creation, fertility, healing and wisdom. They are part of many geographical creation stories of India, like those concerning the origins of regions such as coastal Karnataka, Kerala and Kashmir.

The *Mahabharata* distinguishes between benevolent and malevolent serpents. In the real world, the cobra—deadly yet medicinal—mirrors this duality. Serpents appear frequently in Indian epics, often in the company of deities such as Shiva, Vishnu, Subramanya and Ganesha.

Naagas, a semi-divine race of half-human, half-serpent beings, were believed to roam freely, until they were banished to the netherworlds by Brahma in a moment of divine displeasure (see Part 3, Introduction). Naaginis, maternal figures, have long been relegated to supporting roles, their forms objectified and exaggerated by pop culture, reduced to caricatures with voluptuous curves. This pop culture portrayal contrasts sharply with their role in folklore, however, where they are guardians of treasure, keepers of secrets and potent symbols of divine retribution.

When appeased, these Naagas bless their devotees with fertility, protection, and fortune. When angered, their wrath brings swift and devastating consequences. They are not evil—

they are cosmic arbiters of balance, holding the power to both create and destroy.

In the following pages, dear reader, we will venture deeper into India's complex and ancient serpent traditions, where lore, ecology and spirituality intertwine like the coils of the serpent itself.

III

Etymology of Some Serpentine Terminologies

A few years ago, I found myself at a late film director's Mumbai residence, discussing ideas for a film project which touched on the concept of serpent worship. Among us was an elderly man from Kerala, whose name escapes me now. When someone casually referred to these revered beings as 'snakes', the gentleman quickly corrected us, saying, 'No, you should not call serpent deities mere snakes. The term serpent adds a level of respect to these entities.'

From then on, we always used the term serpent. But what really is the difference between a serpent and a snake? Between Naaga and sarpa? For a lay reader, all of them may appear as a slithering reptile. Before diving into the rich tales of serpents in the later part of this book, it's essential to understand the roots of four significant terms—Ahi, Uraga, Sarpa and Naaga—each carrying deep reverence in Hindu tradition.

Sarpa

The term Sarpa stems from the Sanskrit root word 'srp', meaning 'to glide' or 'to crawl'. This word broadly refers to snakes in Hindu belief, symbolizing their sinuous movement. As discussed in the previous chapter, 'serpent' in other world lore can also denote giant crawling creatures like dragons. However, within the Hindu belief system, sarpas are typically understood as powerful snakes with a single head.

Naaga

Naaga (or naag) has a more complex meaning. Interestingly, the word 'naaga' can also mean 'elephant' in Sanskrit. How did this seeming confusion arise? One theory suggests the link comes via the Sanskrit word 'nagn' meaning 'naked' or 'hairless'. This could apply to a large, relatively hairless elephant, but perhaps more significantly, it could describe the mighty cobra just after shedding its old skin, appearing smooth and renewed.

Adding to this connection, early Indian cosmology features guardian beings protecting the earth's four quarters, sometimes depicted as four great elephants and other times as four great dragon-serpents. While it's debated which motif came first, the idea of sky-serpents seems older in literature. Both elephants and cobras were likely seen as beings of immense power—the elephant for its strength, the cobra for its potent venom. If Vogel's theory is accurate, the term 'naaga', initially meaning serpent/dragon (perhaps the original guardians), might have later been applied to the guardian elephants and then to elephants in general. This shows how cosmological ideas can influence language over time.

Unlike the more general sarpa, Naagas are often depicted as divine or semi-divine beings. They are sometimes shown with multiple heads and are associated with water, fertility and protection, revered across India, especially in the south as guardians of treasure and land. Naagas are more than just snakes; they are mystical entities with immense power.

The *Sanatkumaara Samhita* distinguishes between two types of serpents—Naagas and sarpas. According to this, Naagas are endowed with mystical powers, including the ability to change form at will, aligning with the concept of ichchadaari Naagas popularized in modern cinema and television. They are often portrayed in traditional narratives as semi-divine, multi-headed beings linked to water bodies and capable of assuming human or other forms. Sarpas, by contrast, are described as gliding serpents—earthlier and singular in nature, lacking the transformative and divine attributes of their celestial counterparts.

Further, these serpents fall into three primary categories—Phani, Mandali (hoodless and painted with circular patches or rings of varied colours on their skin) and Rajila (hoodless and striped), corresponding to the forces of wind, bile and phlegm, representing different temperaments. A further class, the Vyantara, emerges with a combination of these traits, making them more unpredictable. As serpents, they are most often depicted with hoods, bearing signs and symbols such as cart wheels, ploughshares, umbrellas, swastikas and goads—iconography steeped in the metaphysical (Gangadharan, 1954, p. 807).

Uragas

There is also another category, uragas, which generally refers to other types of snakes. The word uraga comes from Sanskrit roots 'ura' (chest) and 'ga' (go), meaning 'one who crawls on the chest'. Uragas are part of the serpentine lineage but usually lack the strong divine status of Naagas.

Scriptural origins can be confusing; Valmiki's Ramayana, for instance, states uragas were born from Kadru and Naagas from Surasa (both daughters of Krodhavaasa, wife of Kashyapa). This differs from the more popular Mahabharata version where Naagas are born to Kadru and Kashyapa. Exploring language further, the Tamil word 'Aaravam' for snake comes from root sounds ('ar', 'ara', 'aravu') related to serpent movement and sound, similar to the Sanskrit uraga. The term 'ara' in Tamil can also represent the sound made by a snake, leading to 'arakku', which conveys the idea of wriggling—an action associated with serpents (Rangaswamy, 1958, p. 540).

The similarity between aaravam and the Sanskrit uraga raises an intriguing question about which language might have influenced the other. While it's difficult to pinpoint the direction of influence, the connection between these terms highlights the deep linguistic and cultural ties between Tamil and Sanskrit, both of which have evolved over millennia with shared sacred narratives, religious practices, and symbolic representations of the serpent.

Ahi

Ahi is another significant Sanskrit term for serpent, often appearing in Vedic texts like the Rigveda. The most prominent association is with Vritra, the great sky serpent slain by Indra to release the waters, a figure whose name might even echo in the Greek 'ophis' or Old Norse 'ormr'. It is this Greek 'ophis' which is the root word for 'ophiolatry,' the term for serpent worship. The term 'Ahi' also resonates geographically through Ahikshetra.

Ahikshetra—The Serpent's Domain

Ahikshetra translates to the 'Region of the Serpent'. This name points to a place deeply entwined with serpent lore, though its exact location is debated, often placed somewhere between legend and the historical landscape of ancient India.

Within India's epic narratives (Itihasa Puraanas), Ahikshetra features significantly in the Mahabharata. It is remembered as the place where King Parikshit, Arjuna's grandson, was fatally bitten by Takshaka, the serpent king (this story is detailed in Part 3 of this book). Parikshit's death prompted his enraged son, King Janamejaya, to initiate the Sarpasatra—a massive sacrificial ritual aimed at eradicating all serpents—at this very location. Thus, Ahikshetra became a crucible of legend, vengeance and divine intervention.

Some traditions identify Ahikshetra with Ahichhatra, the ancient capital of the Paanchaala kingdom in modern Uttar Pradesh. Ahichhatra has its own layered history. Old tales mention King Mayuravarma inviting brahmin families from this revered site to settle in Tulunadu (Karnataka).

Ahichhatra is also highly significant for Jains as the place where the twenty-third Tirthankara, Parshvanatha, attained omniscience (Kevala Jnana). Legend tells that while Parshvanatha meditated, his jealous brother from a past life, Kamath, tried to drown him with a magical flood. However, the serpent deities Dharanendra (Naagayaksha) and Padmavati (Naagayakshini) protected him— Dharanendra spreading his hoods like an umbrella and Padmavati coiling around his body. This event is said to have given the place its name, Ahichchhatra—the 'Serpent's Umbrella'.

Archaeological accounts by figures like Alexander Cunningham confirm the site's antiquity and the persistence of serpent legends, linking it back even to the time of the Mahabharata and potentially earlier. The ancient Chinese traveller, Xuanzang (Hiuen Tsiang), also mentioned this city, which he recorded as Ohichitalo. He described the city as naturally strong, being flanked by mountain crags, with an agreeable climate and inhabitants who were sincere, truthful, loved religion and applied themselves to learning. He noted the presence of about ten Buddhist monasteries (sangharamas) and also mentioned nine Shiva temples (Beal, 1884, p. 200).

Yakshas

The mention of the protective Naagayaksha and Naagayakshini in Parshvanatha's story brings us briefly to another class of nature spirits often linked with Naagas—the Yakshas. Like Naagas, these often benevolent (though sometimes unpredictable) spirits are frequently guardians of earthly treasures or associated with trees and fertility. Kubera, the lord of wealth, is the most famous Yaksha.

In certain traditions, they were believed to have an affinity for fragrance and controlled speech, and they were thought to bless offspring to those who worshipped them. They were seen as both bearers of great wisdom and paragons of beauty, frequently associated with music, art and the finer creative arts. Their worship—along with that of Naagas, fertility deities and mother goddesses—likely originated among the early indigenous peoples of India and coexisted alongside the priestly sacrifices of the Vedic period. In fact, Naaga and Yaksha are believed to be of the same rank, being in charge of fertility and rain respectively. The view is that they were the primitive men of the Pre-Vedic era (Tavakar, 1971, p. 72).

As we've seen, the language surrounding serpents in ancient India is rich, complex, and sometimes even contradictory. The terms Sarpa, Naaga, Uraga and Ahi are more than just synonyms for snake; they connect to specific traditional lineages, linguistic roots spanning different regions, sacred geographies like Ahikshetra, and even other divine beings like the Yakshas. While sarpa might refer to a powerful snake, Naaga may imply a being with divine potential, immense power, and a deeper connection to cosmic forces.

Having untangled some of these terminological threads, we are better prepared to explore the nature of these fascinating serpentine entities themselves—particularly the revered Naagas—and the vital roles they play in India's ancient stories, legends and living traditions. Moving forward, while acknowledging these distinctions, this book will often use the terms 'Naaga' and 'serpent' somewhat interchangeably when referring generally to these revered, often divine beings central to Indian lore, unless a specific term like sarpa or uraga is required by the context.

IV

Divinity and Danger—Naaga in Indian Lore

My earliest memories of snakes are threaded with fear. At six years old, in the quiet village of Kanjikode, Kerala, I stumbled upon a cobra coiled near an old well. Its presence was terrifying, igniting a primal terror in my young heart. My instinct was to run, but my mother's calm voice cut through my trembling, 'Don't run. It will anger them. These are gods, the Naagadevatas. Do not disturb them, do not fear them. When you see one, do not retaliate. Instead stand back and let them pass. They won't harm you. Pray.'

I prayed not just for the cobra to pass, but that I might never encounter another one in my life.

That year, my father's job took us from the lush fields of Kerala to the sprawling urban chaos of Delhi. For the next two decades, snakes became distant memories, surfacing only in unsettling dreams. There was one fleeting encounter at a fair in Haryana—perhaps Suraj Kund or Badkhal—where I saw a cobra swaying to the tune of a snake-charmer's flute. A small crowd of onlookers, oblivious to the cruelty, watched in delight.

'Appa, are they praying to Naagadevata?' I asked, wide-eyed at the spectacle.

'No,' he replied, 'they're making it dance to the man's tune.'

'Aren't they afraid? Why doesn't the serpent god bite them?'

With a shrug, my father said, 'Its fangs have been removed. Now, it cannot bite anyone. It is just a voiceless creature.'

In that moment, I felt no fear, only a strange sadness for the cobra—an erstwhile god stripped of its power, robbed of its primal essence by man.

Fear and fascination intertwined, casting serpents in a spectral light—creatures that slipped between the realms of gods and men. Yet a question has always lingered in my mind—are all serpents worthy of worship? Do they possess the mystical powers and the ability to transform into humans, as legend suggests? Or have the popular stories and bad YouTube videos taken liberties with ancient tales? We may never get a conclusive answer, but seeking clarity in traditional texts offers a starting point. Let us explore our scriptures and folklore to understand the types of serpents recognized in this chapter.

Divine Serpents and Earthly Kin (Divya vs. Bhauma)

Starting with ancient medical and religious texts, we find that not all serpents are considered of divine origin. The *Sushruta Samhita*, for instance, broadly classifies serpents into two categories—Divya (Divine or Celestial) and Bhauma (Earthly, terrestrial, or ordinary). The Divya serpents include the great Naagas of Puraanas—Vasuki, Takshaka, Ananta Shesha and others. These are beings of immense power, said to shine like fire and capable, when angered, of incinerating worlds with their breath or gaze. Their bite, legend holds, is beyond any earthly cure.

However, the bhauma serpents, which are born on the earth, possess venom in their fangs and can bite humans. According to the *Sushruta Samhita*, there are eighty types of these earthly serpents, divided into five categories—Darvikara, Mandali, Rajiman, Nirvisha and Vaikaranja. Altogether, this brings the total number of serpents to eighty (Bhishagratna, 1911, p. 703). The venom of serpents is called visha.

Origin of the word Visha

In the ancient Sanskrit lexicon, *visha*—poison—comes in two distinct forms—*sthaavaram*, deriving from immobile objects such as plants, minerals, and flowers, and *jangamam*, originating from mobile creatures like animals. The venom of serpents falls under this latter category, though a significant distinction is drawn between the divine (divya) and the terrestrial (bhauvma) serpents. The poison of divine serpents lies in their very breath and gaze, while their earthly counterparts carry it in their fangs.

The origin of visha itself is tied to profound cosmic events in Puranic narratives. One well-known story traces it to the churning of the ocean (Samudra Manthana), where the deadly kaalakoota visha emerged before the nectar of immortality. Another account links it to Brahma's overwhelming rage during creation, a fury so potent it had to be distributed among creatures, both mobile and immobile. In both stories, the gods, witnessing this raw, uncontrollable force, were consumed by a profound *vishaada*—a grief or depression of the spirit. From this *vishaada* arose *visha*, now synonymous with substances born of divine wrath and cosmic disturbance, capable of bringing forth sorrow and destruction. Thus, in the Puranic scriptures, poison was not merely a physical toxin but a manifestation of the gods' anguish and their creation's primal tumult (Bishagratna, 1911, p. 698).

Sacred Times—Aashlesha and Naagapanchami

Given this potent mix of reverence and potential danger, traditional culture established specific times and rituals to honour serpents and seek their favour. The nakshatra (lunar mansion) known as Aashlesha (or Aayilyam in Malayalam) is deeply connected with serpent deities, particularly in Karnataka and Kerala, sometimes linked to the birth stars of great Naagas like Vasuki or Shesha.

More widely celebrated is Naagapanchami, typically observed on the fifth day (Panchami) of the bright lunar fortnight in the month of Shraavana (monsoon season, when snakes often emerge). While traditions vary—some link it to the creation of Naagas, others like the Varaha Puraana mention it as the day Brahma relegated them to Paataala—the core purpose remains honouring the serpents. Across the subcontinent, from Nepal to Kerala, people make offerings at shrines, pour milk over idols (Naagakallus), and pray for protection, fertility and prosperity.

Regional customs add unique dimensions to the celebration. In parts of rural Maharashtra, for instance, Naagapanchami is reportedly celebrated with great reverence. Women may consider the Naaga a symbolic brother and gather for festivities. Certain activities are traditionally avoided in some villages on Panchami, such as chopping vegetables, cooking using a pan (tava), and ploughing or digging the ground. This last prohibition often stems from reverence and practicality—snakes help farmers by controlling rodents, and avoiding digging prevents accidental harm to snakes or potential snakebites.

Naagapanchami endures as a living expression of an ancient pact, a time when reverence seeks to balance the inherent power, both protective and dangerous, embodied by the serpent.

Echoes from Antiquity—Serpents in the Indus Valley

The serpents' presence is woven deeply into the fabric of Indic religions, often coiled around the pillars of ancient temples, guarding sacred waters, or standing sentinel over long-lost treasures. Their symbolism straddles creation and destruction, reflecting the duality of their nature as both protectors and harbingers of death. This complex relationship with serpents finds its earliest visual echoes in the Harappan Civilization, circa 2000 BCE. A handful of serpentine depictions have been discovered over time. The serpents in these Harappan discoveries—possibly cobras, naturalistically rendered with a single head—hint at a deeper, older reverence. The image of the cobra, poised and ready to strike, is one deeply embedded in the collective memory of Indians (Parpola, 1994, p. 252).

In the Harappan amulets, human worshippers offer sacrificial vessels also to anthropomorphic deities who resemble the 'Proto-Siva' and who are attended by serpents. Strong drinks and fish were also integral parts of sacrifices to fertility spirits (Yaksha) and serpent gods (Naaga) in the early popular religion of North India (Parpola, 1994, p. 194).

Given that the serpent's role in Indian lore is far more complex than simple fear or worship might imply, we are now prepared to investigate the most revered of these serpentine figures—the cobra—and how its reality aligns with the legends of the Naaga more closely.

V

Naaga and Cobra: Belief Meets Reality

The ancient stories hum with tales of God-like Naagas—powerful, sometimes multi-headed beings dwelling in hidden realms. But how much of this legendary figure connects to the reptile sharing its name, the familiar, fearsome cobra of the Indian landscape? This chapter felt crucial to my exploration—to bridge the gap between the divya serpents of scripture and the bhauma (earthly) reality of the Indian cobra (*Naja naja*). Where do belief and biology overlap? Where do they diverge?

To navigate this complex terrain, I sought insight from someone who has dedicated his life to understanding these creatures—renowned herpetologist and conservationist Romulus Whitaker, founder of the Madras Snake Park. His expertise, shared graciously via email correspondence, illuminates the scientific facts that sometimes intertwine with, and sometimes challenge, the deep-rooted folklore surrounding the cobra.

Among the approximately 300 species of snakes that roam India's vast and varied landscape, the cobra holds a place of singular significance. It wasn't just a snake—it was the embodiment of both life's sacred mysteries and death. The Indian cobra (Naja naja), one of the 'big four' venomous snakes responsible for the majority of snakebites in the country, was not merely feared but revered and woven into the fabric of Indian spirituality. Its form finds prominence in the iconography of temples, its image curling around the deities of Hindu tradition and its very biological name traces its roots to the ancient Sanskrit word *naaga*, meaning serpent.

The cobra's venomous strike, its lethal efficiency, and its ubiquitous presence across the subcontinent—India, Pakistan, Sri Lanka, Bangladesh, Nepal and even Afghanistan—make it both an object of worship and fear. For centuries, across temple murals and sacred texts, the cobra has been enshrined as Naagaraaja, Naagadevata, Naagaradevata, or Naagathaanmaar depending on where in the region one invokes its name.

The cobra's habitat mirrors the diversity of India's landscapes. Whether coiled in the underbrush of tropical rainforests or slithering through the dust-laden paths of villages, its domain spans from verdant mangroves to cultivated savannas. Its prey—black rats (particularly the Lesser Bandicoot, Bandicota bengalensis, found commonly in paddy field bunds), frogs, lizards, birds and other snakes—becomes paralyzed by its venom, offering itself to the cobra's slow, deliberate consumption. The snake's hood, fanning out in moments of tension, serves as both an evolutionary defence and a symbol of its power. The 'spectacled cobra', as it is often called, wears an unmistakable pattern on the back of its hood, resembling two eyes connected by a curved line.

The Lifespan and Size of Cobras

The Agni Puraana says that the Naagas shed their skins every six months, and that they live for up to one hundred and twenty years. I recall, vividly, a story shared with me by an elder during a drowsy Kerala afternoon, the kind where the heat slows time, and the rhythmic hum of insects lulls you into a state where myths and reality begin to blur. 'Naagas,' she said with reverence, 'outlive humans. They live for centuries, standing vigil over families, watching as generations rise and fall, as though time itself bends to their will.'

However, science dictates a much shorter maximum lifespan for an Indian cobra, around twenty to thirty years, based primarily on records from captivity. Though they may reach lengths of five feet (generally 1.5 metres), whispers of seven-foot cobras circulate in the oral traditions of the land, while the verified maximum length for *Naja naja* is closer to two metres. Where might the myths of extreme longevity originate? Expert insight suggests that snake charmers historically were a primary source of 'snake facts' and would sometimes resort to deception, such as inserting animal hair into a cobra's head to claim great age, complete with a 'moustache'.

The notion that these serpents transcend the limits of human mortality—that they are silent witnesses to the inexorable passing of time—underscores their legendary stature. In traditional accounts, they seem immortal, their existence only threatened by the few predators capable of challenging them—the mongoose (Nevla in Hindi) and mankind's encroaching settlements.

Serpent and the Mongoose

The lore of Kerala and Tulunadu is rich with tales of these two sworn enemies, eternally entwined in their deadly struggle, a relationship immortalized in the Malayalam phrase 'keeriyum-paambum', a metaphor for adversaries bound by fate, neither able to vanquish the other fully.

The English word 'mongoose' itself, I was once told, originates from the Marathi 'mungus' or its Kannada/Tulu counterpart 'mungusi', a reflection of the creature's long-standing presence in the Indian imagination.

Revenge of the Cobra

Another popular belief in India (solidified by those ichaadaari naagin movies and serials) is that cobras can keep the face of a wrongdoer in their memory for up to twelve years and actively seek revenge. According to some folktales, a serpent when it lives for a hundred years, can become so powerful that it can assume the form of any living creature. It becomes an all-powerful ichchadaari (roughly translates as shape-shifter), and if someone wrongs it, then it will avenge either by biting the person or inflicting misfortune upon the wrong doer. By wrong-doing, I mean catching a cobra, stomping on its hood, spitting, chasing or hitting it with a stick.

From a herpetological standpoint, however, the idea of cobras recognizing specific individuals to exact premeditated revenge is considered a myth. Mr Whitaker reveals that while cobras possess cognitive abilities related to knowing their territory and having homing instincts, they are generally scared of humans. Recognizing specific individuals is unlikely, except perhaps in captive situations where a snake might grow accustomed to a non-threatening caretaker. Vengeful behaviour is not part of their known cognitive capacity.

Pointing at a Cobra

There is another popular belief in rural parts of the country that one should not point at a cobra as that may enrage it. This action, like any perceived threat when the snake feels cornered and unable to escape, could indeed elicit a defensive response such as hooding, hissing or even a bluff strike (often with the mouth closed). The idea that pointing might specifically trigger spitting venom, however, needs clarification. Expert insight clarifies that the Indian Spectacled Cobra (*Naja naja*) does not typically spit venom. While the related Monocled Cobra (*Naja kaouthia*) has a limited spitting capacity, it's not comparable to some African or Southeast Asian spitting cobras.

Inhabitation and Mating Taboos

Indian cobras, elusive yet present in every shadow, seek refuge in the hidden corners of the earth—burrowed into ancient tree hollows, termite mounds, or concealed among rocks. These homes, as varied as the landscapes they inhabit, are crucial for their survival.

A popular belief in Indian lore holds that witnessing cobras mating is a grave omen, foretelling that the observer will not live to see the next sunrise. Cobras, after all, deserve some privacies too, don't they? Jokes aside, this belief likely emerged from a deep respect for nature and the understanding of boundaries. Our ancestors carved this warning into folklore to instil the importance of keeping one's distance.

So, if someone ever accidentally stumbles upon cobras entwined in their mating ritual, the tradition advises to cover one's eyes and turn away immediately. But if someone deliberately observes, the consequences according to such lore are believed to be far more dire—the serpent is said to seek them out later in the night, and bite them. Another variant of this belief claims that the naagin, the female cobra, will follow the observer home, cursing the household with misfortune.

Ancient Buddhist myths also speak of a similar taboo. If one were to witness cobras intertwined along a roadside, it is believed they must immediately tear off a button or shawl as an act of repentance, for watching cobras mate is considered a grievous sin. Whether a spiritual consequence or simply a cultural warning to leave the wild undisturbed, these stories reinforce the enigmatic and powerful presence of the cobra in Indian lore.

Reproductive Cycle and Maternal Care

The reproductive cycle of naagas, as detailed by the Agni Puraana (Chapter 294), begins in the months following Aashaadha (June–July). The serpents lay 240 eggs, incubating them for four months until they hatch. After seven days, the young serpents' eyes open, and within a month, their black skin begins to form. By twelve days, their senses sharpen, and their venomous teeth—known by fearsome names like Karali, Makari, Kaalaraatri and Yamadutika—begin to appear within twenty to thirty-two days, growing first in the left and then the right jaws.

Scriptures aside, science reveals that the Indian cobra's reproductive cycle is intricately connected with the rhythms of nature. As the cold mists of January sweep across the land, cobras begin their mating rituals. Soon after, the female retreats to her chosen hiding spot, where she lays her eggs—anywhere between ten and thirty. This mother cobra, fierce and vigilant, becomes a guardian over her brood, embodying the ancient maternal archetype of the Naagayakshi Amma or the protective naagini from south Indian lore, figures who defend their young and devotees with unwavering intensity. This 'nest guarding' behaviour, where the female stays with the incubating eggs, is observed in cobras, king cobras, pythons, kraits and checkered keelback water snakes, among others. Typically, however, a guarding snake will attempt to escape if disturbed. While recent studies show extended maternal care after hatching/birth in some snake species, this has not specifically been documented for cobras.

For fifty to seventy days, the mother cobra remains on high alert, leaving her nest only when hunger demands it, always returning swiftly to her eggs. She is the silent force, her presence a symbol of both nurturing and danger. When the time comes, the eggs break open, releasing tiny snakelets into the world—already venomous and ready to strike.

Cobra Venom

When the cobra feels threatened, it rises with an almost regal posture, lifting the upper third of its body, its iconic hood unfurling like an ancient banner of defiance. The hiss that escapes its mouth is a warning, sharp and unmistakable. Unlike the viper, whose retractable fangs offer a fleeting danger, the cobra's bite is committed—its venomous fangs, once sunk into flesh, begin their lethal work immediately. What follows is a grim procession of symptoms—searing pain, blurred vision, nausea, paralysis, and for the unfortunate many, the slow, inescapable descent into respiratory failure or cardiac arrest—unless swift medical intervention saves them from the cobra's kiss.

Venom—Power, Exploitation, and Reverence

In bygone times, this venomous power was both feared and coveted. The cobra's venom, believed by some to hold medicinal properties, was sometimes exploited by those who understood its perceived value. Snake charmers, once a ubiquitous sight in India, capitalized on the cobra's hypnotic presence. With their wicker baskets and the haunting notes of the pungi, a double-reed instrument, they seemed to make the cobra dance. In truth, it was not the music that enchanted the snake but the rhythmic sway of the charmer's instrument, to which the serpent responded in kind.

Yet, the cobra paid a price for this spectacle. Charmers would often cruelly defang their cobras or milk them for venom, which sometimes fetched high prices as an intoxicant. Even its scaly hide was once sought after for leather goods. This practice of defanging or removing venom glands is exceptionally cruel and often amounts to a death sentence for the cobra. Although it might survive for months or even years in some cases, its ability to properly digest food is compromised, leading to starvation.

Furthermore, the removal isn't always permanent; fangs can grow back, and according to Mr Whitaker, there are documented cases where charmers were fatally bitten by snakes they believed were defanged. Today, the Indian cobra enjoys protection under the law, spared from the fate of mass exploitation. The king cobra (*Ophiophagus hannah*) is India's national reptile and rightfully protected under Schedule 1 of the Indian Wildlife Protection Act. The Indian Cobra (*Naja naja*) itself is also protected under Schedule 2. But perhaps it is not just legal barriers that protect these serpents; perhaps it was the foresight of our ancestors, who elevated the cobra to the status of deity, embedding within us a deep reverence that tempered our material desires. In this way, the cobra—Naagadevata—remains a symbol of both life and death, a force to be respected, not consumed.

Snakeskin

A snake sheds its skin; the process called molting is a regularly recurring event which helps the snake grow and adapt to changes in the environment. Many cultures associate snakeskin with superstitions, such as the belief that hanging a snakeskin on a door will keep the house disease- and sorrow-free. Diseases bring sorrow, and pests like rats are known carriers. Such rodents, when they see a snakeskin, might mistake it for a predator and stay away from the house. Some believe that snakeskin will protect the house from fire and lightning. People in olden times reportedly tied snakeskin around a pregnant woman's waist at the time of labour to reduce pain.

Some people believe that one should not see a snake or feed it while it is shedding its skin. It was thought to be a supernatural process because the snake would change its eye colour while molting. However, there is some truth grounded in science here, not the supernatural. As a snake grows, its skin stretches. Snakes shed this stretched skin every couple of weeks or once a month, depending on age and conditions. The process starts with the formation of a new skin layer under the existing one. The snake's eyes turn milky or bluish because the skin that forms the eye cap (spectacle) has loosened in preparation for shedding, impairing its vision. It may get defensive at such times and strike at anyone that comes near. So, snakes often remain in hiding and may fast until the process is complete. Once it sheds its skin, the snake immediately hunts for food.

Milk Offerings—Ritual vs. Reality

The practice of offering milk to serpents, common during Naagapanchami, involves pouring it over idols or near anthills, but sometimes directly to live snakes. From a biological standpoint, cobras are carnivores. What is the biological reality behind this act of devotion? From a herpetological perspective, it is unlikely that a cobra will voluntarily drink milk unless extremely thirsty and lacking access to water. While consuming milk probably won't harm the snake directly, it is certainly not a natural part of its diet.

The Myth of the Splitting Snake

Another enduring belief is that cutting a snake in half creates two living, vengeful entities. Elders in my family warned against this, advising not to kill a cobra, but if absolutely necessary, never to cut it in the middle lest it return as two. This belief likely arises because the severed head and tail sections can continue to move reflexively for some time due to residual nerve signals, giving the terrifying illusion of two living beings, especially if they disappear into undergrowth while still writhing. As Mr Whitaker explains, this phenomenon, combined with the reptile's slower metabolism meaning the head portion takes time to die from trauma or blood loss, easily gives rise to the appearance of two wriggling beings. It remains, needless to say, an exceptionally cruel way to kill any animal.

Encountering a Cobra—Recommended Action

Given the blend of fear and reverence surrounding cobras, what should one actually do if they encounter one unexpectedly? Traditional advice, as our ancestors taught us, often suggests standing still or praying. From a safety and snake behaviour perspective, this holds some truth. Mr Whitaker confirms that standing still or slowly retreating while keeping an eye on the cobra are indeed best practices. The key is not to make the snake feel cornered or threatened. However, a crucial point often emphasized by experts is—if a cobra seems insistent on moving towards your location (likely because its retreat or hole is where you are standing), the wisest action may be to simply move away quickly. Humans may easily outrun a cobra, and the snake is not charging aggressively but probably trying to get to safety.

Ecological Role and Conservation

Beyond the layers of myth and the realities of venom, the Indian cobra plays a crucial ecological role that underscores the wisdom potentially embedded in ancient reverence. Cobras are vital predators, particularly effective in controlling rodent populations that damage crops and spread disease. As highlighted by conservationists, they thrive on pests like the Lesser Bandicoot rat in rice paddies, potentially consuming creatures responsible for destroying 20–30 per cent of grain stores. Their presence contributes significantly to the balance of the agricultural ecosystem.

Therefore, understanding the cobra requires moving beyond simplistic fear or romanticized myth. Recognizing its ecological importance provides a strong rationale for conservation and respectful coexistence. Perhaps, as Romulus Whitaker suggests, the rest of India can learn from regions like the village in Burdwan District, West Bengal, where communities have achieved a remarkable harmony with cobras, demonstrating that scientific understanding and deep-seated cultural respect can indeed replace fear-based myths.

Beyond Biology: The Enduring Divinity of the Naaga

However, even understanding the cobra's biology and ecological importance doesn't fully capture its significance in the Indian spiritual context. To view it merely as a reptile is to miss its sacred dimension. Across the subcontinent, it remains Naagadevata—a revered deity, a symbol of divine authority, embodying the eternal cycles of nature. The Naaga is a custodian of life, a force whose power transcends simple good and evil, representing cosmic balance. Celestial serpents are believed to command the monsoons, control fertility and dispense both blessings (prosperity, rain, progeny) and wrath (disease, drought, hailstorms). This enduring reverence, seeing divinity manifest in the serpent's tangible form, provides the foundation for the diverse practices of ophiolatry across India, which we are now ready to explore through its most iconic figures.

VI

The Cosmic Serpents—Naagaraja
Shesha and Vasuki

According to the scriptures, Ananta Shesha and Vasuki—two of Kadru's most illustrious sons—stood apart from the rest of their serpent kin. Shesha and Vasuki redefined their legacy—not as agents of chaos, but as cosmic serpents, embodiments of balance, endurance and celestial order. It is through their stories that the Indian serpent ceases to be merely an inhabitant of the netherworlds and instead becomes a pillar of the universe itself. While this chapter focuses on their prominent roles described in major scriptures, it's worth remembering that, like many figures in religious traditions, varying accounts and regional folktales offer further diverse perspectives on these powerful beings. In many Indian temples, the title Naagaraja (Serpent King) is often applied to either Ananta Shesha or Vasuki.

Ananta Shesha

Shesha, the eldest son of Kadru and Kashyapa, is revered as Adishesha or Ananta Shesha. Unlike his many brothers, who were marked by cruelty and malice, Shesha was repulsed by their malevolent actions, especially towards his cousin, Garuda, the noble son of Kashyapa through his aunt, Vinata. Disturbed by their unkindness and the discord it bred, Shesha chose to renounce his kin and the privileges of his lineage, seeking refuge in austere penance. Sustaining himself on air alone, he meditated in sacred places in the Himalayas, distancing himself from the darkness of his brothers.

In the Bhagavata Puraana, Lord Vishnu entrusts him with the responsibility of supporting *Bhoomandala*, the cosmic plane of existence. Naming him *Ananta*—the endless—Vishnu assures Shesha that he will bear the universe until the final syllable of Vishnu's thousand names (Sahasranaamam) is uttered.

Now, in Hindu cosmology, the genesis of creation begins with the *Hiranyagarbha*—the golden womb—floating in the primordial waters. From this cosmic egg, Vishnu reclines upon the infinite ocean, and from his navel, a lotus blooms, giving rise to Brahma, the creator. Brahma's emergence marks the birth of time and matter, as he constructs the heavens, the Earth, and all forms of life. But creation is not linear—it is cyclical. At the close of each *kalpa* (one day in the life of Brahma), the cosmos dissolves back into the void, awaiting its next rebirth.

Between these cycles of creation and dissolution rests Ananta Shesha—the endless serpent. His coiled form is both cradle and cornerstone, supporting the dormant universe like a bridge suspended over the abyss of non-being. Shesha embodies the eternal principle that survives beyond destruction—a symbol of continuity, stability and cosmic rhythm.

The Sanskrit root of his name, *shesha*—meaning 'that which remains'—reveals this essence. At the end of time, when galaxies are believed to be unmade and worlds collapse, it is Shesha who remains, coiled beneath the void, holding space for what is yet to come. According to Hindu scriptures, Adi-Shesha, the primordial remainder, is the first and last witness to the universe.

In Vaishnava tradition, Shesha is revered as the king of all Naagas, a thousand-headed serpent central to the very fabric of creation. Lord Vishnu rests on the coiled form of Ananta Shesha in the primordial waters of Vaikhuntha. When Vishnu incarnated as Raama, Shesha, the divine serpent who serves as Vishnu's constant companion, is believed to have taken birth as Lakshmana, Raama's devoted younger brother. In another of Vishnu's incarnations, as Krishna, Shesha was born as Balaraama, Krishna's elder brother. In both incarnations, Shesha's role was to provide unwavering support and protection to the divine incarnations of Vishnu, continuing his eternal bond with the God across different lifetimes.

The Shiva Puraana elevates Shesha to cosmic grandeur. He is described as a colossal being with a thousand radiant hoods, each bearing a jewel that shines like a sun. His coils are wrapped in garlands, his breath thick with divine fragrance. His eyes roll with the intoxication of eternal power. He is the mountain, the river, the fire and the void—an embodiment of paradox.

When time collapses at the end of a kalpa, it is Shesha's mouths that release the final flame, reducing the three worlds to ash before drawing the fire back into himself. Even the gods cannot comprehend his full form. In *Paataala*, he bears the weight of the world like a divine ploughman, holding both the ploughshare and the threshing rod—a guardian of life and a harbinger of endings. The ploughshare, a symbol of agriculture and sustenance, further connects Shesha with Balaraama, Krishna's elder brother. This association underlines the nurturing aspect of Shesha, who is believed to hold the universe as effortlessly as a farmer tends to the soil.

In modern interpretations, his thousand heads are sometimes seen as metaphors for the multiverse—each head holding a different universe, coiling through dimensions known and unknown.

Vasuki

Vasuki, one of the most revered and significant Naagas in Hindu tradition, is a central figure among the serpent deities that populate ancient Indian lore. According to the Vaayu Puraana, Vasuki resides on the Nishaadha mountain, where he presides as a chieftain of Naagaloka, the realm of serpents. In many accounts, he is depicted as the eldest son of Kadru, the progenitor of the Naagas, which emphasizes his prominent role within this mystical hierarchy.

Vasuki's most renowned appearance in Hindu Puraanas is his participation in the *Amrita Manthana*, the churning of the cosmic ocean, which was orchestrated by Devas and Asuras in their quest for amrita, the nectar of immortality. In this grand event, Vasuki was employed as the churning rope, coiled around Mount Mandara, which served as the churning rod. The Devas and Asuras pulled on Vasuki from either side, creating immense friction and releasing various treasures and eventually the coveted nectar. His involvement in this cosmic event underscores his immense strength and vital role in the universe's balance.

Vasuki has a special connection with Shaivite traditions. He is often depicted adorning Shiva's neck, coiled around him like a garland. This iconography represents Shiva's mastery over the natural world and his transcendence of fear and death. Vasuki here represents both the destructive and regenerative aspects of life, which are central to Shiva's identity.

In another fascinating narrative, Vasuki is identified as the serpent who heard the Vishnu Puraana from Dhritarashtra—another serpent, not to be confused with the Kaurava king of the Mahabharata. Vasuki, imbued with wisdom, later narrated this sacred text to Vatsa, demonstrating his role as a transmitter of divine knowledge. This aspect of Vasuki's legend underscores the importance of Naagas not only as powerful subterranean entities but also as keepers and conveyors of spiritual wisdom.

Vasuki is sometimes described as having a svastika on his head, a symbol that carries deep spiritual significance in Hinduism, representing auspiciousness and well-being (not to be confused with the German Hakenkreuz). In some Buddhist traditions, Vasuki is portrayed as a white serpent with a blue lotus on his head, an image that denotes purity, enlightenment and divine grace.

In Balinese mythology, there is a benevolent dragon deity called Naaga Besukih, who lived atop Mount Agung, known for his immense wealth and generosity. Those who pleased him were rewarded with countless treasures, reflecting his role as a guardian of prosperity. Besukih's character is vividly portrayed in the well-known tale of Manik Angkeran (which I have presented in the fourth part of this book).

Dual Pillars of Serpent Cosmology

Together, Shesha and Vasuki form the dual spine of serpent cosmology in Indian thought. If Shesha is the stillness beneath all things, the axis upon which time turns, Vasuki is the motion that catalyses change—churning, guiding, transmitting. One is the unshakeable support, the other the willing sacrifice. Both embody the sacred paradox of the Indian serpent—protector and destroyer, cosmic and earthly, silent and wise.

VII

Naagini–The Serpentine Feminine

The concept of the female serpent deity is one of the most intricate and captivating figures in South Asian traditions. Terms such as naagini, naagayakshi, naagakanya, naagi and naagin are often used interchangeably, yet each holds some unique resonances shaped by region, belief system and time. While all evoke the powerful image of the serpentine feminine, they inhabit distinct cosmologies—some local, some scriptural and some shaped by modern fantasy.

Across these diverse portrayals, the feminine serpent—sometimes depicted as a full-bodied woman, sometimes as a hybrid with a serpent's tail—depicts a bond with elemental forces—the earth, the water and the unseen realms. This deep connection often manifested in folklore, as Vogel notes, through rich tales of mortal men enticed by the allure of serpent women, often culminating in romance or marriage. Even Kalidasa, in his epic *Raghuvamsa*, couldn't resist this potent theme; he tells of Kusa, Raama's own son and heir, whose destiny became entwined with Kumudvati, the youngest sister of the Naagaraaja Kumuda, through marriage. Travel north to the mist-shrouded mountains, and Kalhana's *Rajatarangini* breathes life into a poignant Kashmiri legend—the whispered story of love igniting between Visakha and the ethereal

Chandralekha, fair daughter of the Naaga Susravas (Vogel, 1926, p. 34).

Oldham speculates these stories might reflect historical mingling between serpent-worshipping tribes and Aryan or Dravidian settlers—or perhaps they are simply projections of a deeper human fascination with the mystery and perceived power of the feminine divine or natural form.

Beyond these narrative speculations, the historical worship of serpent deities itself has ancient roots. There is no doubt that ophiolatry existed in India long before Buddhism spread widely. Before the ninth century, female serpent deities were often not portrayed in human-like forms but rather represented through simple, potent objects like earthen pots (perhaps representing the womb) or basic effigies made from stone and clay. It wasn't until around the ninth or tenth century that major sectarian traditions began personifying these snake goddesses more explicitly. In Hinduism, Manasa emerged in human form; in Jainism, it was Padmavati; and in Buddhism, Janguli took shape as the protector against snakebites (Shaw, 2006, p. 225).

Naagayakshi—Guardian of the Sacred Grove

In the southern states of India, particularly in Kerala and Tulunadu, the naagayakshi is a revered household deity often found enshrined within the cool, damp earth of serpent groves (sarpakaavus). These sacred spaces merge the worship of tree spirits (Yakshas) and serpent deities, forming a deeply ecological and spiritual tradition. Here, the naagayakshi is invoked as a maternal guardian—a protective presence watching over the family, the land and the ancestral order in exchange for shelter and ritual reverence.

While male serpents are identified as naagaraajas, the female serpent deity is worshipped under names like naagayakshi, naagamma or naagi. And yet, her specific identity often remains elusive. Although Vasuki and Ananta are frequently named as presiding deities in these groves, the naagayakshi herself—her precise origin, her individual story—can be uncertain.

I have often sought clarity on the true identity of the naagayakshi venerated in a specific family's serpent grove, yet the answer has frequently eluded me. Perhaps she was inspired by Puranic Manasa or the Jain figure Padmavati, or maybe she is a goddess whose distinct story has been lost to time, her origins blurred by centuries of cultural assimilation and shifting traditions. No conclusive answers have been given, for the nature of truth, especially concerning the divine, is often shrouded in layers of belief and memory. Perhaps only the ancient idols, standing watch through the ages, hold the key to these mysteries. The gods, after all, rarely reveal all their secrets, leaving us to ponder the intricate web of story and history surrounding their enigmatic forms.

Naagakanya—The Radiant Maidens of Paatala

The naagakanyas, or serpent maidens, are celestial beings described in the Shiva Puraana with skin like polished gold, radiant inhabitants of the subterranean realm of Paatala. They surround Ananta Shesha in constant veneration and are celebrated for their ethereal beauty and divine poise. Unlike naagayakshis, they may not be generally tied to specific groves or households but exist as part of a luminous, cosmic court.

Buddhist iconography adds an unexpected feature to these maidens—wings. These winged naagakanyas hover in the symbolic space between serpents (Naagas) and celestial birds (Suparnas like Garuda, traditionally their foes). The wings might represent a bridging of elements—earth and sky, water and air—or perhaps symbolize a deeper metaphysical transcendence. Their perpetual virginity is often emphasized in lore, adding to their otherworldly mystique.

Naagin—The Shapeshifter of the North

In north Indian folklore, naagins are typically conceived as ichchadhari beings—shape-shifting female serpents who can assume human form, often said to be attained after centuries of penance. These naagins are deeply embedded in the cultural imagination, portrayed as figures of formidable power, both dangerously fierce and deeply alluring. They are believed to revert to their serpent form at least once a day, even while living among humans.

While rooted in folk tradition, these tales mirror the inherent duality of the serpent woman—mystical yet mortal, ascetic yet seductive. They often appear in stories as powerful protectors of treasure (like the fabled naagamani) and potent agents of vengeance when wronged or betrayed. In a folktale from Maharashtra, we get to see the benevolent side of the naagin as well, which you will find in Part II - Chapter IV of this book, under the section, 'The Naagin and the Farmer'.

Corruption of Naagin

For most modern Indians, the word naagin conjures images not primarily from scripture or deep folklore, but from cinema—Sridevi in shimmering costumes, or stylized television heroines with glowing eyes and dramatic transformations. The female serpent has often become a melodramatic trope, primarily focused on vengeance, her sacred nuance stripped away, reduced to a simplified echo of her former power. These portrayals sometimes echo a broader pattern seen across world mythologies—the occasional vilification or simplification of figures embodying feminine power.

Like the Yakshas—once revered guardians of nature, later sometimes cast as demonic beings—the naagin too has, in some popular narratives, been subtly recast from a multifaceted divine protector or powerful spirit into a primarily seductive or vengeful threat. What was once a potent symbol of fertility, elemental balance, spiritual guardianship and righteous power has sometimes been flattened into a caricature.

However, this modern simplification contrasts sharply with older literary traditions, which often depicted more complex interactions. Pop culture has sometimes unwittingly contributed to the erosion of the sacred feminine aspect represented by the traditional naagin. But even within these modern tropes, if we look closely, a recurring pattern often emerges—it is frequently the sapera, the snake-charmer (reminds me of the late Amrish Puri in the iconic black robe)—driven by greed or ignorance—who disturbs the naagin's world, perhaps seeking the naagamani, the fabled jewel of wisdom and power. It is this act of intrusion, this disruption of balance, that often unleashes the naagin's fury. This trope arguably mirrors a deeper reality where human interference often disrupts the natural world, leading to retaliation, yet the blame in the story sometimes falls on the protector rather than the provocateur.

In essence, the serpentine feminine weaves through the lore of the Indian subcontinent in varied and powerful forms. She is the nurturing, place-bound guardian embodied by the naagayakshi, the radiant celestial maiden or naagakanya dwelling in otherworldly realms, and the formidable, shapeshifting naagin of folklore, embodying both allure and peril. While modern interpretations may sometimes overshadow their deeper significance, these figures collectively represent profound connections to nature, divinity, ancestral power and the complex mysteries of feminine energy. Having explored the concept of the serpentine feminine, we now turn to meet some of these powerful figures individually, including notable female serpent deities described in the Puraanas and related lore of the subcontinent.

VIII

A Pantheon of Serpents–Key Naaga Deities Across Traditions

As my journey into the world of serpent worship deepened, I realized that the Naagas weren't just a monolithic concept but a vast and diverse pantheon. These powerful, semi-divine serpent beings coil through Hindu, Jain and Buddhist traditions alike, their presence felt everywhere from the grand epics and Puranas to intimate local village tales. Getting acquainted with some of the most prominent figures felt essential to understanding the breadth and depth of this reverence.

Progenitors of the Serpent Race—Kadru and Surasa

In Hindu Puraanas, the origins of the serpent race are deeply entwined with two powerful maternal figures—Kadru and Surasa. Both are traditionally counted among the many wives of the sage Kashyapa, and both are venerated as progenitors of serpents, though their roles diverge across different texts.

Kadru, often depicted as a naagini of orangish hue, is best known as the mother of the Naagas. Said to be the daughter of Daksha, Kadru is also portrayed as the sister of Vinata, mother of Garuda. Their rivalry forms the basis for several traditional narratives, most famously the wager over the colour of the celestial horse Ucchaishravas, which led to Vinata's subjugation. This tale showcases Kadru's cunning and strategic mind, balancing her role as a nurturing mother with that of a shrewd matriarch.

Surasa, by contrast, occupies a more ambiguous space in puranic literature. Like Kadru, she is often described as a serpent and is sometimes identified as the mother of Rakshasas as well as serpents. The Aranya Kanda of Valmiki's Ramayana suggests that Naagas were born of Surasa, while Uragas emerged from Kadru. However, this distinction is contested across texts, further blurring the lines of their genealogies. Some traditions even propose that Krodhavaasa, another of Daksha's daughters, was Kashyapa's first wife, with Kadru and Surasa born from her, thus reclassifying them as sisters rather than spouses.

The Ashtanaagas—Eight Pillars of the Serpent Realm

Among Kadru's most illustrious offspring are the Ashtanaagas, or the eight principal serpents, who occupy a revered and fascinating space in Indian lore. These serpents—Vasuki, Takshaka, Karkotaka, Shankha, Kulika, Padma, Mahapadma and Ananta Shesha—are frequently invoked in the Puraanas and Hindu epics. All these great serpents should have two tongues and two arms and a hood with seven heads held over their human heads bearing on them gems (Rao, 1916, p. 557).

Takshaka

While Shesha and Vasuki usually wear the crown of Naagaraaja (King of Serpents), Takshaka also holds this title in some traditions. Unlike Shesha (linked to Vishnu) and Vasuki (linked to Shiva), Takshaka has a unique connection to Indra, king of the gods. This places Takshaka under the protection of the Vedic pantheon's most powerful deity and sets him somewhat apart. He made his home in the Khandava forest near the Yamuna River with his family, and Indra's fierce defence of this forest highlights their strong bond.

Takshaka steps dramatically onto the stage in the Mahabharata, playing the key role in the tragic death of King Parikshit, Arjuna's grandson. Fulfilling a sage's curse brought on by Parikshit's disrespect, Takshaka delivers the fatal bite. His presence isn't confined to the Mahabharata, though; he appears in various Puraanas and is known as Takshan or Tassan in south Indian languages. Interestingly, even today in Bihar, the beautiful ornate flying snake (Chrysopelea) is sometimes called Takshaknaag.

Karkotaka

Karkotaka holds a special place among the Naagas, particularly through his connection to the royal lineage of Kashmir. The powerful Karkota dynasty, which produced the great ruler Lalitaditya (founder of the Martand Sun Temple), proudly traced its ancestry back to this serpent king.

He's also a major figure in Nepal's lore. Legend holds that when Manjusri drained the Kathmandu valley, Karkotaka was the only Naaga who remained, dwelling in the great lake Tau-dahan. The Skanda Puraana brings him into the story of Kadru's curse upon her children; frightened by the curse, Karkotaka cleverly wrapped himself around the tail of the celestial horse Ucchaishravas to alter its appearance—a tale we'll explore more in the third part of this book.

Kulika

Kulika is depicted as a red-coloured serpent whose hood bears the mark of the crescent moon. His identification as Guliga in southwestern India is especially significant in the context of

Daivaaradhane (spirit worship), where Guliga serves as one of the most prominent guardian spirit deities. This association becomes even more intriguing when considering the etymology of the word 'Guliga'. During my research for *Daiva*, I encountered texts where some scholars suggest that Guliga may be derived from the Malayalam word for 'tablet', possibly referencing the shape of the deity's idol. Yet, it remains entirely plausible that these two figures—Guliga and Kulika—share a deeper, common origin, with their mythological identities converging as local and cosmic elements blend together over time.

Shamkha, Padma and Mahapadma

Shamkha, Padma and Mahapadma often step into the role of guardians, especially watching over wealth and treasure. Shamkha, also called Samkhapala, is sometimes depicted as a multi-headed, fiery serpent, powerful yet not necessarily malevolent. Iconographic texts like the *Mayasilpa* give him a yellow hue with a white streak on his hood, while a Jataka tale features a compassionate Naaga king named Samkhapala.

Padma is described with fittingly rosy colours, a white streak and coral adornments. He's sometimes linked to the north-west direction or said to dwell near Vasuki. Mahapadma (or Shankhapadma) is portrayed as white, bearing a trident mark on his hood. The *Nilamata Purana* specifically mentions a Naaga Mahapadma taking refuge with Nila Naaga after being attacked by Garuda.

Shamkha and Padma are named among Kubera's principal attendants. This role as lords of wealth likely eased their integration into Buddhist traditions outside India. In ancient Sri Lanka, for example, figures identified as Shamkha and Padma guarded the entrances to Buddhist shrines. Their presence suggests that even as people embraced Buddhism, they still sought worldly prosperity from these traditional guardians, who found a new role as revered gatekeepers in the Buddhist sacred space.

Naagas from the Puraanas and Regional Folklore

Beyond the progenitors and the well-known Ashtanaagas, the great epics and Puraanas are filled with other compelling serpents whose stories reveal much about their nature and interactions with gods and humans. The Mahabharata, for instance, specifically in the Udyoga Parva, highlights the sheer number of these beings when the sage Naarada recites an extensive list of prominent serpent names to Maatali, Indra's charioteer. Alongside these pan-Indian figures, there are also numerous Naaga deities who hold particular sway in specific regional traditions, deeply influencing local worship and folklore across the subcontinent. Let's explore some of these significant figures.

Ulupi

Ulupi, a captivating character in the Mahabharata, is a naagini who plays a pivotal role in Arjuna's epic journey. Appearing in her serpent form, she lures the hero into the depths of an underwater palace. Scholars like Wheeler theorize that Naagas could have been descendants of Scythians who migrated from Iran, intertwining the threads of history and myth (Wheeler, 1867, p. 148). This theory gains further intrigue when compared to Scythian mythology, where a similar figure named Drakaina Skythia is found. She is depicted as the first ruler of Scythia, a woman with the torso of a human and the tail of a serpent. Her myth parallels that of Ulupi. When the Greek hero Hercules journeyed through her land with the cattle of Geryon, Drakaina Skythia stole some of the herd and demanded that Hercules mate with her before returning them.

Their union gave rise to a line of Scythian kings, much like how Ulupi's union with Arjuna resulted in the birth of the serpent prince, Iravan.

Iravan

Iravan, a significant character from the Mahabharata, is the son of the Pandava prince Arjuna and Ulupi, connecting him to both heroic and Naaga lineages. He grew up in the realm of the Naagas with his mother but later reconnected with Arjuna, promising his aid in the great war to come. True to his word, Iravan arrived at Kurukshetra with celestial horses capable of trampling the enemy. In the Bhishma Parva of Mahabharata, Iravan is revered for his ultimate sacrifice during the Kurukshetra war, where he volunteers to give his life to secure victory for the Pandavas. He is the only one, after Krishna and Arjuna, who possessed all the thirty-two gunas or qualities.

In Tamil folklore, Iravan is venerated as Aravan. This legend is further enriched by a poignant narrative wherein the Pandavas sought divine intervention for their victory in the Kurukshetra war. They were instructed to offer a life in sacrifice to Goddess Kali. In response to this, Aravan selflessly volunteered. His final request was to experience the joys of marital life before his impending sacrifice.

Faced with the challenge of finding a bride for a man condemned to die the following day, Lord Krishna, ever the divine orchestrator, assumed the form of Mohini. In a miraculous and poignant twist, Krishna's guise enabled the marriage to take place overnight. With his wish fulfilled, Aravan met his fate the following day. This sacrifice, known as *Kalappali*, is dramatically re-enacted in traditional Therukoothu or Kattaikkuttu performances in Tamil Nadu.

This compelling tale has given rise to the Koovagam festival, an eighteen-day celebration that resonates deeply within the transgender community of Tamil Nadu. Held at the revered Koothandavar Temple in Koovagam village, the festival commemorates the symbolic marriage of Aravan and the subsequent mourning observed by transgender women, known as Aravanis.

During the festival, the ceremonial head of Aravan is hoisted on a post, reflecting his ability to witness the entire war through his severed head, as granted by Krishna. Aravan is worshipped in the form of his severed head, often depicted with a moustache, pronounced eyes, and a conical crown. His iconography frequently includes Vaishnava symbols and sometimes features a cobra hood or snakes, reflecting his Naaga heritage.

Kaaliya

Kaaliya, one of the serpents portrayed with a villainous character in the Puraanas, has an intriguing backstory that intertwines with divine blessings and curses. It is believed that in a previous life, Kaaliya was blessed by Vishnu, which ultimately led to his encounter with Krishna.

Legend goes that once upon a time, a sage named Vedashira, a descendant of Bhrigu, was performing austerities in the Vindhya Hills when another sage, Ashvashira, arrived to practice penance at Vedashira's ashrama.

Vedashira, with fiery eyes, confronted Ashvashira, demanding, 'Do not perform your austerities in my ashrama.'

Ashvashira, equally angered, retorted, 'This world belongs to Lord Vishnu, not to you or me, who are merely temporary guests in this material realm. Your anger is misplaced. You hiss like a snake.' In his fury, Ashvashira cursed Vedashira, saying, 'Become a snake! You shall live in fear of Garuda.'

Vedashira, not one to back down, responded, 'For such a minor offence, you seek such severe revenge. On this earth, you are like a crow. Fool, become a crow!'

Both sages' curses took effect until Vishnu intervened, consoling them. He acknowledged their devotion and declared, 'I could make my own words false, but I will not allow the words of my devotees to be in vain. Your curses shall stand. Vedashira, in another life, I will place my footprints on your head, ensuring that you never fear Garuda.' Turning to Ashvashira, Vishnu added, 'You will take the form of a crow but will possess transcendental knowledge, siddhis, and the highest wisdom in the three worlds.'

Thus, Vedashira became Kaaliya, the serpent in the Mahabharata, and Ashvashira transformed into Kaakabhushundi, who is said to have heard the Ramayana from Garuda. Kaaliya was born to Kadru, a connection that deepens his ties to the ancient lore.

In the Tulu region, researchers have uncovered a unique tribal dance ritual called Kaadyanaatta, which centres on a primitive serpent deity, a black cobra known as Kaadya. The name Kaadyanaatta is believed to have derived from Kaadya and Aatta (dance). This Kaadya may have its origins in the Puranic figure of Kaaliya, reflecting the deep cultural connections between puranic narratives and regional traditions.

Rahu and Ketu

The dramatic churning of the ocean (Samudra Manthana) for the nectar of immortality (amrita) gave birth to two other serpentine figures. The Asura Svarbhanu cleverly disguised himself as a Deva to sneak a drink of the amrita. But Surya (the sun) and Soma (the moon) spotted him and alerted Vishnu (in his enchanting Mohini form). Vishnu hurled his discus, severing Svarbhanu's head. Because of the nectar, however, both parts remained immortal—the head, growing a serpent's tail, became Rahu; the body, sprouting a serpent's head, became Ketu. Forever separated, these two parts of one being are eternally in conflict.

As two of the nine Navagraha (celestial bodies believed to influence destiny), Rahu and Ketu wield serpentine power over human lives. Rahu, the head, still nursing his grudge against the sun and moon, perpetually tries to swallow them, was believed to cause eclipses. Ketu, the body or tail, represents a force guiding towards spiritual detachment and liberation from worldly desires. Buddhist stories also feature Rahu attempting to devour the sun or moon, only to be calmly commanded by the Buddha to release them. In astrology, an unfavourable placement of Rahu and Ketu is associated with the affliction known as Kaal Sarpa Dosha. Even in kola and theyyam traditions of Tulunadu and Kerala, Rahu figures as an important deity, sometimes known as Rahuguliga.

Nila Naaga

No discussion of Kashmiri Naagas would be complete without mentioning Nila (pronounced as Nee-la) Naaga, the central figure in the region's serpent lore. According to the Nilamata Purana, which derives its name and core teachings from him, Nila was the chief king of the Naagas who originally inhabited the Kashmir valley when it was the primordial lake of Satisaras. He played a crucial role in the valley's origin story, interceding with the gods to make the land habitable and later negotiating the terms for permanent human settlement alongside the Naagas. Revered as the primary guardian of Kashmir, Nila Naaga was specifically worshipped in various rituals, such as during the first snowfall, embodying the deep connection between serpent deities and the land itself.

Manasa

I've always been fascinated by mother goddesses in folklore and sacred narratives, and Manasa is one who draws me in, urging me to understand her deeper. She's not an elusive naagini, hidden in shadows, but rather a figure of persuasion, embodying both power and grace. Her story demands attention, like the legend of Kannaki in my hometown.

Manasa is a Hindu goddess of snakes, revered primarily for her role in preventing and curing snakebites, as well as for bestowing fertility and prosperity. Worshipped predominantly in Bihar, Bengal, Jharkhand, south Assam and parts of north-eastern India, she holds particular significance in rural communities, where snakebites are a real threat.

In Puranic accounts, she is the sister of the serpent kings Shesha and Vasuki and the wife of sage Jaratkaaru. Manasa is also the mother of the sage Astika who plays a crucial role in the Mahabharata, famously intervening to save the Naaga race from King Janamejaya's great snake sacrifice (sarpasatra), a story we will delve into in Part 3 of this book. She is often called Vishahari, meaning 'the destroyer of poison'.

I must clarify that there are two distinct origin stories for Manasa. One account, found in the Mahabharata, describes her as a creation of Kashyapa, born from his mind as an antidote for venom. In contrast, another narrative portrays Manasa as the daughter of Shiva, born when Shiva's semen fell onto a lotus leaf in Vasuki's kingdom. A further legend tells of a sculptor who carved a statue of a girl at the behest of Vasuki's mother. When Shiva touched the statue, it transformed into Manasa, whom Vasuki accepted as his sister (Rhyzakova, 2020, p. 33).

Now, it is difficult to say which version is definitive, but these are the stories that have been passed down. Some scholars suggest that Manasa was originally a local deity, who was gradually side-lined as Shiva's influence grew in the region. The folktale of Behula and Lokhindar (Lakshmindra), which illustrates Manasa's fierce determination to gain recognition from a devout follower of Shiva, reflects this tension. You can find this story in the fourth part of this book.

In some places, Manasa is also known as Padmavati. Brahmani, linking her to Brahma, is another of Manasa's names. Ketaka, Totola, Jaguli or Janguli, Jagati and Jagatgauri, are some of her other names, but their usage is restricted to one or another region (Haq, 2015, p. 47).

Celestial Serpents in Cross-Cultural Lore

Beyond Hinduism, these serpent figures also extend their influence into Buddhist and Jain mythology. In Buddhist beliefs, much like the Ashtanaagas in Hindu Puraanas, there is a similar pantheon of eight great dragon kings said to exist, living deep within the oceans. These dragon kings—Nanda, Upananda, Sagara, Vasuki, Takshaka, Anavatapta, Manasvin and Utpalaka—share striking parallels with their Hindu counterparts. Legends surrounding figures like Naagarjuna, the renowned Buddhist philosopher said to have retrieved sacred texts guarded by Naagas in their underwater realm, further underscore the role of these beings as keepers of profound wisdom within Buddhist tradition. This overlap points to a shared cultural heritage, where the mighty serpents transcend geography and time, weaving through different belief systems.

In Tibetan Buddhism, these Ashtanaagas are referred to by various titles, such as Naagaraaja, Naagesa, Naagendra and Bhujagesa, each name carrying the weight of their divine status. According to Luipada's *Smasanavidhi*, they are adorned with white ornaments, signifying their celestial nature, and depicted with human torsos, coiled serpent tails, and crowned with cobra hoods bearing distinct markings and colours. These dragon-serpent figures reflect ancient cultural exchanges and the common reverence for serpents as symbols of power, mystery and protection. Let us now look at some prominent serpent deities from Buddhist and Jain traditions.

Elapatra

Elapatra (also Erakapatta) is a significant Naaga king featured prominently in Buddhist stories. He was a monk in his previous life who, due to the minor, unconfessed transgression of tearing an *eraka* (cardamom) leaf, was reborn as a mighty Naaga. Longing for the appearance of the next Buddha, Elapatra devised a riddle, proclaimed by his daughter, knowing only a Buddha could solve it. Eventually, Shakyamuni Buddha revealed the answer to a young brahmin, allowing Elapatra to recognize the enlightened one and receive his teachings. Elapatra is also mentioned in the Mahabharata as having advised Vasuki on how the Naagas could be saved from Janamejaya's sacrifice, linking him to Astika's birth.

Janguli

Janguli is one of the most unique deities in the Mahayana Buddhist tradition, known primarily for her role in protecting people from snakebites and granting immunity to poison. In ancient Buddhist practice, killing snakes was forbidden, so instead of harming these creatures, monks and followers relied on rituals, mantras and prayers to keep themselves safe. Janguli's name reflects her special connection with snakes who live in the 'jangal' or jungle.

She is often depicted holding a snake, representing her control and mastery over the serpentine world. Janguli has a 'poisonous kiss' and a 'poisonous glance', but these traits are not meant to harm. Instead, they represent her immunity to poison and her ability to grant this same protection to others. Her power over poison is symbolized by the nectar she pours from a pitcher, which has the ability to neutralize deadly venom.

In rituals, this nectar is sometimes compared to water blessed through mantras, used to treat snakebites. Janguli, through her association with both poison and healing, plays the role of a guardian, offering safety to those who seek her help against the dangers of snakes (Shaw, 2006, p. 224).

Janguli is typically portrayed as a sixteen-year-old girl with a green body, depicting her youthful vitality and connection to the trees of the forest. She is shown with four arms and seven snakes crowning her head, representing her close association with serpents. In her upper right hand, she holds a trident, or trishula. In the same hand, she grasps a snake.

Her upper-left hand holds a peacock feather, which signifies her power to cure snake bites and neutralize poison, much like how the peacock consumes snakes despite of them being venomous. Her lower left hand is shown in the gesture of granting boons, reflecting her readiness to offer protection and antidotes to those afflicted by snake-related dangers.

Janguli is sometimes depicted with different body colours, such as green, yellow or white, and carrying various symbols depending on the tradition. These diverse forms all highlight her role as a protector, offering her divine intervention against snakebites and poison across different Buddhist traditions (Rinpoche, 2016).

Apalala

Apalala, a dragon serpent, is associated with the region of Magadha. Originally a brahmin, he took the form of a serpent after being angered by losing the people's offerings, which were once given to him for subduing a destructive dragon-serpent named Sundara. When the Buddha arrived in Rajagriha, his presence neutralized

Sundara's destructive powers, leading the people to stop rewarding the brahmin. In retaliation, the brahmin vowed to become a dragon-serpent, along with his family, and began ravaging crops, leaving only straw, earning him the name Palala, meaning 'without straw' (Vogel, 1926, p. 121).

Muchalinda

In Buddhist tradition, Muchalinda or Mucilinda is revered as the Naagaraja, the serpent king who protected the Buddha during a pivotal moment of his enlightenment. After Siddhartha Gautama had attained enlightenment beneath the Bodhi tree, a fierce storm began to unleash torrential rains. Muchalinda, emerging from the depths of the earth, coiled his immense body around the meditating Buddha, shielding him from the downpour. With his multi-hooded form spread wide like an umbrella, Muchalinda provided shelter for seven days, ensuring the Buddha remained undisturbed until the storm passed.

Naagaraaja Dharanendra

In Jain traditions, Naagaraaja Dharanendra emerges as a revered serpent deity, closely linked to the esteemed twenty-third Tirthankara, Parshvanatha. Dharanendra, the formidable king of the Naagas, is immortalized in Jain tradition for a similar gallant act of protection. When Parshvanatha was deep in meditation, a malevolent ascetic named Kamath conjured a torrential storm to disrupt him. Responding to the Tirthankara's plight, Dharanendra is said to have emerged magnificently from the earth, unfurling his numerous hoods like a vast canopy to shield Parshvanatha from the relentless downpour. This selfless act of devotion highlights the nurturing and protective essence attributed to the Naagas within Jain belief.

Padmavati

Padmavati, a revered naagayakshini and the divine consort of Dharanendra, holds a significant position as a guardian goddess within Jain tradition. In iconography, she is depicted with a snake's hood gracefully covering her head, seated upon a blossoming lotus flower. A small image of Parshvanatha is often nestled within her crown, reinforcing her connection to the twenty-third Tirthankara. Frequently shown as four-armed, Padmavati carries a noose, a rosary (japamaala), an elephant goad, a lotus and a fruit, each symbolizing various aspects of her divine attributes. Her vaahana, or mount, is the rooster, further enhancing her unique character.

Ultimately, the protective impulse embodied by serpents towards figures of immense spiritual significance reveals a striking consistency. Just as Muchalinda sheltered the Buddha and Dharanendra shielded Parshvanatha, we witness a powerful parallel in the well-known account of Ananta Shesha forming a protective canopy over the infant Krishna during his perilous river crossing. This shared motif across Hindu, Jain and Buddhist traditions underscores a deep-seated reverence for serpents as divine guardians within the subcontinent. This particular depiction of a hooded serpent safeguarding a deity is, therefore, a crucial piece of Naaga iconography, evident in temples and serpent idols throughout the region. In the next chapter, we will explore the diverse range of Naaga iconography found across the subcontinent, with this significant motif of the hooded serpent protecting a deity—as seen in the examples of Muchalinda, Dharanendra and Ananta Shesha—serving as a key point of discussion and comparison within that broader visual landscape.

IX

Naaga Iconography

The serpent is not merely an animal but an archetype in Indian culture—found in temple sculptures, intricate floor designs known as *kolam*, and even in dancers' crowns in the ritual performances of the south like Kola and Theyyam. Far from mere decoration, Naagas embody divine protection, and their hooded heads resonate across Hindu, Jain, Buddhist and folk traditions. From Shiva's serpentine ornaments to the protective canopy over Vishnu, from ancient stupas to modern *kaavus*, Naaga iconography bridges nature and divinity, inviting devotees into a timeless dialogue with the sacred.

Scriptural Depictions

Although representations exhibit variability, specific iconographic prescriptions are detailed in some ancient textual sources. The *Amsumadbhedagama*, for example, delineates the characteristics of Naagadeva, presumably the principal Naaga figure. This deity is described as possessing a comely, red-hued countenance, three eyes, and four arms. Embellished with a karanda-makuta (crown) and various other adornments, the figure is situated upon a padmapeetha (lotus pedestal). The anterior hands are represented in the varada (boon-granting) and abhaya (fear-dispelling) mudras, whereas the posterior hands each grasp a serpent. Furthermore, a pentacephalous, or five-headed, cobra hood provides shelter above the Naagaraaja's head, and the figure is attired in white.

The *Silparatna* adds that Naagas are often depicted therianthropically—human above the navel, serpentine below—with one, three, five or seven hoods, bifurcated tongues, and sometimes carrying a sword and shield. Regarding the Naagini, variations exist wherein a crown may be absent, and the number of hoods might be limited to approximately three (Rao, 1916, p. 556).

The Serpentine Hood—A Defining Motif

Perhaps the most central and recognizable element in Naaga iconography is the serpentine hood, often signifying divine kingship and protection across traditions. This is a very popular way to represent Vishnu in my part of the country. I was born in the temple town of Tripunithura (Cochin), in a hospital just a stone's throw from the revered Poornathreyeesha temple. Here, the main deity is 'Santhaanagopala Moorthy', a form of Lord Vishnu celebrated for his protection of infants. Legend holds that Lord Vishnu presented the idol of Poornathreyeesha to Arjuna when he sought divine intervention to revive the ten dead babies of a brahmin. At this ancient temple, the idol of Vishnu sits upon the coiled form of Ananta, its five hoods forming a protective canopy over Santhaanagopala Vishnu's head. If we travel further south to the capital of Kerala, Thiruvananthapuram, we come to the royal temple of Shri Anantapadmanaabha Swamy. The name of the town is connected with the story of the origin of this temple, which is venerated as one of great antiquity.

According to one legend, the site of the temple was once believed to be a wild, jungle-covered plain amidst which a couple lived, earning their living by cultivating a small paddy field. One day, while the wife was working in the field, she heard a cry and discovered a beautiful baby whom she dared not touch, deeming it to be divine. She fed the child and laid him in the shade of a tree. As soon as she left, a five-headed cobra placed the child in a hole in the tree and spread its hood to provide shelter from the sun. This child was believed to be an incarnation of Lord Vishnu (Hatch, 1933, p. 171).

Thiruvananthapuram literally means Thiru (Sri—sacred), Ananta (the great serpent Shesha), and puram (place), or the sacred place of the serpent Ananta. At the ancient temple here, Vishnu is depicted in his Anantashayanam posture, and the idol is a massive, 18-foot-long figure reclining on Ananta Shesha.

Such depictions featuring a deity adorned in royal attire and shielded by the elegant arches of serpent hoods represent a common theme. This striking imagery evokes the likeness of iconic figures like the Jain Tirthankara Parshvanatha, safeguarded by the multi-hooded serpent Dharanendra, or the Buddha, protected by the five-headed Muchalinda—images encountered in the previous chapter. In these moments, one cannot help but feel the profound connections woven through time and tradition, where serpentine guardians stand watch over the divine and the sacred. In Kerala, this serpent iconography permeates sacred groves known as kaavus, where stone idols called naagakallu are dedicated to serpent deities like Naagaraaja, Naagayakshi, Sarpayakshi, Sarpachaamundi and Ananta. These stone idols serve as protectors and embodiments of divine energy, and similar representations can be found in Tulunadu, reflecting a shared spiritual heritage.

Serpentine Ornaments

Beyond serving as protectors, Naagas also feature prominently as adornments for deities, signifying their connection to primal forces.

Ganapathy or Ganesha may be depicted as wearing a serpent around his waist. The story goes that Lord Ganesha, returning from a feast with a very full belly of Modaka (a sweet), tumbled from Mooshak, his mouse-mount, when it was startled by a snake, causing his stomach to burst open. As Ganesha gathered the spilled sweets, Chandra, the Moon God, arrogantly mocked his appearance. Infuriated, Ganesha cursed the Moon to lose its light and, in some versions, threw his tusk at it. Upon Chandra's repentant pleas, Ganesha modified the curse, decreeing that the Moon would henceforth wax and wane, creating its monthly phases. Often, it's said Ganesha then used the snake that caused the mishap to tie around his own belly.

In the Skanda Puraana, serpent symbolism comes alive in the depiction of Lord Shiva, seated in meditation and surrounded by his bhuta-ganas. In these texts, he is depicted as adorned with various serpents as his bodily ornaments. Shiva wears Vasuki, the king of serpents, as a naaga-yajnyopaveetam (sacred thread), while the serpents Kambala and Ashvatara drape his chest. Karkotaka forms his earrings, Pulaha wraps his arms like bangles, and his ankles gleam with Shamkha and Padma. This intricate serpent imagery captures Shiva as an embodiment of primal energy and mysticism, entwined with serpentine power.

Vyaalimukham

Naaga influence also extends into architectural motifs. I remember my father taking me to a temple in Kannur when I was a child—though the exact name escapes me now. A stone carving of a fierce, beastly face caught my eye, and when I asked my father, he introduced me to the concept of Vyaalimukham—the 'beast face' or 'serpent face'. This motif, deeply embedded in the temple architecture of southern India, merges the forms of beasts and serpents, suggesting a symbolic bond between them. The vyaali or yaali, as he described it, was a mythical creature with immense power. In its iconography, the yaali has a sleek, cat-like body, the head of a lion, tusks reminiscent of an elephant, and a serpent-like tail. To an untrained eye, some of these carvings might resemble dragons, hinting at ancient visual connections across cultures that are echoed elsewhere.

Serpent Elements in Buddhism

Naagas in Buddhist lore are frequently described as 'water spirits with human forms adorned with serpent crowns' or 'snake-like entities controlling the clouds', embodying a mystical connection with nature, water and the celestial.

Among the eight classes of deities who protect and revere the Historical Buddha, Naagas play a crucial role. The chronicles of ancient Chinese pilgrims recount a fascinating ritual in the storied city of Takshasila. When the inhabitants sought rain or fair weather, they would journey with Buddhist priests to the sacred tank of the Naagaraaja Elapatra. Here, in the shade of stupas and amidst the incense of prayer, they offered their supplications to the serpent king. Remarkably, it is said that their wishes were swiftly granted—whether for rainfall or clear skies—as if the very forces of nature bent to the will of this revered deity.

Interestingly, archaeological and epigraphical evidence indicates that Buddhists often established their monasteries and worshipped at sacred sites already associated with Naaga deities. Instead of eliminating or diminishing the Naagas, these serpentine beings were incorporated into Buddhist cosmology. However, in this new context, Naagas were often depicted as subservient to the Buddha, now cast as protectors and vassals of the Buddha rather than objects of direct worship themselves. Their presence, while significant, became more ornamental than central, reflecting a process of assimilation and subjugation where ancient beliefs were integrated yet subtly transformed to fit within the Buddhist worldview. This delicate balance reveals how Buddhism both revered and redefined the role of Naagas, maintaining their mystical power while reorienting their spiritual significance.

Naagas as Dragons

As Buddhist concepts and texts journeyed across Asia, the iconography and understanding of Naagas underwent further transformation. When translated into Chinese, for instance, the term 'naaga' may have become 'long', or dragon. In Chinese tradition, dragons were revered as guardians of Buddhism, often depicted as benevolent beings associated with rain, wealth and good fortune, capable of shapeshifting—characteristics strongly paralleling their Indian Naaga counterparts. Their mythical adversaries even included the bird-man Karura, an echo of the Naagas' traditional foe, Garuda. An anecdote recorded by the pilgrim Fa-Hien tells of a white-eared dragon serpent revered as a patron by monks in Sankassa, ritually honoured each year. Interestingly, this dragon was believed to be responsible for rain and at the end of every season, it would turn into a tiny snake with two white edges over the hood (Legge, 1971, p. 52).

Beyond Ornament—The Deeper Meaning of Naaga Iconography

For devotees encountering these serpent figures at religious sites, scholarly discussions of power dynamics—such as the subjugation or assimilation of these ancient deities—often fade into the background. What stands out instead is the potency of these serpentine forms. Their presence visually connects the viewer to nature, while also signalling the sanctity of the site, a sacred space where devotion would bear fruit. In the early Buddhist stupas, where the Buddha was absent in anthropomorphic form, it was the enigmatic presence of Naagas—serpentine deities from an ancient, more primal belief system—that served as a tangible connection to the divine.

Or consider the case of Shiva, around whose blue neck Vasuki winds himself like a sacred ornament. Were these serpentine beings mere attendants, decorative fixtures in the presence of figures of immense spiritual significance like Shiva on the icy Himalayan peaks, or the Buddha seated beneath the bodhi tree? Indeed, the very presence of these powerful, potentially dangerous beings serving as protectors or companions arguably enhances the aura of veneration surrounding the central figures; if such primal forces offer reverence, it underscores the immense spiritual authority of the deity they attend.

However, the answer, it seems, is simpler yet far deeper. Naagas, with their coiled bodies and hooded heads, were far more than just ornamental figures; they represented primal forces as guardians of sacred spaces and symbols of sanctity. Their silent, watchful gaze at these holy sites imbued the places with a spiritual gravitas, making the unseen forces of divinity almost palpable to the common devotee. It was as if the very elements of nature, embodied in these serpents, had aligned themselves in reverence to the higher powers at work.

This intricate fusion of natural forces and divine kingship reveals how Naagas transcended their original role, becoming embodiments of both spiritual guardianship and cosmic authority. Whether depicted standing tall, adorned in royal regalia beneath a canopy of serpent hoods, or coiled protectively around a deity, their imagery resonates across geographies and religious traditions. From the sacred serpent groves of the southwest coast of India to the towering temples of Nepal, from the stony remnants of Mathura to the pagodas of Japan, the Naagas endure—silent and eternal—reminding us of an ancient, forgotten world that still hums beneath the surface of the faiths that followed. Beyond their visual representation as protectors and symbols of sanctity, Naaga lore is also rich with tales of their connection to hidden wisdom and earthly treasures—mysteries we will explore next.

X

Naagamani and the Guardians of Treasure

It was late in the summer of 1897 when an English scholar with a fascination for local legends, arrived in some remote village in Farukhabad, Uttar Pradesh. The land, bathed in the thick, unrelenting heat of northern India, sprawled with ancient mounds and ruins, remnants of long-forgotten civilizations. The Englishman had heard of one such termite mound from passing travellers—an odd, desolate rise of earth that the locals avoided with an almost superstitious dread.

Curiosity piqued, he decided to investigate.

One afternoon, he found himself seated in the shade of a neem tree, speaking with a weathered old villager whose face bore the lines of many seasons under the harsh sun. The Englishman inquired in the local dialect about the strange mound, casually at first, hoping to elicit the old man's knowledge of its history.

At first, the villager remained silent, merely shaking his head and muttering under his breath. But the Englishman persisted, pressing gently for details, until the man—perhaps swayed by the foreigner's relentless questioning or perhaps relieved to share the burden of an old story—finally spoke.

'They say,' the villager began, his voice barely above a whisper, 'that beneath the mound lies a palace from a time long forgotten, buried deep in the earth. It is filled with treasures, more gold than a man can dream of. But no one dares to go near.'

The Englishman leaned forward, intrigued. 'Why not?' he asked, expecting some tale of curses or wrathful gods.

The old man's eyes grew wide. 'Because it is guarded,' he said. 'Guarded by the Cobra King.'

'A king cobra, you mean?'

The villager nodded solemnly. 'No, not king cobra. He is the king of all cobras, Naagaraaja. He lives within the mound, waiting for those foolish enough to dig for the treasure. There was once a man, years ago, who thought himself brave enough to claim the wealth buried below. He took his shovel one night, when the village slept, and he began to dig.'

The Englishman felt the hair on the back of his neck prickle as the story unfolded.

'The man dug for hours,' the villager continued. 'He toiled through the night, deeper and deeper into the earth, eager to find the gold. But as he returned to his home, satisfied with his progress, he was unaware that he had awakened the Naagaraaja.'

The villager's voice grew softer, his gaze distant, as though the memory of that night still haunted the village.

'At midnight, the Naagaraaja emerged from the mound, his army of serpents at his side. They slithered silently through the village, their eyes glowing in the darkness. They surrounded the house of the man who had dared to disturb their treasure. And before dawn, they struck. The man was found dead in his bed, his body cold, his face twisted in terror, and the marks of the snakes' fangs all over him.'

The Englishman remained silent, taking in the vivid image conjured by the villager's words. The old man shifted uncomfortably, casting a wary glance toward the distant mound.

'They say the Naagaraaja still guards the treasure,' the villager murmured. 'He and his army haunt the strange trees around the mound, watching, waiting. No one has dared go near it since.'

Naagas emerge as spiritual guardians of hidden treasures in Indian folklore. These serpentine figures inhabit a space between the mortal realm and the supernatural, vigilantly safeguarding hoards of wealth buried deep within the earth, often in remote or sacred locales. The motif of snakes as treasure-keepers weaves through countless folktales, with serpents fiercely defending their riches, refusing to yield without a fierce struggle. The imagery of a female cobra protecting its eggs comes to mind here.

Consider the tales from the *Panchatantra*. In one, a prince suffering from a mysterious ailment (revealed to be a snake dwelling within him) is saved when his wife overhears two serpents conversing—one inside the prince, the other guarding treasure beneath an anthill. Their dialogue reveals the cures—cumin and mustard soup for the internal snake, hot oil for the anthill guardian. By applying this overheard wisdom, the wife heals her husband and secures the hidden wealth. Another tale, set in Bhinmal, echoes this—a king tormented by an internal snake is saved when a clever clerk eavesdrops on its conversation with a treasure-guarding serpent at the town gate, learning the remedies needed to expel the first and defeat the second to claim the riches.

In these narratives, Naagas transcend mere protectors of wealth; they embody the mystical forces that govern fate and fortune. Their treasures are not easily accessible, demanding intelligence, perseverance, and often a touch of divine insight to obtain. This complexity is echoed in the Balinese origin story of Naaga Besukih (Vasuki) and Manik Angkaren. Legend holds that the Padmanabhaswamy temple's immense wealth, stored in underground vaults, is divinely protected. When state officials attempted to access these funds some hundred years ago, their torchlit descent revealed the vaults were infested with guardian cobras. The terrified men fled, convinced the serpents were placed by the gods to safeguard the treasure against appropriation (Hatch, 1933, p. 173).

W. Crooke, in his *Religion and Folklore of Northern India*, recounts an intriguing incident involving two elderly women living in adjoining houses. They formally requested that a wall separating their houses be excavated, claiming to have heard a treasure-guardian snake imploring for someone to relieve it of the treasure it protected. Despite digging up the wall, no treasure was found. It was later explained that this particular snake, capable of transforming every hundred years into a man or a bull, had likely vanished along with its hoard due to the disturbance.

Crooke also notes of snake-charmers reputed to possess the ability to identify such serpents who guarded treasures. These charmers would stealthily follow the snakes back to their burrows, compelling them to reveal hidden treasures. According to the folk beliefs, the serpents would only agree to disclose their riches on the condition of receiving a drop of blood from the little finger of a first-born son. Such tales abound in old Indian folklore, reflecting the mystical and elusive nature of these treasure-guardian snakes, eternally entwined with the mysteries of wealth and knowledge that lie beneath the surface of both the physical and metaphysical realms.

Naagamani

Among treasures, there is one that almost every Indian must have heard at least once in their lifetime, either through movies or from their grandparents—the naagamani. It is sometimes also known as nagina or phaniratnam as well. It is a gem of inestimable worth and power, said to emerge on the hood of a rare male cobra during the moment of mating. This luminous stone is thought to draw fortune and prestige to its bearer, and those who come into possession of it are said to be impervious to the lethal venom of any serpent. In some regional folklore, it is believed that the naagamani is hidden deep within an anthill, fiercely protected by a Naaga, often depicted as spitting fire. The fire-spitting serpent reminds me of the dragon.

Radiance of the Naagamani

It seems there is no corner of this vast country whose folklore does not extol the mystique and allure of the serpentine stone. The naagamani appears in various regional traditions, including the folklore of Kerala, as seen in the story of the Namboothiri from Pambumekattu Mana (a detailed account of which can be found in the fourth part of this book). I recall a Bengali folktale from my childhood, where a king's son and his minister cleverly gain possession of a brilliant naagamani concealed in the hood of a monstrous cobra. To obscure its gleaming radiance from the serpent and successfully claim it, they shrewdly cover the gem with horse-dung.

This naagamani or hood-jewel, known for its extraordinary radiance, plays a pivotal role in such folklore. There's one in which its radiance guides the hero on his journey to a palace where a silver-jewelled tree can be found.

In the olden times, some even believed that the rainbow was

created by the resplendent jewel on the serpent's head. Legends whispered that if one were to reach the place 'where the rainbow ends' and dig at the nearest anthill, treasure awaits—provided, of course, one can withstand the wrath of the guardian serpent. According to some beliefs, especially in the south, the naagamani appears on the serpent when it is mating with a naagini in their serpentine forms.

A late uncle once shared with me an ancient tale about the naagamani, one he had heard from his great-grandmother in his youth—though, of course, it was the tale, not the gem itself, that had been passed down. He spoke of the serpents that protected gold coins and hidden treasures, who would exhale their fertile breath over a stone of gold for so long that it became enveloped in their very essence, transforming it into the naagamani. Once their task was complete, the serpent would grow wings and take flight, carrying the precious stone. Thus, in the distant past, people linked this serpent, its radiant stone and wings with the appearance of comets streaking across the sky. Every time a comet appeared; they believed it was the serpent soaring through the heavens with its coveted gem. Now, this image of a winged serpent may be born of vivid imagination, but when I picture it in my mind, I am reminded of the imagery of naagakanya, the winged serpent-maiden.

Miracles of the Naagamani

Beyond these specific tales, the naagamani is revered as a potent amulet, capable of fulfilling one's deepest desires. It is often equated with the philosopher's stone or 'paras pathar' too. Its power is believed to be so vast that it can part waters, allowing a person to cross rivers without getting wet. This legendary jewel, deeply tied to the Naagas, exemplifies the transformative power and allure of treasure-guardian serpents in Indian folklore and tradition. There is so much power associated with this jewel that it was believed to cure any illness or even bring back the dead.

In a south Indian folktale, which also has a variant in Sri Lanka, a Naaga—typically known for guarding treasures—willingly grants his naagamani to a king as a token of gratitude for his kindness. Unlike other tales, where the jewel is obtained through deception or struggle, this story highlights the Naaga's benevolent nature, offering the coveted naagamani willingly as a gesture of goodwill. This act emphasizes a different portrayal of Naagas, not just as vicious protectors of hidden wealth but as beings capable of compassion and generosity. You can find this story in the fourth part of the book, where it sheds light on the more benevolent aspects of serpent lore in south Indian traditions.

According to our folklore, once the naagamani is taken, the Naaga guarding it perishes, sacrificing itself for the precious stone. Driven by greed, people in ancient times would watch cobras during mating seasons, hoping to seize the coveted gem when it was said to appear on the snake. Tragically, many of these individuals were bitten in their attempts, succumbing swiftly to venomous bites, their deaths marked by frothing at the mouth and violent convulsions. In other instances, people even went so far as to kill the cobra in their desperate pursuit of the stone.

The Tragedy of Cobra Poaching

In modern times, cobra poaching has taken on a different, yet equally cruel form. It may not always be for the naagamani, but it could be for illegal reasons or plain 'entertainment'. Snake charming, long associated with tradition and religious reverence in India, continues to be practiced, but the underlying reality is far darker than the enchanting spectacle many associate with it. Unlike the conservation efforts in sacred groves of southern India where

Naagas are venerated and protected, snake charmers may actually exploit this cultural reverence to profit from the suffering of the cobras they display.

These cobras, often poached from the wild, endure unspeakable brutality. Their fangs may have been crudely crushed using metal pliers, and in many cases, their venom glands may be painfully gouged out or punctured. In most cases defanging and venom gland removal are death sentences for the cobra though it may live for months or occasionally even years. As I mentioned in Chapter V, Cobras need their venom for digestion, and without it, they are unable to process their food properly, leading to prolonged suffering and death by starvation.

This inhumane treatment is not only unethical but stands in clear violation of the Prevention of Cruelty to Animals Act, 1960, which expressly prohibits the needless infliction of pain or suffering on animals. Yet, despite these legal safeguards, the abuse of cobras persists, in the guise of tradition. It is vital to bring to light the grim reality behind snake hunting, encouraging people to acknowledge the cruelty involved and urging law enforcement to take decisive action against these unlawful practices.

As you will discover in a later chapter, our ancestors, with their profound understanding of the natural world, urged us to venerate the cobra. They passed down strict instructions—if ever you encounter a cobra, do nothing to provoke it, simply let it pass. The wisdom here is clear—Hinduism, with its deep reverence for life, forbids the killing of a cobra, seeing the snake as both a protector and a divine being. Yet, the modern world may have little regard for such ancient teachings. Greed has replaced reverence, and poachers, driven by profit, show no hesitation in defiling these sacred beings.

Cobras are not their only victims. Snakes like the red sand boa, valued for their supposed mystical properties, are also captured and sold, smuggled across borders to places like China, where snake meat fetches a high price. The delicate balance between man and nature, once nurtured through centuries of ritual and respect, is being eroded by those whose only concern is the weight of gold in their pockets (*Deccan Herald*, 2018).

It is my understanding that most religious practices, in their essence, do not involve disturbing live cobras or any snakes. In southern India, for instance, offerings are primarily made to stone idols called Naagakallu or Naagaprasthishta, or it may simply involve meditating upon the form of the Naaga and chanting mantras. Occasionally, a person, or paatri, is worshipped when the spirit of the serpent is believed to enter their body. The true reverence lies in respecting the serpent, both as a powerful symbol and a vital part of the natural world.

XI

Naagaloka–The Anthill and the Netherworlds

One languid January afternoon, I found myself in my spouse's ancestral village near Karkala, Karnataka. The warm breeze lazily stirred the coconut palms, their long fronds casting rippling shadows on the surface of the ancient well into which I had been staring.

'This well is as old as time itself,' came a voice from behind me, belonging to a pot-bellied man, his tone full of gravity as if the well's age held some great secret.

'Someone must have built it,' I replied, still peering down at the weathered bricks lining its interior. 'I can see the masonry. It can't be more than a hundred years old.'

'True, we renovated it,' he admitted, 'but our ancestors believed this well was once a gateway to the netherworld.'

Intrigued, I encouraged him to continue. He obliged with a tale that seemed to belong more to sacred lore than to the quiet, sleepy village that surrounded us.

'The Naagadevatas—the serpent deities—are the true owners of this land,' he began, his voice lowering. 'This estate once had a puncha—an anthill, where a mighty Naagaraaja and his consort would often come and go.'

'And where did they go?' I asked.

He leaned in closer, as if sharing a clandestine truth. 'An oracle once revealed that a portal to the kingdom of the Naagadevatas exists beneath this well, leading to a world of serpents and precious stones. Naagaloka. To protect them, someone built this well, sealing the entry so that no human could disturb their realm.'

I couldn't resist asking the obvious question. 'Have you ever seen one? A Naaga?'

He nodded solemnly. 'They reveal themselves on rare occasions—always during moments of great fortune. In fact,' he added, his gaze growing distant, 'the last time a Naaga appeared was just before your engagement.'

Goosebumps prickled my skin at his words. I recalled the day, the rush of events surrounding my engagement, and realized I hadn't given the remark much thought at the time. It had seemed like a quaint superstition, the kind of folklore that cloaked much of rural southern India. But now, after having spent more time in these lands where Kannada, Konkani, Tulu and Malayalam were spoken, I had encountered countless similar tales—mesmerizing stories of the Naagas and their ancient anthills, or puncha as they say in Tulu.

The Anthill—Nature's Subterranean Castle

Anthill worship is a cult as old as the land itself, surviving in pockets across the subcontinent even today. This ancient practice once held a prominent place in Hindu rituals, and over centuries has seeped into popular belief. Anthills are revered as the dwelling places of serpentine deities, playing an important role in temple consecrations, warding off evil and securing material prosperity. When Alexander's forces stepped into the territories of greater

Punjab, it was the sight of these sacred mounds that must have greeted them, standing as guardians of the ancient world.

Strictly speaking, what we call 'anthills' in English are not the work of ants at all, but termites—sometimes misleadingly called 'white ants'. These tiny creatures, unrelated to ants, are remarkable engineers of the natural world, constructing towering mounds from soil, water, and their own saliva (Irwing, 1982, p. 339). These structures are as intricate as any human-made fortress, perhaps even more so. Termite mounds can rise up to six feet tall, their durability and strength matched by their complexity—porous enough to ventilate the underground nests, maintaining the perfect balance of temperature and humidity. In a sense, they are nature's air-conditioned palaces.

The earthen mounds, those towering monuments to the industriousness of termites, are not mere heaps of dirt but, in fact, intricate constructions of soil, water and the saliva of their tiny architects. So ingeniously crafted are these structures that they rival, and perhaps even surpass, human-made castles in their complexity. These enigmatic fortresses have long fascinated biologists, inspired architects and captured the imagination of robotics experts, all drawn to the remarkable engineering of these minuscule creatures. Termites, often dismissed as mere pests, are revealed here as sophisticated builders who construct not just a home, but a subterranean kingdom.

Beneath the surface of these towering mounds, often rising to heights of six feet or more, lies a hidden metropolis—vast colonies of millions of termites that are workers, soldiers, larvae and at the heart of it all, the royal chambers of the queen termite. Alongside them, the termites tend to their fungal gardens, intricate ecosystems in themselves, which feed the colony in a complex symbiosis. These mounds, despite their impressive durability and strength, are not rigid fortresses but breathing, living structures. Their porous walls allow for the ventilation of the underground nests, ensuring that the temperature and humidity within remain perfectly regulated. In this way, the mounds function like natural air-conditioned palaces, with a level of architectural genius that even modern builders can admire (*Mongabay*, 2020).

As with many other natural wonders, these termite nests play host to a variety of creatures, some of which are incapable of living independently of their termite hosts. Known as termitophiles, these species have evolved in tandem with the termites, becoming utterly dependent on the nests for survival. Among them are beetles, flies, bugs and caterpillars, some of which have developed specialized glands that secrete substances sought after by the termites. The relationship is symbiotic, a dance of life within these hidden earthen realms. Furthermore, the warmth and protection afforded by the termite mounds also attract larger occupants—lizards, snakes, scorpions and even birds find shelter in these subterranean homes (*Britannica*, 2024).

In a feat of remarkable engineering, fungus-growing termites excavate materials from deep within the earth, often digging as far as fifty metres down—an astonishing 164 feet—to reach the water table (Jouquet, 2017, p. 190). It is here, in the darkness of the earth, that we may encounter the mystery of the Naagas and the legends they seem to inspire.

It was then, staring down into that well in Karkala, that I wondered—could these ancient stories, passed down through generations, hold some truth? Is it possible that if we dig deep enough, we might reach Naagaloka, the hidden realm of the serpent gods? Could the Divya Naagas, the celestial serpents, with their shimmering hoods and celestial jewels, truly reside below, guarding treasures that mortals could scarcely imagine? Was it in such a place that Ulupi, the Naaga princess, lured Arjuna into the depths, or where the relics of Buddha were hidden at his request until received by Naagarjuna?

As we explore the concept of Naagaloka in the coming pages, we will draw upon both ancient texts, medieval folklore and modern scientific discoveries, searching for the thread that ties these sacred worlds to our own. Could this well, or the anthill that it is still believed to house underneath, truly be a portal to another realm, sealed off by the Naagas to protect their sacred treasures? The answer, as always, lies somewhere between belief and wonder, in the rich kaleidoscope of India's Puranic past.

Mapping the Netherworlds—Where is Naagaloka?

According to legend, the hidden world of the Naagas, also known as Paataala, is very difficult for humans to access, though a few like Uttanka in the Puraanas have managed it. It's believed there are many entrances to this realm (Vogel, 1926, p. 34).

One specific example, drawn from the *Kathasaritsagara* collection of folktales, describes a famous entrance in Kashmir. This gateway was created by the legendary architect Maya, the father-in-law of Raavana. It was famously used by Usha to secretly bring her lover Aniruddha into the realm of the Daanavas (offsprings of Danu). Later, Pradyumna enlarged this entrance and placed the goddess Durga there, under the name Sarika, to guard it. Because of this story, the location is known as both the Peak of Pradyumna and the Hill of Sarika (Vogel, 1926, p. 35).

This intriguing question leads us through the subterranean realms that pulse beneath the surface of our world. I will take you back to a story from our Puraanas. In the quest for a suitable groom for his daughter, Maatali is guided by the sage Naarada into the netherworlds. Their journey begins with a crossing of Varuna's domain, before arriving at Paataala, a vibrant realm inhabited by the Naagas. Ultimately, they reach Bhogavati, the magnificent capital of Naagaraaja Vasuki. This underground city, resplendent and enchanting, captivates with grand palaces encrusted with jewels and lush gardens bursting with fragrant flowers and abundant fruits.

In a similar vein, the tale of Ulupi and Arjuna reveals the Naaga princess escorting the Pandava prince to the serpent kingdom hidden beneath the river. This realm is portrayed as a treasure trove, brimming with aquatic life, precious stones and unimaginable riches. Another enchanting abode of the Naagas mentioned in the Mahabharata is Ramanaka or Ramaniyaka Island, a shimmering place created by Brahma amidst the vastness of the Lavana Samudra. This tropical paradise, draped in lush forests, is alive with the melodies of winged choirs, each note a celebration of the Naagas' existence in this vibrant domain.

The landscape unfolds as a vivid fabric of colours, with clusters of fruit-laden trees and fragrant blooms mingling their scents in the air, carried by gentle breezes that waft refreshing incenses from the ocean's depths. Towering trees stretch skyward, while sparkling lakes, filled with blooming lotuses, mirror the heavens. Scattered throughout are fair mansions that invite all who enter to bask in their charm. This thriving forest is a haven of life, home to bees intoxicated by nectar and an array of birds whose melodious songs enchant the atmosphere. Ramaniyaka Island offers not merely a visual feast, but a sanctuary of delight, cherished by the Gandharvas and steeped in an aura of holiness.

The Shalya Parva of the Mahabharata further introduces another captivating location linked with the serpents—Naagadhanwana, a sacred *tirtha* teeming with snakes and revered as the splendid abode of Vasuki, the illustrious king of the serpents. This mystical realm serves as a sanctuary, where 14,000 Rishis are believed to have taken up eternal residence, intertwining the lives of serpents and sages in a unique harmony. In ancient times, celestial beings descended upon this sacred site, performing rituals that led to Vasuki's anointment as the ruler of all serpents. Interestingly, within this divine habitat, despite the multitude of serpents, there exists no fear, underscoring the sanctity of the place and the protective grace of Vasuki.

Yet, the most pervasive belief, echoing through our folktales, is that serpents dwell in the netherworld, with Naagaloka situated in Paataala, the lowest of the seven lokas that lie beneath our own.

Paataala—The Subterranean Serpent Heaven

The Puraanas, like the Vishnu Puraana and Devi Bhagavata Puraana, detail these seven netherworlds—Atala, Vitala, Sutala, Talaatala, Mahaatala, Rasaatala and Paataala. It's crucial, as I learned, not to confuse these with Naraka (hell) or Western concepts of fiery underworlds. The sage Naarada, having visited, proclaimed Paataala more delightful than Indra's heaven. These Vila-Swargas (subterranean heavens) are realms of immense pleasure, filled with lavish gardens and opulent palaces, inhabited by Daityas, Daanavas and Naagas living in delight. Perpetual light emanates from the naagamanis (serpent jewels) on the Naagas' hoods.

Of particular note is Mahaatala, the fifth realm, where the formidable Naagas—Kuhaka, Takshaka, Sushena and Kaaliya—are believed to reside according to Puraanas. These great serpents, with their wide hoods and fierce tempers, live in constant vigilance, wary of Garuda, the eternal predator. Here, they indulge in the pleasures of life, surrounded by their loved ones.

Lower still lies Rasaatala, where the Daityas, Danavas and Pani Asuras make their home. Beneath this, in Paataala, dwells Vasuki and his kin, including Shamkha, Kulika, Shweta and Dhananjaya, their fearsome forms adorned with multiple hoods—some bearing five, others seven, ten or even a thousand. The jewels that crown these serpents shine with a brilliance that cuts through the deep gloom, though their tempers are as fiery as their surroundings.

Beyond Paataala—The Realm of Ananta Shesha

According to the Devi Bhagavata Puraana, at the very base of Paataala, thirty yojanas or roughly 384 kilometres below the earth, lies the region of infinite darkness. Here rests the thousand-headed Ananta Shesha, as Sankarshana, the essence of 'Aham' or 'Self', where the boundary between the seer and the seen dissolves. The physical manifestation or reality meets the eternal consciousness. The Vishnu Puraana says that Lord Vishnu rests here in deep yogic slumber, taking the form of Sheshashaayi, reclining on the great serpent Shesha. This sacred site is untouched by the 'laws and flaws' of physics. Time halts at its threshold. The gods, sages and celestial beings frequent this realm, where the seasons never change, and the very air seems to carry the scent of immortality.

Here, Ananta Shesha is believed to support the universe as effortlessly as a mustard seed upon his head, holding all that moves and all that is still. Yet, when the time for destruction approaches, Sankarshana Rudra (Shiva) emerges from him, trident in hand, his three eyes blazing, ready to set the universe ablaze in the flames of dissolution.

Metaphorical Realms and Ancient Peoples

Can we reconcile these vivid Puranic descriptions with our scientific understanding of the Earth? Imagining thriving worlds deep underground echoes science fiction like Jules Verne's *Journey to the Center of the Earth* or the pseudoscientific Hollow Earth Theory.

While intriguing, science confirms Earth's core is not hollow but intensely hot and pressurized, making literal subterranean civilizations impossible. Perhaps, then, Naagaloka holds significance as a symbolic or metaphorical realm, not a physical location.

Scholars like Oldham proposed alternative interpretations: could these 'netherworlds' actually represent the sophisticated cities of ancient inhabitants—Naagas, Yakshas, Rakshasas—who flourished before the arrival of Vedic culture? Were the Naagas literally serpents, or were they serpent-worshipping tribes whose reverence predated their integration into broader Hinduism? Conflicts described in epics, like the burning of Khandava forest or the Sarpasatra, might be read metaphorically, representing cultural clashes or assimilation rather than literal events.

Or perhaps the search for Naagaloka need not only look outward or downward into the earth. What if the concept of a hidden realm, guarded by serpentine power and holding immense potential, also resonates within the human form itself? While sacred narratives and folklore place Naagaloka in the subterranean depths or forgotten cities, another ancient tradition points inward, exploring the potent symbolism of the serpent as a fundamental energy coiled within our own consciousness.

XII

The Coiled Serpent Within— Kundalini and Consciousness

I am far from being an expert in Kundalini, or indeed in any form of Yoga, but the serpent symbolism that entwines itself with this ancient practice of awakening the mind is too fascinating to ignore. The concept of Kundalini as a coiled serpent at the mooladhara chakra, ready to unfurl along the spine, is deeply evocative—yet, when viewed through the lens of anatomy, it acquires an unsettling, perhaps even more profound resonance. Allow me to delve into this idea, which may challenge the conventional imagery associated with this spiritual energy.

At its core, Kundalini is about energy ascending the spine, passing through the chakras, those mystical centres of consciousness, until it reaches the crown of the head—the Sahasrara—where enlightenment is said to be achieved. But consider for a moment the possibility that consciousness itself, as I briefly alluded to in my previous book, *Daiva*, is not merely some ethereal force, but intrinsically tied to the physical nervous system. Without the brain, spinal cord and nerves, our very sense of awareness—our being— would simply not exist.

With this in mind, an anatomical parallel struck me as visually resonant, though it stands apart from traditional yogic philosophy—picture the body stripped of its flesh, leaving only the spinal cord and brain. In my understanding, what remains is quite strikingly serpent-like. The spinal cord forms the long, sinuous body of a snake, while the brain assumes the shape of a cobra's hood. The spinal cord carries the impulses that give rise to our most primal instincts as well as our most refined thoughts. Interestingly, Carl Jung made a related observation, suggesting that the serpent form could be seen to personify the spinal cord and ganglia, linking primal energy directly to the nervous system (Jung, 1980, p. 667).

The image of the snake thus becomes a symbol of profound transformation and awakening. The Kundalini serpent, coiled at the base of the spine, represents a potential shift in perception—a movement towards higher understanding. However, this awakening is often described as potentially disruptive, pushing the boundaries of what we know and forcing confrontation with deeper truths about the self and reality.

Shesha and Kundalini

The primordial serpent, Ananta Shesha, residing deep below Paataala, offers another layer to this symbolism. The coiled Kundalini serpent evokes the imagery of Ananta Shesha, the eternal serpent who holds up the earth on his thousand hoods. In this metaphor, the earth can be seen as representing our physical self, our material existence, while Shesha could signify the underlying consciousness that upholds it. Just as Ananta Shesha sustains the universe in cosmic balance, the awakened Kundalini serpent is believed to sustain and elevate our awareness, pushing us towards higher realms of understanding.

Yet, this awakening is often associated with fear—not necessarily fear of malevolence, but the profound fear of entering the unknown, of venturing into realms of consciousness that lie beyond our familiar conceptions of self and the dissolution of ego. It compels us to recognize that our perceived world and selves, our joys and sorrow, might be fragile constructs, and exploring deeper layers of consciousness means stepping into a domain where such constructs dissolve. It is a fear of dissolving boundaries, where the self as we know it feels insignificant in the face of truths that may defy conventional reason and comfort. Thus, the Kundalini serpent embodies a powerful, transformative potential that invites both reverence and trepidation.

The Quest Continues

As we journey through Naagaloka, the symbolism of the serpent, and the parallels between lokas and chakras, a question emerges— Could these ancient motifs hint at a deeper understanding of existence? Though merely a speculative theory and not reality, one can't help but wonder if our ancestors intended these symbols as clues to a larger mystery.

The serpent—revered across different Indian sub-cultures as protector and guide—represents hidden knowledge and realms beyond ordinary perception. From the coiled Kundalini energy within us to Ananta Shesha, who is believed to hold the universe in balance, the serpent suggests a hidden interconnectedness between the material and the mystical. Maybe the treasure serpents guard in our folklore is the treasure of knowledge of the true nature of consciousness? Could these traditional stories, passed down through generations, preserve insights that science has yet to explore?

In Hindu cosmology, the seven lokas (realms) may seem to align with the seven chakras, suggesting both an inner journey and a layered understanding of the universe. Might our ancestors have perceived hidden dimensions that interact with life's energies? While science regards such tales as metaphor, the connection between lokas and chakras, serpentine wisdom and cosmic balance raises the possibility that these ancient symbols offer a map to understanding the unseen.

As you continue this journey with me, let these pages ignite curiosity and wonder, inviting you to reflect on the deeper meanings embedded within ancient lore and symbolism. The path to Naagaloka, whether seen as sacred tradition or metaphor, beckons us to explore the realms of consciousness itself. Could the serpent represent more than a creature of folklore—perhaps the human nervous system stripped of flesh, striving to bridge the physical and the vast subconscious, interconnected with a super consciousness that sustains all existence? Are these ancient symbols mere relics, or do they hold preserved messages, challenging the limits of what we know? This question remains open, inviting those who seek truth to embrace both wonder and discernment on their journey.

PART 2

Naagaaradhana: Ophiolatry in India

I

Ophiolatry in North India

Many millennia ago, when the mighty Alexander swept across the far reaches of the known world, his armies found themselves in a land where the dust of war mingled with the whispers of gods. As they marched deeper into the heat and haze of northern India, they were no longer just conquerors of men. Here, in this ancient land, they encountered forces far older, forces that slithered beneath the earth and commanded the fear and reverence of the people.

In the baking plains of the Punjab, under a sun that seemed to weigh down upon them with each passing day, Alexander's men stumbled upon something they could neither conquer nor understand—a Naaga, one so venerated that it held dominion over the very air the villagers breathed. Word spread quickly through the camp—this was no mere snake. It was believed to be a guardian of the earth, and its home, a cave not far from the village, was shrouded in legend.

The locals approached the Macedonian king with offerings of fruit and flowers, their voices trembling as they begged him to spare the creature. This serpent, they said, was no ordinary beast but a living god, whose hiss could carry across the plains like a thunderclap. Over a hundred feet long, they whispered, it's very

97

breath could halt the winds and bring the rains. To kill it would invite the wrath of the land itself.

Alexander's soldiers, hardened by the battles of a hundred lands, set out to see this creature of myth for themselves. Their footsteps grew hesitant as they neared the cave, and from its depths came a low, menacing sound. It was unlike anything they had heard in their long march from Greece to the edge of the world. The hissing grew louder, more threatening, as if the serpent itself was warning them to stay away. The air thickened with an otherworldly tension, and for the first time in their many campaigns, they stood before an enemy they could not face with sword or spear. The serpent, though unseen, seemed to watch them—its presence a force beyond their comprehension, a reminder that this land belonged not just to men, but also to the gods of the earth, and serpents of the netherworlds.

The Greeks, who had followed their king into these strange lands, would later recount these stories with a mixture of awe and superstition. Aelian, the chronicler, wrote of the 'bane of snakes', describing how serpents were worshipped and revered in the old Punjab (now most of it is in Pakistan). He told of a belief that if a snake killed a man, the earth itself would banish it—severing its connection with the natural world in a symbolic act of justice. The Naagas, it seemed, held a dual power—to protect the land and bring ruin upon it, a balance of life and death that left even Alexander's mightiest warriors questioning their place in this foreign, sacred land.

While serpent worship may not be mainstream anymore in the region, but, like the story above mentions, long ago, even people in present-day Afghanistan, Pakistan and Punjab worshipped the

Naagas. Colonial writers, such as Oldham, have even gone on to speculate that the Naagas were the original people of the land who used the serpent as their totem. The people of the country between Kabul and Kashmir, down to the time of the foreign invasion, still worshipped the Naaga demi-gods (Oldham, 1906, p. 45).

Takshasila—Crossroads of Serpent Worship

The ancient city of Takshasila (modern-day *Taxila*) was not just a crossroads of empires but a melting pot of spiritual traditions, a city where knowledge flowed as freely as the great rivers of the Indus Valley. Known for its great university, which drew students from across the ancient world, Takshasila's rich intellectual and cultural history often overshadows an even older, more primal layer of reverence—serpent worship. For long before the arrival of Buddhism or the spread of Hellenistic influence under Alexander, the people of this region were believed to have held the serpents in a position of divine reverence.

The Greeks who came with Alexander referred to the inhabitants as the *Takhas* or *Kathas*—a people whose very identity was intertwined with their veneration of serpents. The name Takshasila itself is believed to derive from *Taksha*, a legendary Naaga ruler whose kingdom stretched across these northern plains (Oldham, 1906, p. 113). Taksha was not merely a king, but venerated as a demigod—a protector of his people who governed with wisdom and the power of the earth. Even in the ancient texts, Takshaka is mentioned alongside other powerful Naagas, immortalized in the *itihasa puraanas* as one of the ashtanaagas. Of course, it can be debated (like many scholars have) that the serpent Takshaka in the Puraana and this king Taksha may not be one and the same.

Historians and scholars have drawn connections between the serpent-worshipping people of Takshasila and surrounding regions, such as *Uraga* and *Abissara*, where similar traditions persisted. The very name *Uraga*, as we have seen in an earlier chapter, translates directly to 'snake' in Sanskrit, highlighting the deep-rooted veneration of the Naaga.

Alexander's soldiers, fascinated and terrified by these beliefs, documented their encounters with serpent worship in the region. The Greek historian Arrian, writing on Alexander's campaign, recounts the awe the Macedonian soldiers felt upon witnessing the Naaga temples. To these men of war, used to subduing foreign lands with sword and shield, the reverence for serpents seemed both exotic and intimidating. The local people believed that the serpents were not mere animals, but deities who could not be conquered by man (Vogel, 1926, p. 2).

Buddhism, particularly in the northern regions, also incorporated elements of Naaga worship. Pilgrims like Fah Hian and Hiouen Tsiang recorded instances where sacred lakes associated with Naaga deities became pilgrimage sites. The symbiosis between Buddhism and Naaga reverence was particularly evident in places like Udyana, where the Buddha, was said to have converted a malevolent Naaga into a devout follower.

Oldham mentions that in Gandhara (Kandahar, Afghanistan), Buddhist monks were believed to have acted as intermediaries between the local populace and Naaga deities, offering prayers on behalf of the people for rain and prosperity. The stupa built by the Kushan emperor Kanishka in the region was reportedly destroyed multiple times by an enraged Naaga, demonstrating that even royal authority was sometimes powerless against the will of these ancient serpent gods (Oldham, 1906, p. 121).

Despite the rise of new religions and the arrival of Muslim rulers, traces of serpent worship remained resilient, at least, up until the last century. In regions like Baluchistan, serpent-related traditions persisted, even in areas converted to Islam. The mountain of serpents, Koh-i-Maran, and the grave of a great serpent near Mazar in Afghanistan were testaments to the continued veneration of serpent myths (Oldham, 1905, p. 117).

Mathura

Further east lies Mathura, Uttar Pradesh—a city eternally famous as the birthplace of Lord Krishna. Yet, beneath its profound connection to Vaishnavism, layers of history suggest an older reverence. Scholars like Vogel have speculated that long before Mathura became synonymous with Krishna, the region was a vibrant centre for the worship of serpent deities. Striking archaeological evidence supports this, notably the numerous Naaga images recovered in the district, such as an inscribed statue found in Chhargaon. Interestingly, these ancient serpent icons are often locally identified as Dau-ji or Baldeo—names for Balarama, Krishna's elder brother.

Balarama—An Avatar of Ananta Shesha

This blending of traditions is not difficult to explain. Balarama, Krishna's elder brother, was long considered an agricultural deity—a figure closely tied to the fertility of the land and its rhythms. As an incarnation of Ananta Shesha, he came to embody the protective power of the Naagas, becoming a natural bridge between the older serpent cults and the burgeoning popularity of Krishna.

In the first century BCE, as Hindus began to adopt Naagaraaja iconography, sculptures of Samkarshana Balarama—depicted with the characteristic serpent hood—began to appear across northern India, most notably in Uttar Pradesh and Madhya

Pradesh. The earliest of these, found in Jansuti and dated to the first century BCE, represents one of the first visual manifestations of Vaishnavism in the Mathura region, and stands as a testament to the enduring legacy of serpent worship in these lands (Quintanilla, 2007, p. 92).

From an iconographic perspective, the ancient Naaga images in Mathura offer intriguing insights. The serpentine figures, often depicted with hoods of seven snake heads, evoke a sense of awe and power.

Remnants of Ophiolatry in Bihar

Interestingly, Mathura was not unique in its dedication to serpent deities. Excavations at Maniyar Math in Rajgir, Bihar, unearthed another Naaga shrine, dating from the second century BCE to the fifth century CE. Ritual paraphernalia from the site, including spouted jars adorned with cobra hoods, along with inscribed sculptures paying homage to Mani Naaga, further highlight the pervasive nature of serpent worship across northern India (Bloch, 1909, p. 103–106; Chandra, 1938, p. 52–54). The serpent deities, it seemed, were everywhere at some point in time.

In the case of Mathura, colonial writers have speculated that what began as a localized serpent cult may have gradually evolved over the centuries, merging with and ultimately becoming absorbed by dominant traditions. However, relying solely on the studies of British scholars, we should avoid hastily concluding that the Naaga cult predated Vaishnavism, or vice versa; the truth of such origins may be far more nuanced, rooted in complex exchanges and assimilations across eras.

Yet, even as the Naagas faded into the background of popular imagination, their influence endured, their iconography and symbolism subtly woven into the spiritual fabric of the region. Today, as pilgrims gather at the temples of Mathura and Vrindavan to offer prayers to Balarama, the elder brother of Krishna, few may realize that this mighty wielder of the plough is also the inheritor of an ancient legacy—the legacy of the Naagas, whose dominion over land and waters once captivated the hearts of Mathura's earliest inhabitants.

Goga Chauhan—The Serpent Hero of Rajasthan

In the arid landscapes of Rajasthan and neighbouring states, a unique figure embodies the confluence of hero-worship and ophiolatry—Goga Chauhan. His followers, lost in the deep rhythms of devotion, are believed to fall into trance-like states to commune with the demigod, seeking his guidance and protection. The figure of Goga stands as a striking evidence to the syncretic fabric of Indian devotion. His followers—spanning across the boundaries of Hinduism and Islam—come from all walks of life, bound together by the wrath of one common fear—the snake.

Born into the Chauhan lineage, Goga's story begins in the eleventh century in a village located in Rajasthan's Churu district. According to legend, his birth was blessed by the great Nath Yogi, Guru Gorakhnath. Raised in a family of high esteem, Goga's life was shaped by the agrarian culture of his homeland. His marriage to Kelmade, a princess from Kolamand, was cut short when his betrothed was bitten by a snake. Furious, Goga is said to have begun reciting powerful mantras, slaying snakes in his path until a Naagadevata appeared before him, offering him the boon of becoming the protector of snakes, thus transforming him into the Devta (deity) of serpents.

Goga's devotion to his land and people is immortalized in the tales of his sacrifice to protect cattle and his nation from invasions. His martyrdom elevated him to the status of a folk deity, worshipped as Jaharpir or Gogapir. His samadhi—his final resting place—is known as Goga Medi in Nohr-Hanumangarh, where an annual fair is held every year on Goga Navami.

Across the countryside, small shrines dedicated to Goga can be found beneath the sacred khejdi tree, where stone carvings of serpents are worshipped. Farmers, particularly in Rajasthan, pay homage to him before ploughing their fields by tying a sacred thread known as Goga Rakdi to their ploughs and oxen, invoking his protection against snake bites.

The devotion to Goga is not limited to Hindus alone. He is venerated by Muslims as well, who regard him as a saint and call him Gugga or Gogapir. His shrine in Goga Medi bears an inscription of 'Bismillah' on its doorway, and the faithful, whether Hindu or Muslim, gather in unison.

Goga's figure, often depicted as a warrior on a blue horse, spear in hand, and accompanied by the symbol of a serpent, is offered traditional fare such as kheer, lapsi and choorma in devotion.

Goga Chauhan's enduring popularity, especially among rural communities, stands as a fascinating example of how a singular figure can unite disparate communities, creating a shared heritage of faith, mysticism and protection against the ever-present dangers of nature.

From ancient crossroads like Takshasila to the heartland of Mathura and the folk traditions surrounding figures like Goga Chauhan, north India reveals a complex history of serpent worship.

Here, Naagas were once perceived as primordial rulers, powerful deities integrated into Buddhism and Vaishnavism, and syncretic protectors bridging religious divides. This deep-rooted reverence, though perhaps much less visible today, laid the groundwork for diverse practices that continue to echo across the subcontinent, taking different forms as we move into the hilly regions of the Himalayas.

II

Serpents of the Hills and Valleys

There are landscapes that call to you long before your feet touch their soil. For me, Uttarakhand—the high, craggy realm known as Dev Bhoomi, the Land of Gods—had begun to exert such a pull, whispering of ancient folk beliefs tangled amidst its peaks and valleys. The path towards understanding its specific spiritual contours, however, unfolded unexpectedly, prompted by echoes from a different journey altogether. Following the publication of *Daiva*, which delves into the spirit worship traditions of Tulunadu, I was invited for several podcast interviews. During one such discussion at the Aaj Tak studio in Noida, the conversation naturally shifted towards potential similarities between the Daiva Kola and Uttarakhand's own devata worship, specifically mentioning the ritual of Jaagar. It was a compelling connection I hadn't fully considered until the very next interview, this time with a renowned literary figure in Delhi NCR, who, being from Uttarakhand herself, was eager to share insights into her region's deities.

Through these conversations and further research, I learned that many villages have serpent deities and while travelling on the road, one may find stones on the side depicting village serpent deity. She spoke with great pride of the Jaagar ritual, which, like the Kola,

106

Naagamandala, and Thullal traditions of the south, is a sacred practice carried out in the rural parts of Uttarakhand. The purpose of Jaagar is to awaken the local deities, seeking their blessings and ensuring the well-being of the community. It strikes at the heart of the people's deep-rooted spirituality, much like the serpent worship I've explored throughout the southern parts of India.

The conversation naturally led to the subject of Naagadevatas—serpent deities.

Naagadevatas of Uttarakhand

Uttarakhand, with its hills and valleys, is home to several temples dedicated to these serpent gods, the most notable being the temples of Naagaraaja. Among these, Sem Mukhem and Danda Naagaraaja stand out, drawing devotees from far-flung corners of the state to pay homage to the serpent king. These temples, with their architecture and rich folk narratives, offer a treasure trove of stories and spiritual significance to anyone willing to delve deeper.

Sem Mukhem Naagaraaja Temple, perched 7,000 feet above sea level in the Tehri Garhwal district, is particularly fascinating. Surrounded by towering peaks and dense forests, this ancient temple is dedicated to Lord Krishna, revered here in the form of Naagaraaja, the king of serpents. It is believed to be one of India's oldest pilgrimage sites, known as the fifth Dham of Uttarakhand and referred to as the Dwarka of the North. According to local lore, Lord Krishna once visited this region disguised as an old sage and sought a place to stay from the local king, Gangu Ramola. When the king refused, the land fell into turmoil—drought, disease and death plagued the kingdom. Realizing his mistake, the king begged the sage to return, thus restoring prosperity to his people. Today, the temple stands as a reminder of this divine intervention, with an idol of Krishna enshrined on the hood of the serpent king, symbolizing the eternal connection between man and the gods (Etv Bharat, 2023).

But Sem Mukhem is just one of many serpent temples in Uttarakhand. The state also houses temples dedicated to Karkotaka, Manasa, Vasuki and other prominent Naagadevatas, each with their own legends and histories, waiting to be explored. This intersection of the sacred and the serpentine in Uttarakhand's spiritual landscape beckons. Much like the groves and temples of the southern coasts, it feels as if these hills hold countless more hidden stories waiting to be uncovered.

Deities of Himachal

The deep connection between the hilly landscape and local deities isn't unique to Uttarakhand; it resonates strongly as one travels northwest along the Himalayan range. I recall this vividly from my time spent in Himachal Pradesh during the location scouting and filming for the web series Bhram. As our team journeyed through the winding roads and remote villages, conducting reconnaissance for suitable locations, we frequently came across small, unassuming shrines and sometimes more elaborate temples tucked away, dedicated to deities whose presence felt deeply interwoven with the mountains themselves. Vogel notes that the Kullu valley, in particular, was historically a great centre of Naaga worship. There, Baski or Basu, as the ancient Naagaraaja Vasuki is commonly called by local people, is regarded as the father of the other Naagas scattered over the various villages (Vogel, 1926, p. 255). A fascinating local folktale illustrates his connection to the region and explains the dispersal of serpent lineage in the region.

The Scattered Serpent Babies—A folktale from Kullu

Baski Naaga, the mighty serpent king, once gazed upon a woman from the Kullu valley, captivating in her red attire. Smitten, he shed his serpent form, appearing as a handsome man, and swept her away through the air to his celestial realm.

In this upper world, they lived together, but Baski Naaga gave his bride one strict warning, 'You may tend to me as I rest, but never, ever lift the hair upon my head.' For a time, she obeyed. One day, however, as the serpent king slept soundly with his head upon her lap, curiosity, or perhaps a longing for her past life, overcame her. Gently, she lifted the hair on his head.

In that instant, her vision cleared, and looking down from the heavens, she saw her earthly home, her fields, her village spread out below. A wave of homesickness washed over her, and tears began to fall, splashing onto Baski Naaga's face.

He awoke instantly. Understanding her longing and perhaps accepting the consequence of her broken promise, he made her his wife then and there. But before returning her to her world, he commanded her, 'Whatever offspring are born from our union, you must worship them devoutly.' With those words, she found herself standing once more upon the roof of her own house, without experiencing any passage of time.

Nine months passed, and the woman gave birth—not to human children, but to eighteen small snakes. Remembering her husband's command, she treated them with reverence. She placed her serpent children carefully into a large earthen pot, the kind called a 'bhandal' in Kullu, making eighteen small holes around its side. Through these holes, she patiently fed each snake with milk from her breast, day after day, burning incense in worship.

After several months, the woman needed to visit her parents' home. She entrusted the care of her serpent children to her mother-in-law. 'Please,' she instructed, 'continue the worship and feed them while I am away.'

The next day, the mother-in-law prepared the incense on a large iron spoon, lighting the coals to create the sacred smoke. As she approached the bhandal, the eighteen snakes, hearing her footsteps, poked their heads eagerly through the holes. Startled by the sudden appearance of so many serpent heads, the old woman gasped and dropped the spoon. The burning incense and hot coals tumbled directly into the pot.

In terror and pain, the young snakes scattered, escaping the pot and fleeing in all directions. It is said that of those eighteen serpent children of Baski Naaga, two fled to the lands of Mandi and Suket, and two others found their way into the district of Lahaul, forever dispersing the serpent king's unique lineage across the hills.

As this folktale suggests, Naaga worship in the region, much like in Uttarakhand, is often tied to specific locales. Usually, each Naaga belongs to the particular village near which its temple or shrine stands. They function essentially as local deities (devatas). In some instances, the Naaga has no formal shrine but is associated with a sacred lake high in the mountains, visited for ritual bathing. Sometimes, the serpent deity doesn't even possess an individual name but is simply referred to as 'Naaga' (Vogel, 1926, p. 258).

Kashmir: Realm of Nila Naaga and the Karkotas

Further north still, in Kashmir, the lore is dominated by Nila Naaga, revered as the primary guardian of the Kashmir Valley.

Local legends, particularly the Nilamata Purana, credit Nila Naaga with taming the primordial waters of the Satisaras lake, making the land habitable. He played a pivotal role in negotiating the terms for human settlement alongside the Naagas, embodying the deep connection between these serpent deities and the land itself. As Dr Ved Kumari notes, the identification of the Naagas remains complex, as they appear sometimes as snakes and other times as human beings in these narratives (Kumari, 1968, p. 46).

Nila Naaga and the Creation of Kashmir

The Nilamata Purana provides a detailed origin story for the valley. It recounts that Kashmir was initially a vast, beautiful lake called Satisaras, which served as a divine sanctuary. When the Naagas, led by Vasuki, sought protection from Garuda, Lord Vishnu designated Satisaras as their refuge, appointing the pious Nila Naaga as their king and protector, ensuring Garuda would not harm those dwelling within its waters.

However, peace was disrupted by the emergence of the water-demon Jalodbhava, born from the seed of a defeated demon named Samgraha. Raised by the Naagas but empowered by a boon from Brahma granting him invincibility in water, Jalodbhava grew arrogant and began terrorizing the inhabitants of neighbouring lands, forcing people to flee and leaving the region desolate. Seeing this devastation, Nila Naaga appealed to his father, the sage Kashyapa.

Kashyapa, after witnessing the destruction, sought the intervention of the primary gods—Brahma, Vishnu and Shiva. They descended upon the mountain peaks surrounding the lake, but Jalodbhava, secure in his watery domain, refused to emerge. To force the confrontation, Vishnu commanded Ananta Shesha (in his Balarama aspect) to drain the lake. With his mighty plough, Ananta

Shesha broke open the surrounding mountains, allowing the waters to rush out. Despite Jalodbhava creating magical darkness, Shiva illuminated the world with the sun and moon, allowing Vishnu to engage and finally slay the demon.

Following the demon's defeat, Kashyapa wished for humans to settle the now-fertile valley. The Naagas, led by Nila, initially objected to living alongside humans. An angered Kashyapa cursed them to coexist with the fierce Pisachas. Nila pleaded for mercy, and Vishnu modified the decree—the Naagas would share the land cyclically with Pisachas for a period, but eventually, humans would inhabit the valley permanently, provided they honoured and worshipped the Naagas according to customs established by Nila. This ensured the Naagas' protection and the land's prosperity.

According to the Purana, the name Kashmir itself is linked to Kashyapa (Ka) and because water called 'Ka' was taken out by Balarama (the plough-wielder) from this country, it was called Kashmira. This foundational narrative firmly establishes Nila Naaga as the primordial guardian of the valley, whose worship was integral to the very fabric of life in Kashmir. While the historical accuracy of Puranic etymologies is debated by scholars, the story itself remains central to the region's identity.

This connection to Naagas was further solidified by the Karkota Dynasty, which rose to power in the seventh century CE. This influential dynasty, proudly traced its lineage back to the serpent deity Karkotaka, one of the Ashtanaagas. The Karkota rulers were thus seen not just as earthly kings but as inheritors of a divine mandate, protectors of the land following their serpentine ancestor. These beliefs permeated the erstwhile Kashmiri culture beyond royal lines. Sacred groves, stone idols, and serpent shrines were common, often situated near springs, streams and lakes—bodies of water believed to be inhabited and protected by Naagas. This reverence is reflected in place names like Anantnag (spring of Ananta) and Verinag (often linked to Nila Naaga). Offerings were made to ensure prosperity and appease the Naagas, whose dual nature as protector and potential bringer of calamity (floods and hailstorms) was deeply respected.

The Chinese pilgrim Hiouen Tsiang, who travelled through the region in the seventh century CE, described numerous instances where prayers to serpent deities resulted in rain or fair weather, reinforcing the belief in their power over nature. In Kashmir, Vasuki Naaga is particularly revered in Bhaderwah, where a temple dedicated to him houses two ancient black stone idols of serpent deities, uniquely placed at a slant without any visible support.

Thus, across the Himalayan arc, from the valleys of Kashmir and Himachal to the foothills of Uttarakhand, serpent worship reveals a profound connection between the people, the mountainous landscape and powerful local deities, often blending Puranic figures with indigenous traditions. The Naagas here were guardians of springs and rulers of ancient lineages. Having explored these northern heights, our journey now moves eastward, to the plains and deltas where traditions like the worship of Manasa Devi hold sway.

III

Serpents of the East

Serpent worship has long been a powerful undercurrent in the religious life of eastern India, entwined with both the spiritual and everyday realities of its people. The *Mangalkaavya*, or 'auspicious poems', an important literary tradition in Bengal that eulogizes gods and goddesses, offers not only a window into religious practices but also glimpses into the social, political and economic fabric of the time. These texts, particularly the *Manasamangal* and *Chandimangal*, devoted to the goddesses Manasa and Chandi respectively, paint a vivid picture of life in Bengal. Through them, one can trace the ebb and flow of landscape, trade, food and even the delicate balance between the human and divine. Within this context, the serpent goddess Manasa emerges as a central, compelling figure.

The Serpent Goddess of the Bengal Delta

We encountered Manasa briefly in Part 1 as one of the prominent Naaga deities, but her worship in Eastern India warrants closer examination. She is a deity who was not born into power but had to seize it. Unlike many goddesses who are bestowed with their status, Manasa's rise is fraught with struggle, much like the Bengal delta she presides over, a land constantly reshaped by the shifting waters of the Ganga and Brahmaputra. Known as the daughter of Shiva in some traditions, and in others, an incantation created by the sage Kashyapa to protect humans from snake bites, Manasa's name itself—meaning 'of the mind'—carries metaphysical weight. But her role as a goddess is far more corporeal, rooted in the raw fear of snakes that dominates rural life, especially during the monsoon.

For many scholars, Manasa represents the remnants of an older, pre-Aryan serpent cult that once thrived in the Sundarbans before being subsumed by Shaivite traditions. The goddess's struggle for recognition from Shiva's devotees, or shivbhaktas, reflects deeper power dynamics between older indigenous deities and the ascendant gods. Some historians even suggest that she may have supplanted an earlier Buddhist Tantric deity, Janguli. Her worship, however, remains distinct in Bengal, where she is revered not only as the protector from snakebites but also as the guardian of fertility and prosperity.

Manasa's Iconography

Manasa's iconography is as striking as her mythology. Images of Manasa, crafted from stone, bronze and terracotta and recovered from various regions, share common features. Typically, she is depicted with two or four arms, wearing a crown with five or seven expanded snake hoods, symbolizing her dominion over serpents. She often appears seated between her husband, Jaratkaaru, and her brother, King Vasuki, with her son Astika on her lap. In her left hand, she either cradles Astika or holds a snake. Some representations show her seated on a lotus platform or standing triumphantly upon a serpent, enveloped by snakes in her divine form. Her festivals, particularly in the month of Shravan (July–August), are deeply tied to the agricultural calendar and the fear of venomous bites during the rainy season.

Manasa's Veneration

In the Sundarbans, her worship is often simple, with mud idols erected in her honour, reflecting the raw, elemental nature of the region itself. A temple dedicated to Manasa in Jakpur, for instance, notably has no roof. Legend holds that centuries ago, farmers of a small village called Mahisha, plagued by snakes, worshipped Manasa for protection and bountiful harvests, offering grain bundles post-harvest. Around 400 years ago, a zamindar of the region, guided by a divine vision of Manasa in her four-armed form, formalized her worship on a concrete platform adorned with a red lotus. Devotees pray there on Tuesdays and Saturdays, especially during the monsoon, seeking safety and prosperity.

Manasa's reach extends beyond Bengal, but she may not be the same goddess everywhere. In Haryana, Punjab and Uttarakhand, where temples dedicated to her exist, she may not be the snake goddess known as Monosha in Bengal or Monoha in Assam. These regional variations reveal the fascinating ways in which deities are shaped and reshaped by geography and culture. But in Bengal, Manasa remains a crucial figure for certain communities, particularly the Rajbansis and the tribal communities of North Bengal and Assam. For these groups, her protection is not just a religious act—it is an integral part of life in a landscape teeming with danger.

The Jhapan Festival

In Bishnupur, West Bengal, the Jhapan festival, held on the last day of Shravan, celebrates Goddess Manasa with snake-handling performances by Jhapanias. People pray to Manasa during this time for good rains and fertile land, vital for the farmer's survival. This ancient tradition, believed to bring blessings for a bountiful harvest, includes local fairs, plays and snake shows by charmers. Over 400 years old, the festival faces concerns about snake welfare. To address this, efforts are made to release snakes after the event and follow wildlife laws, preserving both cultural heritage and ecological balance (*The Times of India*, 2020).

Manasa's story is one of resilience, a testament to the power of belief in a land defined by its relationship to the natural world. Like the rivers that snake their way through the delta, her worship has twisted and turned through centuries, absorbing and being absorbed by the people who call this land home.

Regional Beliefs and Taboos

Beyond the specific worship of Manasa, various folk beliefs surrounding snakes persist in eastern India. An interesting belief dictates that one should not dispose of a killed snake by throwing it out through a door. Instead, a hole should be made in the wall, or an open window used, lest malevolent spirits enter the house. An old friend from Bhubaneshwar (Odisha) once shared another local superstition—if a guest utters the word for snake or cobra, the creature itself will make an appearance that night. Similarly, some believe one should never call a snake by its name upon seeing it, but rather refer to it euphemistically as a 'keeda' (worm), supposedly causing temporary paralysis in the snake (though attempting this is strongly discouraged). These beliefs highlight a widespread cultural sensitivity and deep-seated awe regarding serpents in the region.

Similarly, in the northern and central parts of India, it was believed that snakes should be referred to euphemistically. People often called them 'mama' (maternal uncle) or 'rassi' (rope) to avoid offending them. Crooke also notes that Sonjhara women, much like how they avoid naming their male relatives aloud, follow this tradition and refrain from speaking the snake's name, emphasizing the cultural taboos and deep-seated reverence surrounding snakes in these regions.

Naagavanshis of Chota Nagpur

The *Mahabharata* is vast enough on its own, but once we account for the countless folktales and local legends that have spun out of its central narrative across the Indian subcontinent, we step into a labyrinth of myth, history and cultural memory that stretches into infinity. According to beliefs, the Naagavanshis of Chota Nagpur trace their lineage back to the aftermath of the Mahabharata's Sarpasatra, the infamous snake sacrifice.

The tale revolves around Pundarika, a Naaga prince who sought to escape the fiery doom planned for his kind during the yajna of King Janamejaya. Refusing to meet his end, Pundarika fled to Kashi, adopting the guise of a human. It is here that this shape-shifting serpent found refuge in the home of a brahmin, studying under him, hiding his serpentine nature beneath layers of intellect and scholarship. The brahmin grew fond of Pundarika whose brilliance in study seemed almost superhuman. As the brahmin's trust deepened, he eventually offered his daughter, Parvati, in marriage to this extraordinary disciple.

However, beneath the veneer of humanity, Pundarika's true nature could not be entirely hidden. At night, when he slept, his tongue would slip out, forked and serpentine. Poisonous fumes escaped from his breath, leaving his wife Parvati unsettled. She repeatedly asked him the cause of this strange phenomenon, but Pundarika, bound by fear or shame, kept his secret.

It wasn't until they embarked on a pilgrimage to the southern holy lands that Parvati's persistent questioning bore fruit. As they reached Sutiambe near Pithoria, Parvati, now heavy with child, went into labour. In the throes of pain and perhaps sensing her own mortality, she decided to press her husband once more for the truth. Pundarika, perhaps knowing he could no longer keep his secret, confessed that he was not a human at all but a serpent in human form. Having revealed his secret, Pundarika disappeared into a nearby lake, his serpentine body slipping beneath the still waters as if he had always belonged to that otherworldly realm.

Parvati, left alone, gave birth to their son in the wilderness. In a desperate bid for survival, she gathered firewood and lit a pyre, perhaps hoping to reunite with her husband in death, or maybe simply to end her suffering. She immolated herself in the flames, leaving the newborn child behind.

The story takes an even more poignant turn when local woodcutters, seeing the baby beneath the protective hood of a cobra, informed a nearby brahmin. He took the child home, naming him Phanimukuta Raya, 'the one crowned with a serpent hood,' raising him as his own.

In another version of the tale, Phanimukuta was entrusted to a local chief named Madar Munda, who noticed that the boy's brilliance far surpassed that of his own son. Madar Munda, with a keen sense of justice, declared Phanimukuta as his heir, and thus the Naagvanshi lineage was believed to be established. This tale, set around the year 121 CE or 64 CE depending on the version, marks the beginning of the Naagvanshi dynasty in the Chota Nagpur region (Goswami, 1902, p. 3).

From the complex goddess Manasa reigning over the Bengal delta to the intricate origin myths of the Naagavanshis claiming descent from a Naaga prince, Eastern India offers unique and powerful expressions of serpent reverence. These traditions, interwoven with distinct folklore and rituals, highlight the enduring legacy of ophiolatry in this region, distinct yet connected to the practices found elsewhere on the subcontinent. While my own exploration for this work did not extend deeply into the diverse traditions of north east India, it's worth noting that this region also holds potent serpent lore, such as tales I have heard of U. Thlen, a figure often described as a demonic serpent in Khasi folklore. Our journey now circles back towards the heartland, to explore the serpent traditions of western and central India.

IV

Serpents Worship in Western and Central India

In the heartlands of India, serpent worship manifests in unique local legends, vibrant rural and tribal festivals, and extraordinary examples of human-snake coexistence across the western and central regions. My own understanding of these traditions deepened during a visit with a couple in Pune for their housewarming. When I mentioned my research on serpent worship and about the revered Mannarasala temple in Kerala, the wife immediately spoke of their family's Naagadevata in Goa, whose temple is nestled somewhere on the Konkan coast, revealing how deeply these practices remain woven into family life.

Maharashtra—Reverence and Unique Coexistence

Indeed, serpent stones (*naaga shila*) are commonly found in smaller temples across the Maharashtra countryside. On one road trip from Pune to Mulshi along the Maan road, I came across just such an example—a village deity's temple with a dedicated stone idol for Naagoba (serpent deity) placed respectfully outside. In rural Maharashtra, Naagoba is often worshipped by farmers, who consider the snake a friend for preying on crop-damaging pests.

Naagapanchami remains a special occasion in the region, celebrated with particular reverence by women.

The importance placed on Naagapanchami and respecting serpents, especially the taboo against harming them or disturbing the earth on this day, is vividly illustrated in a common folktale from the region.

The Naagin and the Farmer

Once, a farmer lived near an anthill inhabited by serpents. On the day of Naagapanchami, he went to plough his field. Tragically, his ploughshare struck the anthill, killing the young serpents within. When the Naagin (mother serpent) returned to find her children dead, she was consumed by grief and rage. Seeking vengeance, she went to the farmer's house and bit him and his entire family, sparing only a married daughter who lived in another village.

Intent on finishing her revenge, the Naagin travelled to the daughter's village. There, she found the young woman devoutly worshipping serpent deities, offering milk and prayers, unaware of the Naagin's presence. Moved by the woman's piety despite her own loss (as she explained her family had been killed by a serpent), the Naagin revealed her identity and the reason for her wrath against the farmer.

However, seeing the daughter's genuine devotion, the Naagin relented. She offered the woman drops of amrita (nectar of immortality) to revive her family. The farmer and his household were restored to life, and the daughter instructed her father henceforth to always observe the fast and respect the sanctity of Naagapanchami, ensuring no plough disturbed the earth on that sacred day.

This deep-seated reverence finds its most extraordinary expression further south in Shetphal, a village in the Solapur district, approximately 200 kilometres from Pune. Shetphal has gained fame, often highlighted on social media, for its unique and intimate relationship with cobras. In this remarkable village, snakes are not merely tolerated or worshipped from afar; they are reportedly considered members of the household. Each home is said to have a designated resting place (*devasthan*) for a cobra, often a hollow space in the ceiling. Snakes allegedly move freely through houses and the village itself, coexisting peacefully with the human inhabitants who treat them with respect rather than fear. This exceptional situation showcases a profound cultural acceptance and veneration of serpents as integral parts of the community.

Bordering Traditions—The Naagoba Jaatra

This reverence extends across state borders, particularly evident in the vibrant tribal traditions found where Maharashtra meets Telangana. Here, the Naagoba Jaatra, a major tribal festival dedicated to the serpent deity Naagoba (a term also used for serpent deities in parts of rural Maharashtra), unfolds annually in Keslapur village, Adilabad district, Telangana. The Naagoba Temple is situated significantly at the confluence of the Pranahita and Godavari rivers. This ten-day event is the second-largest tribal gathering in Telangana, drawing Gond communities (particularly the Mesaram clan) and other tribes not only from Telangana but also significantly from neighbouring Maharashtra, as well as Chhattisgarh and Madhya Pradesh.

The festival commences with elaborate rituals, including the ceremonial bathing (abhishekam) of the Naagoba idol with sacred water fetched by priests from the Godavari River, a journey covering 70 kilometres. A highlight of the Jaatra is the energetic Gusadi dance performance. Thousands congregate at the temple to honour Naagoba, who is revered as a powerful protector and sometimes maybe identified with Ananta Shesha. This large, cross-border gathering underscores the deep spiritual significance of Naagoba and the strong cultural bonds among the tribal communities of the region (*The Hindu*, 2025).

Madhya Pradesh – The Naagdwari Pilgrimage

Deep within the dense Satpura forests of central Madhya Pradesh, near the hill station of Pachmarhi, lies Naagdwari. This site is revered by folk beliefs as a sacred gateway to Naagaloka, the mythical subterranean realm of serpents. Accessible only during a brief period around the Naagapanchami festival (typically in July/August), reaching Naagdwari requires a challenging 12-kilometre trek through monsoon-soaked jungles, traversing steep hills and rugged terrain within the Satpura Tiger Reserve. Despite the arduous journey and potential risks from wildlife, devotees undertake this pilgrimage each year. The main sites of worship are natural caves, including the 100-foot-long Chintamani Cave and the nearby Swarg Dwar (Heaven's Gate) cave, which house idols of Naagadevatas. Pilgrims offer prayers here, seeking blessings and the fulfilment of wishes, their chants echoing through the forests in a powerful display of devotion to the serpent deities believed to reside within these sacred hills.

Nagpur – City of the Serpent King

Concluding this survey of the central regions, an interesting historical note comes from Nagpur in Maharashtra. The city was apparently originally known as Fanindrapura. This name translates to 'City of the Serpent King', with 'fani' (or *phani*) specifically referring to a serpent's hood. This ancient name reflects the deep-seated reverence for serpents in the region's history, a legacy that, while perhaps less visible today, remains embedded in the etymology of this major central Indian city.

From the unique coexistence in Shetphal and the reverence seen in Maharashtrian village life, to the grand cross-border tribal gathering for Naagoba drawing devotees from Maharashtra and beyond, and the arduous pilgrimage to Naagdwari, the western and central regions of India showcase diverse expressions of Naagaradhana. Here, serpents are integrated into village life, honoured through large-scale community festivals, sought in remote natural sanctuaries. Sometimes they are remembered in the very names of cities like Nagpur and Bhuj (named after Bhujanga Naaga). These heartland traditions highlight both the deep antiquity and the living vibrancy of serpent worship, distinct from yet connected to the practices found elsewhere. Our journey next leads southward, specifically to the southwest coast of India, where Naagaaradhane takes on perhaps its most concentrated and deeply rooted forms in the sacred groves and temples of the Tulunadu and Kerala.

V

Naagaaradhane in South India

In the Tulu speaking region of coastal Karnataka, the cobra is revered, elevated to the status of pratyaksha devata or 'a god who is visible'. In the Tulu language, the word uchchu signifies 'snake,' and to utter 'edde ithno uchchu'—the good (potent) snake—is to speak of the cobra imbued with powerful venom and divine power, one whose presence commands respect, even awe. Killing a cobra here is no ordinary act of violence, but considered a Brahmahatya.

Reverence and Taboo on the Southwest Coast

While traveling through Belmannu and Karkala, I encountered a remarkable tale that exemplifies this reverence. The locals spoke of a priest, who for decades has been the one to whom people turn, from far and wide, when they come across a dead cobra. His role is a peculiar one—he is summoned to perform the last rites for these serpentine beings, treating them as one would a deceased family member. Rituals are observed, including 'sutaka'—a period of ritualistic abstinence that lasts fourteen days.

Naturally, I was curious. I asked him, 'Why is such a funeral necessary?'

His reply was as steeped in ancient tradition as the air around us in that beautiful village in Tulunadu, 'It doesn't allow the Naaga's spirit to pass on, and it wanders like an angry restless preta. This brings misfortune.'

Skeptical, I prodded further. 'Most people today don't seem keen on observing sutaka for human beings, forget about a cobra. Is that why they call you?'

The priest nodded gravely. 'Yes, they do. I observe the abstinence for them, just as I would for a family member.'

Astonished by the gravity of the custom, I could not help but ask the inevitable, 'Has there ever been a time when someone ignored a dead cobra and ill fortune befell them?'

His voice dropped to a sombre tone. 'Ten or fifteen years ago, a family was traveling from Bangalore, on their way to a temple. Along the highway, they saw a cobra—dead, lying there in the middle of the road. But they didn't stop. They were in a rush to make it to the temple before it closed.'

'And what happened?' I asked, already sensing the outcome.

'They never reached the temple,' he said, his eyes distant with memory. 'Their car met with an accident. By Lord Krishna's grace, they survived. But they called me afterward to inform me of the dead cobra they had passed. I went immediately to the site and performed the cobra's funeral rites. It was my duty.'

This was but one of many such stories I encountered, tales woven into the everyday fabric of life in this region. Even in Kerala, similar beliefs persist. I was told that when Hindus come across a dead cobra, they cover its body with a clean cloth, an offering of respect and reverence for the divine serpent.

The Legend of Ramabhoja, the Naaga and the Naming of Tulu

The echoes of these beliefs resonate deeply in the myths and legends of the region. Take, for instance, one of the etymological tales behind the word 'Tulu,' the language spoken along the coastlines of Tulunadu in Karnataka. While researching for my book *Daiva*, I encountered many different versions of how the word Tulu came into being. However, one version stood out, entwined with the sacred cobra—a story I am now compelled to share.

The Story of Ramabhoja's Ashwamedham

Long ago, in a land that would one day be known as Udupi, there ruled a powerful king named Ramabhoja. His reign was marked by grandeur and the ancient rituals that affirmed a monarch's dominion in the region. Among these was the *Ashwamedham*, an ancient ceremony through which kings of old asserted their imperial sovereignty. The ritual was as much a test of strength as it was of fate—a horse, accompanied by the king's warriors, was set free to roam for a year, marking the movement of the earth around the sun. Its journey was a silent challenge to neighbouring rulers, a gauntlet thrown down without words. Any rival could stake their claim to power by capturing the horse. But if the horse returned unharmed to the king's capital, it was a sign that no force in the known world could contest his supremacy. The king would then complete the ritual with a yajna, a sacrificial fire, and earn the revered title of Chakravarthi, the emperor whose authority spanned the known world.

During Ramabhoja's Ashwamedham, however, the fates intervened. A cobra, revered as a sacred being in these lands, slithered unnoticed into the ritual fire. It burned in the fire and died a tragic death. This sent waves of fear through the king's court, for in that part of India, a cobra's death was no ordinary event—it was an omen, a portent of the Naagadevata's wrath.

Following Parashuraama's counsel, Ramabhoja performed the *Tulaabhaaram*. This term originates from 'Tula', meaning balance, and 'Bhaaram', meaning weight. It's fascinating to note that the Hindi words *tolna* (to measure) and *bhaar* (weight) stem from these very roots. In Tulaabhaaram, a person is weighed on a large scale against a chosen offering—gold, silver, bananas or grain. The equivalent weight is then given as a donation, symbolizing penance and devotion. In Ramabhoja's case, a silver idol of a serpent, meticulously coated in pure gold, was crafted to appease the Naagadevatas, the serpent deities who wielded power over the land and its fortunes.

It is said that this act of atonement gave rise to the name 'Taulava', a name that may have, over centuries, evolved into what we now call 'Tulu'. Scholars debate the historical accuracy of this tale, but we are not here to dwell on the fine points of history. Instead, we are drawn into the scintillating world of serpent worship that has long permeated this region—a world where myth and devotion intertwine, creating a rich fabric of belief that endures to this day.

Sacred Spaces—Naagabana and Sarpakaavu

Naturally, many people in the southwestern coast have utmost respect for the cobra, and that is why most of them do not kill it when they see one. The primary locus of this reverence is the sacred serpent grove. In Tulunadu, these groves are called Naagabana, while in the neighbouring state of Kerala, they are called

Sarpakaavu. Those who have grown up in these parts would know how much respect serpents receive from the local Hindus. Each family often has a designated serpent grove which is considered the moolanaaga sthaana (root serpent place), bana or kaavu. The word kaavu may have originated from sarpakaaval, where 'kaaval' in Malayalam means protection.

Parashuraama and the Serpent Guardians

An interesting folktale goes back to the times of Parashuraama that I briefly described in my previous book, *Daiva*. Here, I will delve into the mythical creation story of the southwestern coast in a little more detail. Please note that this story is based on *Keralolpatthi*, a treatise that deals with the legends and lore of Kerala and is believed to be based on another Sanskrit language work called *Keralamahaatmyam*. The word is a combination of 'Keralam' and 'Utpaththi' (creation), which means the creation of Kerala. Once again, historians who focus on hard facts debate about the validity of the events, but let us see the story as it is, or perhaps through a metaphoric veil.

The Story of the Creation of India's South Western Coast

One of the most intriguing and awe-inspiring characters of our Puraanas is Raama with the Axe—Parashuraama. Born to sage Jamadagni and Renuka, the sixth incarnation (avatar) of Lord Vishnu occupies a very important position in Hindu scriptures. According to the puraanas, he is the restorer of righteousness, and is considered one of the eight *chiranjeevis* (immortals).

Legend has it that in ancient times, a formidable king named Kartavirya Arjuna, also known as Sahasrabahu Arjuna, ruled from Mahishmati, the capital of the Haihaya kingdom situated along the banks of the river Narmada in present-day Madhya Pradesh. This illustrious ruler is depicted in various texts, having conquered Mahishmati from Karkotaka, a powerful Naaga chief, transforming it into his stronghold.

On one occasion, Kartavirya Arjuna and his retinue visited the ashram of sage Jamadagni. The sage, through the divine cow Kaamadhenu, prepared an opulent feast that astounded the king (Deshpande, 1951, p. 3,215). Envious of the sage's prosperity, Kartavirya Arjuna demanded Kaamadhenu, essential for his sacrificial rites, offering numerous other cows in exchange.

The sage, bound by virtue, declined, stating that such a divine cow, protected by Indra himself, could not be surrendered. Enraged, Kartavirya Arjuna seized Kaamadhenu by force and returned triumphantly to Mahishmati. In the Padma Puraana, the king in his arrogance, kills Jamadagni (Deshpande, 1951, p. 3,218).

When Parashuraama returned to his parents, to his horror he found that his father's holy hermitage had become the scene of tradegy. This act of arrogance enraged Parashuraama, who promptly sought retribution. A fierce battle ensued between Parashuraama and Kartavirya Arjuna, culminating in the demise of the king at the hands of the axe-wielding warrior. Subsequently, Parashuraama embarked on a campaign against corrupt kingdoms, instilling fear among those who abused their power.

The tale continues with the story of Parashuraama, who, in his legendary wrath, annihilated the rulers in twenty-one successive wars. However, once his vengeance was complete, Parashuraama was overcome with remorse. Stricken by the weight of his actions, he convened a council of the great sages, seeking guidance on how to atone for his grievous sin—*Vimhatyadosham*, the sin of having slain so many crowned heads and their armies.

The sages advised him to make a gift of land to the brahmins as an act of penance. Parashuraama, ever obedient to the counsel of the wise, did as they instructed. However, the brahmins, having received the land, warned him that if he continued to reside on it, the act would negate his penance and accumulate as further sin. Convinced of the truth in their words, Parashuraama withdrew to the Western Ghats, seeking once more to cleanse his soul through penance.

During those times, the southwestern coast of the Indian subcontinent was believed to extend only as far as Gokarna. There was no Tulunadu or Kerala as we know it today. It was here that Parashuraama performed intense penance to Varuna, the god of the waters, and Bhumi Devi, the Goddess of the Earth. His devotion earned him permission to claim as much land as could be covered by the throw of his axe from Gokarna into the southern sea. Parashuraama hurled his axe, and it landed in the sea near Kanyakumari. From the depths, a new expanse of land emerged, but it was barren, salty and unstable—unfit for habitation.

To remedy this, Parashuraama sprinkled gold dust and buried coins across the land, which stabilized the earth and stopped its quaking. With the land now secure, Parashuraama brought settlers from the land above and introduced a wide variety of grains, seeds, medicinal plants, and trees, including the coconut, plantain and jackfruit, which have since become synonymous with the region's rich agriculture.

Despite these efforts, the newly reclaimed land remained inhospitable due to its saltiness. Parashuraama then invoked the mighty Naagaraaja Vasuki, who, with a single breath of holy venom, transformed the barren, saline land into a lush and verdant paradise. In the origin tale of Vetticode Sri Naagaraajaswami temple, Parashuraama is believed to have approached Ananta Shesha for the same purpose, and the great serpent directed Naagas to suck out the unwanted elements or contents from the land and thus turned the land into a fertile one (Aayilyam Mahotsavam, Kerala Tourism Official Website).

In recognition of the Naagaraja's valour and loyalty, Parashuraama appointed serpents as the protectors and guardians of the land, honouring the divine origins of the region with this sacred charge (there is another version of this story in the fourth part of this book which contains folktales about serpents).

Parashuraama and Naagaaradhane

According to another version of the story, Naagas may have been fearsome hill tribes who had already established their presence in the region and fiercely resisted the newcomers, driving them back. These tribes were likely devoted serpent worshippers. To resolve the conflict and establish peace, Parashuraama struck a compromise. He ceded a portion of the land to the Naagas, allowing both the settlers and the indigenous tribes to coexist peacefully.

As a gesture of conciliation, Parashuraama instructed his settlers to adopt the Naagas' form of worship, thus sanctioning serpent worship, or *Naagaaradhane*, along the coast. This ancient practice, deeply rooted in both myth and history, continues to hold a significant place in the region to this day.

It is also believed that Parashuraama established 108 fields (parade-grounds) of 42 feet square each, called Kalaris (Garodi in Tulu) for purposes of drill and training in arms, and in each of these he placed an image of the gods who preside over arms and war and then lamps were lit. He also established 108 images of Durga Devi on the seashore, and besides erected shrines for serpents (Aiya, 1906, p. 217).

Pulluvans—Bards of the Serpent Gods

When discussing serpent worship in southern India, one must acknowledge the Pulluvan community of Kerala, bards who have kept the tales of the Naagas alive through generations. The ballads of the Pulluvans, or Pulluvan Pattu, form the core of their spiritual expression. In *Daiva*, I briefly mentioned the Panans, believed by some to be ancestors of the Pulluvan community, who serve as kola dancers in local rituals. Both communities trace their lineage through a patrilineal system, where knowledge, stories and practices are passed from father to son. Edgar Thurston, in his seminal work, describes the Pulluvans as astrologers, healers and singers who traditionally performed in snake groves. Their name, intriguingly, is derived from 'pullu,' a hawk, believed to possess the power to cure disorders caused by evil spirits. Such folklore underscores the Pulluvans' role as both spiritual and physical healers, trusted to treat ailments afflicting pregnant women and infants, thought to be caused by serpent deities or other supernatural forces.

The Pulluvan's primary tool of devotion is their unique lute, often called a pulluvan veena. Crafted from materials like bamboo or wood, sometimes covered with reptile skin, and played with a bow that jingles with a small metal bell, the lute's haunting music is believed to appease the serpents, bringing divine blessings upon the listeners. Both men and women—the Pulluvan and Pulluvatthi— sing these sacred ballads in unison, especially during rituals like Sarpabali and Pambu Thullal (Snake Dance). These ceremonies, presided over by the Pulluvan and his wife, serve to propitiate the serpent gods, making them critical figures in the spiritual life of serpent groves. There is an interesting origin story linking this community with the Mahabharata. Through their ballads, telling the tales of the burning of Khandava or Kaliyamardanam, the Pulluvans serve as conduits between humanity and the divine serpents, preserving an ancient and revered tradition that has captivated and mystified generations.

Sarpam Paattu—A Sacred Song

The Sarpam Paattu or the 'Song of the Serpent' is among the most revered rituals dedicated to the serpents at the famous Mannarasala temple in Kerala. This rare and labour-intensive ceremony is conducted only once every forty-one years, making it a once-in-a-lifetime event for most. Historical records show that Sarpam Paattu has been performed several times, with the ceremony of 1074 M.E. (Malayalam Era) being particularly well-documented.

The deep reverence for serpents, the foundational myths linking them to the land's creation, the dedicated sacred groves, and the specialized communities like the Pulluvans all underscore the unique intensity of Naagaradhana or ophiolatry in south India. This connection manifests most visibly in the numerous sacred temples dedicated to Naaga and Sarpam deities across the region, which we will explore in the next chapter.

VI

Famous Serpent Temples of Southern India

The deep reverence for serpents found across the southwest coast, rooted in foundational myths and expressed through dedicated groves, manifests most visibly in the numerous sacred temples dedicated to Naaga deities throughout the southern regions. These temples serve as major centres of worship, drawing devotees seeking blessings, relief from afflictions and connection to these powerful guardians.

In the monsoon-drenched summer of 2017, I stepped off the train at Harippad's quaint railway station in Alappuzha, Kerala, my heart set on Mannarasala, one of India's largest serpent groves. An autorickshaw carried me through the lush, rain-soaked landscape until a grand archway loomed ahead, flanked by stone idols of serpent deities standing sentinel. As I crossed the threshold, a gentle drizzle mingled with a soft breeze, wrapping me in a sanctity that felt almost otherworldly, as if the earth itself exhaled reverence.

Amid the myriad Naaga idols, I could feel as if the boundary between sacred and mundane dissolved, and the past whispered through the scent of rain-soaked soil. The Naaga holds deep symbolic meaning in south Indian culture, prominently featured in religious iconography and architecture. A vivid example can be

ground and the silence envelops you, truly feels like a return to the womb—a place where time itself stands still. Thousands of granite serpent idols, offered by devotees over centuries, line the paths and cluster around the trees, adding to the unique atmosphere.

Mannarasala draws devotees from far and wide who seek the blessings of Naagaraaja (often considered Vasuki here), particularly for progeny. Childless couples often perform special rituals, including the offering of a serpent image and the famous urali kamazhthal (the ritualistic placing of a vessel upside down), hoping for the gift of a child. The temple also stands out as one of the few major temples in Kerala where the chief priestly duties are performed by a woman, the senior most Namboodiri woman of the resident family, referred to as the Valiya Amma (Great Mother). The name Mannarasala is a compound of three Malayalam words: 'mannu' meaning soil, 'aariya' meaning cool, and 'saalai' meaning house. It was also once known as Mandarasala due to the abundance of Mandara trees in the area.

Aameda Naagaraja Temple

On the banks of Vembanad Lake, 20 kilometres south of Ernakulam, Kerala, the Aameda Temple is dedicated to the Sapthamathrukkal (seven divine mothers)—Brahmani, Maheshwari, Kowmari, Vaishnavi, Varahi, Indrani and Chamundi. Shrines for Naagaraaja and Naagayakshi in the northwest and northeast, respectively, highlight its Naaga worship tradition.

Legend recounts Parashuraama, during his coastal travels, spotting a radiant light in the lake during his sandhyavandanam. Guided by divine insight, he discovered the seven divine mothers traveling atop a tortoise. They halted by his approach. The spot, named Aama-ninna-yidam (later became Aameda), became the temple's site, built where the tortoise paused. Devotees perform sarpabali, with materials available on-site, and partake in daily annadaanam, reinforcing the temple's role as a spiritual haven.

Sri Kalahasti—Devotion Beyond Form

Moving to Andhra Pradesh's Chittoor district, the Srikalahasteeswara Temple, known as Dakshina Kailasam (Kailash of the south), stands as a major Shaivite beacon with significant Naaga connections. A Pancha Bhoota Sthalam representing the element of Air (Vaayu), this magnificent Chola-Vijayanagara era temple derives its name from three unlikely devotees—a spider (sri), a serpent (kala), and an elephant (hasti)—all three are believed to worship the Shiva Lingam here with unparalleled fervour.

According to legend, the spider wove silken temples for the lingam, risking its life to protect its offerings from an altar fire, earning moksha. The cobra, bearing gems, clashed with an elephant that adorned the altar with leaves after bathing in the Swarnamukhi River. Their rivalry ended in mutual sacrifice, but Shiva, moved by their love, granted them liberation, immortalizing their forms—a spider, two tusks, and a five-headed serpent—at the lingam's base.

Kukke Subramanya Temple

Nestled in Karnataka's ghats, the Kukke Subramanya Temple, on the Kumaradhara River's banks, venerates Lord Subramanya as the lord of serpents. Framed by Kumara Parvatha and the serpent-shaped Shesha Parvatha, this ancient shrine celebrates Ganapathy and Subramanya's victory over demons Tharaka and Shurapadmasura and his marriage to Devasena.

According to regional tales, it is here that the divine serpent king Vasuki and other Naagas, seeking refuge from the wrath of Garuda, performed penance and were granted protection by Subramanya. Consequently, the temple became a paramount centre for rituals addressing naagadoshas (afflictions caused by serpents), particularly the famous Sarpa Samskara and Ashlesha Bali pujas. Devotees believe these rites alleviate curses related to serpents, often incurred by harming snakes (even inadvertently or in past lives), and bestow blessings, especially progeny for childless couples.

Ghati Subramanya—Harmony of Deities

Near Bangalore, the 600-year-old Ghati Subramanya Temple, developed by the Ghorpade rulers, unites Lord Subramanya and Narasimha, their idols believed to have emerged from the earth on their own (Swayambhu). Subramanya, depicted with a seven-headed cobra, protected Naagas from Garuda, making it a key snake worship site. Rituals like Sarpa Dosha Nivarana Puja and naaga idol installations aid childless couples, while festivals like Brahmarathotsava and Narasimha Jayanti draw crowds. A December cattle fair unites farmers from Tamil Nadu, Andhra Pradesh and beyond, blending faith and livelihood.

Thirunageshwaram—Rahu's Sacred Abode

In Tamil Nadu's temple town of Kumbakonam, the Thirunageshwaram Naaganaathar Temple is famous as a Navagraha Sthala dedicated specifically to Rahu, one of the serpentine celestial nodes in Hindu astrology. A well-known phenomenon occurs here—during the auspicious Rahukaalam timings, milk poured over the idol of Rahu for abhishekam miraculously appears to turn blue, a spectacle drawing numerous devotees.

This temple, also known simply as Rahu Sthalam, venerates Lord Rahu along with his consorts, Naagakanni and Naagavalli. Believed to have been constructed initially by Aditya Chola I in the ninth century CE, the temple also honours Lord Shiva as Naaganaathar (Lord of the Naagas), who was worshipped here by great serpents including Adishesha, Takshaka and Karkotaka, reinforcing its deep connection to serpent lore.

Karkotakeswarar Temple

In Tirunallur, Tamil Nadu, the Kamarathivalli sameda Karkotakeswarar Temple, built by Sundara Chola over 1,000 years ago, venerates Shiva as Karkotakeswarar. The serpent king Karkotaka worshipped here to lift sage Parishad's curse, granting the region immunity from snake venom—a belief locals affirm. Rathi's prayers for Manmatha's (Kaamadeva) revival named the goddess Kaamarathivalli and the shrine Rathivarapuram.

Naagaraja Temple—Confluence of Faiths

Perched near India's southern tip in Nagercoil, Tamil Nadu, the Nagaraja Temple is a unique site whose very name means 'Temple of the Naaga'. Dedicated primarily to Naagaraja (the Serpent King, often identified with Vasuki or Adishesha), the temple complex remarkably harmonizes Hindu and Jain traditions, with origins possibly predating the twelfth century. The main Naagaraja shrine retains a simple thatched roof, distinct from the grander temple structure built later which houses idols of Vishnu (as Anantakrishna) and Shiva. Adding to its unique character is the presence of Jain iconography along the pillars of the main hall, including images of Lord Mahavira and the Tirthankara Parshvanatha, suggesting a history of interfaith coexistence centered around the serpent deity.

Local folklore, particularly as recorded in Kottarathil Sankunni's *Aithihyamaala*, offers a fascinating origin story for the shrine's humble appearance and special prasadam. According to this account, the revered Paambummekkattu Namboothiri, while travelling through the area, discovered a bleeding five-headed Naaga idol in the forest, accidentally struck by a grass-cutter's sickle. He established worship at the spot in a simple thatched hut ('Naagarukoil'), which gained great fame. The lore continues that although Namboothiri later wanted to construct a magnificent temple building nearby, but the Naagaraja deity appeared to him in a dream, expressing contentment with his original location. Thus, the primary shrine is believed to remain in the spot where the idol was found, slightly below ground level. The *Aithihyamaala* further notes that the soil at this original sanctum is blood-red (attributed to the idol's injury) and perpetually moist, despite surrounding dry ground. This soil is offered as prasadam, believed to cure skin diseases and miraculously replenish itself daily.

Kudupu Anantapadmanabha Swamy Temple

Returning to coastal Karnataka, Kudupu village, just 10 kilometres from Mangalore City along the Mangalore–Moodabidri route, is home to the ancient Sri Anantapadmanabha Temple. The main deity, Lord Anantapadmanabha, is housed in a central sanctum facing westward—a relatively rare orientation. The temple's origins are tied to a poignant local legend about a devout brahmin named Kedar who performed intense penance here by the Bhadra Saraswati Thirtha river, seeking the boon of a child from Lord Subramanya. Though granted his wish, fate delivered three divine eggs containing the essence of Vishnu, Ananta Shesha and Subramanya himself. Following divine instructions, Kedar placed these sacred eggs in a basket (kudupu in the local tongue) at his penance site, over which an anthill later grew, sanctifying the location. To the east of the main sanctum lies an extensive Naaga Bana (serpent grove), containing over three hundred serpent idols. This multitude of idols, scattered amidst the dense grove adjacent to the temple dedicated to Anantapadmanabha, powerfully evokes the site's connection to both Vishnu and Shesha as per its origin story, symbolizing the deep reverence for serpent deities in Tulunadu. The temple remains particularly famous for Ashlesha bali and rituals performed on Naagapanchami.

These sacred groves and temples, each with unique legends, architectural styles and ritualistic focuses—from seeking progeny at Mannarasala and Kukke, to alleviating astrological afflictions at Srikalahasti and Thirunageshwaram, or witnessing unique forms of coexistence and syncretism at Pambumekkattu and Nagercoil—stand as major centres of Naaga worship in the south. They demonstrate the multifaceted roles serpent deities play in the spiritual lives of devotees. Beyond these established shrines, however, reverence also manifests dynamically through ritual performance, particularly the intriguing serpent possession dances found across India, which we explore next.

VII

Serpent Possession Dances in Three States

I began this book with an anecdote from my visit to Khadgeswari Brahmasthana. What I witnessed there was a unique ritualistic serpent dance called Dakkebali. For an outsider, it may appear similar to Naagamandala, another form of ritualistic dance performed in Karnataka. Both Dakkebali and Naagamandala are ritualistic dances that involve a male from the Vaidya community taking on the role of *Naagakanyaka*, while another male priest, known as the *Naagapatri*, assumes the role of *Naagabrahma*. What follows is a spellbinding dance that continues for hours, where the *paatri* becomes possessed by the spirit of the serpent deities.

For those unfamiliar with the traditions of Tulunadu, Dakkebali is a sacred, evocative dance rooted in the region's ancient serpent worship known as Naagaaradhane. The ritual takes its name from the 'dakke', a small handheld drum played by a male from the Vaidya community. And no, despite the sinister connotations the word 'bali' might evoke, this is not a blood sacrifice. I recall mentioning 'Ashlesha bali' during a podcast where I was invited, and the host from Delhi recoiled in shock, asking if it involved slaughter. I had to explain that 'bali' here simply means a ritualistic offering, without violence or sacrifice.

Across the world, from ancient times to the modern age, music, dance and drama have acted as sacred bridges, connecting the mortal with the divine. Since the dawn of humanity, we have sung hymns to the creator, danced to appease the gods and enacted stories of creation and destruction—rituals that express our deepest yearnings for communion with the spiritual realm. These acts of devotion have outlasted the centuries, their essence preserved, even as they evolved into grand spectacles on contemporary stages.

Even today, in the far corners of India, serpent worship continues to embody this timeless bond between the earthly and the divine. Whether it is Naagamandala in Karnataka, Sarpamthullal in Kerala, or the rituals involving Jaagar in Uttarakhand, these ceremonies pulse with ancient spiritual fervour. What ties many of these practices together, beyond their veneration of Naaga deities, is the shared phenomenon of possession. During the rituals, the dancers or designated priests (paatris) are said to be seized by divine spirits, their bodies and voices becoming vessels for the spirits of the serpent gods.

Understanding Possession in Ritualistic Dances

In the context of any possession ritual (not limited solely to serpent worship, but including practices like *kola* or *theyyam*), the process of spirit possession may be seen as a manifestation of an altered state of consciousness or trance. This ethereal state is often induced through rhythmic movements, musical cadences, meditative practices or hypnotic techniques, which are known to produce distinct alterations in perception, cognition, and behaviour (Kumar 2024, p. 78).

When dancers engage in repetitive movements like spinning, swaying or shaking, it induces physical fatigue. This combination of physical exertion, rhythmic motion and sensory stimulation—

enhanced by music and the fervour of the crowd—can transform the medium's state of consciousness, allowing them to become possessed by the spirits believed to inhabit sacred realms. Psychologically, this transformation might be seen as a form of dissociation or absorption. The cultural and religious context of the dance ritual plays a crucial role in shaping how the medium experiences and interprets spirit possession.

Among the older generations, it is widely believed that when a dancer reaches this state, they may be capable of delivering oracular prophecies, perceiving the past or future, or communing with divine entities. We have seen such practices in the Daivaradhane rituals of Tulunadu and in Kerala's Theyyam and Velichapaadu. Similar oracular activities are part of other dance rituals like Naagamandala, Kaadyanaatta, Thullal and Jaagar, making these events not just performances but vital moments of divine communication for the community.

Let us now explore some specific examples of these powerful serpent possession dances across different states.

Dakkebali, Naagamandala, Kaadyanaatta

In Dakkebali, the *naagapatri*—a priest from a special lineage of the Shivalli brahmin community—represents naagabrahma, while a male from the Vaidya community becomes the naagakannike, which is likely a variation of the term naagakanyaka. Together, they embody the male and female aspects of the Naaga deities. The Vaidya, skilled in playing the small drum called dakke, sings along with the dance, while the paatri gets possessed. The devotees watch in awe as this powerful and sacred performance unfolds.

The devotion, however, is not confined to simple offerings; on special occasions, it culminates in elaborate rituals such as Naagamandala, where the faithful gather with hearts full of prayers.

Some seek to break the serpent's curse (*dosha*), while others pray for blessings or the prosperity of their community.

For this sacred dance, a pandal or tent is erected before the shrine, and an intricate mandala is created on the ground. The mandala—reminiscent of the *sarpakalam* in Kerala—is drawn using powders made from natural elements—crushed leaves, saffron, turmeric and rice powder. At its centre is a serpentine figure, coiled in hypnotic patterns, each curve a testament to a larger cosmic order. The serpent, depicted with three, five or seven hoods, stretches within a circle ten to fifteen feet wide, depending on the occasion's grandeur. A full mandala, with its sixteen knots, mirrors the pinnacle of cosmic design—a mathematical precision that reflects the serpentine order.

Viewed from a distance, the mandala stirs awe, offering a glimpse into the hidden world of serpents. Above this artwork rises a fragile yet sacred structure adorned with areca flowers, symbols of purity and blessing.

As the night deepens, the paatri, wild and untamed, his hair loose, holds a bunch of areca flowers, their tender florets sticking to his face, giving him a surreal, otherworldly appearance. Dressed in a dhoti, he becomes both human and spirit, blurring the boundaries between the mortal and the divine. His counterpart, the naagakannike, dressed in half-male, half-female attire, embodies the androgynous nature of serpentine divinity.

As the dance progresses, the paatri moves like a serpent—his body sinuous, fierce and unpredictable. The naagakannike provokes him further, as they dance, knotting and unknotting the lines of the mandala. Their interaction is a delicate balance of reverence and challenge. The crushed areca flowers stick to his body, as if he is moment by moment transforming into the serpent spirit itself. The air fills with the rhythm of drums, cymbals and the scent of flowers, creating a terrifying yet beautiful spectacle—a dance that evokes both fear and devotion.

As the night wears on, the paatri's movements become more serpentine, mimicking a cobra coiling around its prey, while the naagakannike sings praises to the serpent deity. In the final act, the serpent spirit is both enraged and appeased, moving from wrath to grace. The ritual's climax, the 'tying and untying of knots', reflects the duality of life—chaos and order, anger and peace, human and divine (Upadhyaya, 2002, p. 18).

While Naagamandala and Dakkebali hold a revered place in the mainstream religious practices of Tulunadu, a lesser-known, yet equally profound, serpent ritual exists among the Dalit communities of Karnataka. This ancient dance, known as Kaadyanaatta, draws its name from the word Kaadya, meaning the black king cobra, maybe an echo of the legendary Kaaliya Naaga. The shrines of Kaadya are hidden deep within the forests, far from the sanctuaries of more widely recognized traditions. These forest shrines stand as silent guardians of the past, centered on an anthill, where stones representing serpents lie scattered. Surrounding the anthill are hundreds of clay pots, each marked with serpent hoods, varying in number from one to eleven (Navada, 1993, p.14). Each clay pot bears the weight of generations of belief.

The veneration of clay pots is observed in other parts of the country, notably with deities like Manasa (in Bengal) worshipped as a clay pot known as Manasa-ghata (or 'ghot' locally). The pot likely symbolizes the womb, suggesting a connection to fertility rituals, according to scholars. Even in rural Maharashtra, live cobras are kept in earthen pots for reverence. The link between snakes and pots is intuitive—snakes may have been captured and kept in pots, and Tamil beliefs hold that snakes are drawn to pots in summer for their coolness. This association could tie into ancient beliefs about pots containing poison or soma, the puranic elixir (Haq, 2015, p. 26).

Sarpam Thullal

As we move further down towards Kerala, the connection to serpents—both physical and divine—runs through rituals like Sarpam Pattu, Sarpabali and Thullal, where intricate floor patterns, known as Kalams, are drawn using coloured rice powder, charcoal and coconut shells. These serpentine drawings, crafted with artistic precision, are believed to invoke the presence of the serpent deities. Women play a central role in these rituals.

In Thullal, a booth or 'pandal' is erected, covered with a silk or cotton canopy. On the floor, a large snake figure is created using five-coloured powders, and rice is scattered. Incense is burned, and a lamp is placed on a plate as offerings to the snake deity. The male from the Pulluvan community and his wife begin their music, with the wife keeping time by striking a metal vessel. As their songs in honour of the serpent deity rise, young women following ritual baths, begin to sway and quiver in time with the music. Their hair is let loose, and in their heightened state of excitement, they beat upon the floor and rub out the snake figure using palm flowers. After this, they proceed to a nearby snake grove, prostrate themselves before the stone snake idols, and regain consciousness. They are offered milk, tender coconut water and plantains as part of the ritual.

The ceremony is believed to reflect the approval or displeasure of the serpent gods. If the gods do not manifest through one of the participants, the ceremony is extended until they are properly propitiated. Sometimes, the snake figure may need to be destroyed and redrawn many times, stretching the ritual over several weeks. Each time the figure is wiped away, men with torches dance in step with the Pulluvan's music. As a permanent mark of devotion, the family may eventually erect a small platform or shrine, where they continue their worship annually (Thurston, 1909, p. 233–234).

Jaagar

In the hills of Uttarakhand, as briefly mentioned in the previous chapter, the concept of Jaagar is deeply woven into the fabric of local traditions. This ancient form of Indian folklore has coexisted with traditional Hinduism for centuries, serving as a unique bridge between the spiritual world and the mortal realm. Jaagar, meaning 'awakening' in Hindi, is a ceremonial practice meant to awaken the supernatural powers of Puranic gods (devas), folk gods (devatas), or even spirits of the deceased (bhutas). The definition may vary but the ritual, led by a storyteller called the Jagariya, involves invoking these supernatural entities through chants, mantras and ballads, all while accompanied by the rhythmic sounds of instruments like the daunr and thali.

This practice bears a strong resemblance to the paardanas of Tulunadu, particularly in the kola tradition, where ancestral spirits are invoked with song and dance. In both traditions, there is a sacred interaction between the spirit deity and the human, with the chosen Jagariya acting as a vessel for the local deities.

In the case of the Jaagar dedicated to the Naagadevatas or Naagaraaja, the serpent deities, the person selected as the vessel experiences possession, as the deity takes over their physical form. This phenomenon often extends beyond the chosen individual, as others in the gathering may also become possessed, swept up in a frenzy of devotion and ecstasy, dancing wildly in a spiritual communion with the divine. The entire event becomes a powerful, otherworldly experience, where the boundaries between the physical and spiritual worlds blur, and the deities make their presence known through the human form.

These dance rituals, filled with vivid imagery, dynamic movement, and stirring music, leave a lasting impact on those who witness them. They are not simply performances; they are living expressions of an enduring connection between art, religion and the human spirit. Through these sacred acts, we catch a glimpse of humanity's primordial desire to connect with the divine, a bond that has persisted through the ages. In the cases presented in this chapter, the connection is with the serpentine spirit of Naagadevatas. Such rituals are also part of folk traditions of Himachal and Assam as well.

These shared rituals—spanning different parts of the country—reveal common threads in the worship of serpent deities. It makes me wonder what ancient cultural exchanges may have flourished between these regions, or what has been lost over time in the relentless march of history. This deep connection between ritual, belief and the natural world finds its most tangible expression in the sacred serpent groves, which we will explore next.

VIII

Sacred Groves and Importance of Naagaaradhana

According to folklore, when Parashuraama threw his axe to carve the land of coastal Karnataka and Kerala from the sea, he laid down strict mandates—the serpents, guardians of this newly formed land, were to be venerated with the utmost devotion. Along with them, the mother goddesses were also to be revered in sacred groves—kaavu in Malayalam, bana in Tulu—were set aside as sanctuaries for these deities, untouched by human interference, and alive with an almost sentient wildness. The rules were clear. It was forbidden to kill the snakes or disturb the lush flora that encircled their lairs. The groves, in time, became a self-contained wilderness, their dense thickets and towering trees home to an array of serpents, both venomous and benign, their coiled forms adding to the air of foreboding that hung over these enchanted places.

The Cobra's path

It is believed, especially in the southwestern part of the country, that once a cobra takes a path then it will always trace the same route. Sometimes these routes commence from the anthill (mound) in the serpent grove, travel to some point in the village and return to the same place. The route such taken is known to most villagers and they make sure that it is not obstructed even by the shadow of an individual. Similar beliefs are known to exist throughout the western coast of India.

Curiously, in some parts of eastern India, sacred groves known as 'thaans' serve as sites of veneration, where trees are worshipped. The name resonates with the 'sthaana' or 'saana' of Tulunadu, where the Daivas are honoured. In these groves, a branch of the siju plant is placed as a symbolic representation of Manasa.

This, I believe, marks a significant contrast between the southwestern coast of India and the northern regions. I recall watching a video on YouTube where men marched in procession with live cobras. One man, claiming to possess extraordinary power, held multiple cobras in his hands, yet the snakes appeared frail and weak. It is highly likely that their fangs may have been removed—a cruel act that severely impacts their well-being. This does not seem like the form of serpent worship that has been passed down through our ancestors.

Serpent Idols

In the lush landscapes of south India, as well as in the hills of Uttarakhand, the focus is on the reverent worship of serpent idols. Live cobras are neither touched nor harmed, reflecting a deep respect for these sacred snakes and their role in the spiritual fabric of our culture. The cobras, it is believed, wielded immense power over the fortunes of the human families who dwelled near the sacred groves. A small shrine, often crumbling yet adorned with turmeric and flowers during rare rituals, would be erected within the grove to honour these divine deities—Naagaraaja, Naagayakshi and other representatives of the netherworlds. During Naagapanchami, milk would be poured as an offering to appease them, but beyond that, human hands stayed clear. The offering is called 'Thambila' in Tulu-speaking regions and 'Noorum-Paalum' in Kerala. The serpent gods demanded little in terms of direct worship, but their protection and blessing were essential for prosperity. Thus, the sanctity of these spaces, untouched for generations, became inextricably linked not only with the spiritual well-being of the people but also with the conservation of the natural world itself.

The Sacred Ecosystem

These sacred groves, scattered across coastal Karnataka and Kerala like hidden green jewels, still stand as quiet testaments to a more ancient understanding of balance—between man and nature, reverence and fear. Though in many towns much of the land around them has been cleared, scarred by the relentless march of modernity, the groves remain dense and mysterious, their canopies darkened by the thick webs of vines, the ground beneath them overgrown with medicinal plants now rare in the wider landscape. In these mini jungles, life continues in the shadows—snakes including cobras slither unseen, frogs croak in the damp underbrush, birds nest high in the foliage. Eagles, cuckoos and parrots fill the air with their calls, while insects—ants, lizards, earthworms—work unseen, their quiet industry enriching the soil. Monkeys and squirrels play among the branches, all finding refuge in these islands of life.

I encountered a profound tranquillity during my visit to the Brahmasthaana in Padbidri on a balmy afternoon, accompanied by my cousin, who is deeply connected to the place. A similar awe enveloped me at the bana of a mother goddess in my wife's village near Karkala. I stood in reverence before the ancient trees, their gnarled branches intertwining to form a dense canopy that blocked out the light, creating a hushed, sacred atmosphere. Here, the sounds of the outside world faded into silence, much like my experience in the sacred groves of Mekattu Mana in Kerala. A shared custom across these revered sites is the prohibition against wearing footwear, a mark of respect for the sacred ground that cradles the weight of countless prayers and rituals. Should you happen to see a cobra in these sacred groves, it is regarded as a most auspicious sign. In such a moment, one is expected to pause, offer a silent prayer and allow the serpent to glide by unimpeded. As mentioned before, the cobra is the Naaga, revered as 'pratyaksha devatas'—gods made manifest before our very eyes—embodying a divine presence that demands both reverence and humility.

The significance of these groves, however, is not merely ecological. The fear of the serpents—both real and divine—keeps them sacred. Legends warn of dire consequences for families that fail to appease the serpent gods. Childlessness, skin diseases and mental afflictions are but a few of the punishments said to be inflicted on those who disrespect the groves or neglect the annual rituals. The serpent gods, whose power extends across generations, have long been believed to exact their revenge not only on the transgressors but on their descendants, sometimes up to four generations. It is perhaps this deep-seated fear, born of a respect for the unknown and the unseen, that has led to the preservation of these groves as safe havens for countless species.

In my own quest to uncover the remnants of my ancestral grove, I travelled first to a dilapidated naagabana near Kateel, only to find most of the forest cover lost to the onslaught of development. The echoes of ancient chants had long faded, replaced by the sound of bulldozers and trucks. Yet, the stories lingered—of serpent gods long forgotten but still potent, of curses that would not be lifted until the serpents were once again venerated. I followed this trail further, to the old family home near Perumbavoor (in Kerala), a place now leased out to tenants, where I found in the neglected backyard the faint traces of a forgotten kaavu. Overgrown and choked with weeds, the shrine to Naagaraaja and Naagayakshi lay in quiet ruin. Now, one of my cousins performs the necessary rituals there every year to protect the family. I was fortunate enough to join them this year on a rainy day in August.

Serpent Worship and Climate Change

Whether one believes in the power of the Naaga deities or dismisses them as relics of a bygone era, the significance of these groves extends beyond their spiritual dimension. In a time when the world grapples with the accelerating impact of climate change, deforestation and the irreversible loss of biodiversity, the traditions of the sacred groves offer a sobering reminder. The ancestors who decreed that these lands be left untouched might not have known the language of ecology, but they understood the consequences of imbalance. By protecting these groves, they safeguarded not only their own progeny but the future of countless generations to come. If these serpent gods, now threatened with extinction, are forgotten, what will happen to those who inherit the land in their wake?

Perhaps this, then, is the message embedded within the ancient rules governing the bana or kaavu—that the health of the land and the vitality of life itself depend on the balance we maintain with nature. The serpents, coiled in the undergrowth and hidden in the shadows, are not merely gods to be feared—they are the sentinels of an ecosystem that, if destroyed, could take us down with it.

The Rationale

Majority of Indians worship serpents in groves that are maintained with utmost care and sanctity. Truly, snakes are on this planet for a reason. They are a vital link in the food chain. House rats breed fast and they eat our crops. In the natural eco-system, snakes keep a check on such rodents like lizards, frogs, etc. As mentioned before, they are the farmer's friends. However, in the last fifty years, we have invaded homes of these snakes and constructed houses, complexes and resorts over them. Thus, humans are responsible for snake deaths directly and indirectly. With snakes gone, its prey gets a new lease of life and they wreak havoc by damaging crops and spreading diseases. Snakes are mostly harmless and react only when they feel threatened. The religious beliefs and rules prescribed by our ancestors aim at protection of the environment, while smartly replacing fear with respect for the scary serpent. People adhering to the belief system do not touch such areas in their endless conquest for unused lands to build housing. Why? Because serpent groves are sacred and cutting one down is a sin; such a simple supernatural concept that tames the never-ending greed of the humankind.

We have started studying serpent groves and serpent worship from the viewpoint of biodiversity and environmental conservation. The wisdom of the groves challenges us to reflect on our own relationship with the natural world, urging a balance between progress and preservation, use and reverence.

Fear of God will fade away some day, and when that day arrives, only those who care (and realize the importance of snakes) will protect these beautiful serpents who are in every way divine.

PART 3

Naagapuraanam

Stories of Naagas from the Itihaasa Puraana

Introduction

The Puraanas, our ancient collections of lessons and legends, offer a captivating origin story for the Naagas, one that intertwines with other narratives like beads on a sacred thread. This tale, far removed from any explanations offered by the natural world, unfolds within the vast canvas of karma, the law of cause and effect that governs our lives. Each story unravels a piece of this intricate web, revealing how actions in one life determine the fate of the next, and how the echoes of the past continue to resonate in the present. So, prepare to be enthralled by a world where serpents hold a position of power, where destinies are intricately linked, and where the past, present and future is forever intertwined.

Brahma's Wrath

A Tale from the Varaaha Puraana

In the dawn of creation, Brahma, the Grand Creator, first brought forth the sage Kashyapa from his mind. To Kashyapa, Daksha gave his beautiful daughter Kadru in marriage, and from their union sprang countless valiant sons—the Naagas. Ananta, Vasuki, Kambala, Karkotaka, Padma, Mahapadma, Shamkha and Kulika were chief among them, but their progeny soon filled the world.

Yet, these children were born with crooked natures, fearsome forms, and fangs full of venom. They were violent, striking down humans and beasts alike with their deadly fangs, reducing many to ash. Day by day, the population of humankind dwindled under their relentless attacks.

Seeing their numbers diminish so drastically, the terrified humans sought refuge with Brahma, the Creator himself. Flocking to him, they pleaded, 'Protect us, O Lord! Your creation is being undone by these venomous serpents. Soon, no human will be left. Do what is necessary to avert this doom!'

Brahma, moved by their plight, assured them of his protection and sent them home with hearts eased. Then, summoning the chief Naagas, Vasuki and his brothers, Brahma's face darkened with anger. 'You destroy my children, the humans!' he thundered. 'For this transgression against creation, hear my curse—in another age, by your own mother's doing, you shall face a devastating decline!'

The Naagas, trembling before Brahma's fury, fell at his feet. 'Great Father,' they implored, 'it was you who made us crooked by nature! You gave us venom, cruelty and eyes that strike like weapons. We only act according to the nature you bestowed. Reduce the intensity of our power, perhaps, but do not condemn us entirely!'

'Even if I created you thus,' Brahma countered, 'what right have you to devour humankind?'

'Then prescribe us limits, O Lord!' the serpents cried. 'Assign us realms where we may dwell apart.'

Hearing their plea, Brahma relented slightly. 'Tathaastu, so be it,' he declared. 'I shall forge an agreement between you and humankind. Listen well. The netherworlds—Paataala, Vitala and

Sutala—shall be your domain. Dwell there, enjoy your pleasures, and remain until the seventh Manvantara. At the dawn of the Vaivasvata Manvantara, you shall become kin to the Devas and wise Garuda. Then, many of your progeny will perish by fire, fulfilling your mother's curse, though you yourselves shall be spared.'

He set the conditions, 'Those among you who remain fierce and insolent shall surely meet their end. You may bite only those destined by fate to die thus, or those who injure you first. Flee from any human who carries potent herbs, recites protective mantras, or wears the Garuda yantra, lest you invite your own destruction.'

Thus, decreed by Brahma, the Naagas retreated to the subterranean worlds assigned to them, finding solace in the Creator's tempered judgment. The pact between Brahma and the Naagas, the banishment and blessing, occurred on the auspicious fifth day, i.e., Panchami. Therefore, that day remains sacred, capable of washing away sins according to the twenty-first chapter of the Varaha Puraana.

It's helpful to understand that Hindu cosmology operates on immense, cyclical timescales (involving units like Yugas, Manvantaras, and Kalpas), vastly different from human perception. A 'Manvantara' signifies a huge epoch of time, lasting millions of years, presided over by a specific progenitor of humanity for that age (known as Manu). There are fourteen Manvantaras within a single Kalpa (a 'day' of Brahma). Because these timescales are so vast, stories in the Puraanas might describe events occurring millions of years apart or in different cosmic cycles, sometimes grouping them by theme rather than strict chronological order. Brahma's decree here places the Naagas' confinement and eventual change in fate within this immense cyclical timeline. His words in this early pact also foreshadow events, like the specific curse Kadru will later deliver and the great snake sacrifice, which are destined to unfold across these subsequent vast ages. According to scriptures, the Vaivasvata Manvantara is the current age we are said to live in.

I

Kadru and the Colour of the Horse's Tail

A Tale from the Mahabharata

CHAPTER 1

Kadru and Vinata

In the ancient times when gods walked among men, nestled amidst the sprawling forests of Meru, lived two sisters, Kadru and Vinata. Daughters of Daksha, they were as different as the sun and moon. Kadru, fiery and ambitious, yearned for power. Vinata, gentle and wise, sought balance and strength. Both were wives to the great sage Kashyapa, serving him with devotion.

One day, as the sage basked in the warmth of their love and service, he declared, 'My dear wives, ask of me any boon you desire, and it shall be granted!'

Kadru, her eyes gleaming with ambition, spoke first. 'Swami,' she said, her voice ringing with power, 'grant me one thousand sons, mighty serpents who will rule the earth's depths!'

Kashyapa, unable to deny her wish, blessed her with, 'Tathaasthu!'

Vinata, ever mindful, countered, 'Swami, I crave not a thousand, but two sons, as powerful as her thousand combined, their strength born of wisdom and righteousness.'

Kashyapa, impressed by her wisdom, granted her wish too, with another, 'Tathaasthu!'

Thus, the boons were granted and fates sealed. Kadru soon hatched a thousand serpent eggs, each writhing with potent venom and sharp minds. Vasuki, Takshaka, Elapatra, etc. were born thus.

Vinata, however, waited patiently for her two children to hatch from the eggs. But months turned to years, and her hope began to flicker. Half a millennium elapsed. In the passage of time, a moment emerged when Vinata, driven by desperation and envy, succumbed to the temptation of cracking open one of her eggs. From within emerged a peculiar sight—a baby boy, his upper body formed, yet his lower half incomplete. Casting a gaze upon his mother, the infant uttered a curse wrought by the anguish of his condition. 'Your impetuous act to crack open the egg has condemned me to an existence askew. Thus, I bestow upon you a penance of servitude for the ensuing five centuries.'

Tears welled in Vinata's eyes as she pleaded, 'Forgive me, my child. Spare me from such a fate. I am your mother.'

But the curse, once uttered, could not be retracted. The child, with solemn resolve, continued, 'My words stand, yet there is a caveat. Exercise patience, refrain from repeating this folly with my brother within the other egg. If you heed this counsel, upon the conclusion of five hundred years, he shall emerge and deliver you from bondage.'

And so, with this pronouncement, the miraculous child ascended into the heavens. In time, he would be known as Aruna and serve as the charioteer of Surya, and from his lineage would spring forth Jataayu and Sampaati.

Vinata then waited for five centuries. Then at the end of five hundred years, bursting open the other egg, out came Garuda, who went on to become the vahana (mount) of Lord Vishnu.

CHAPTER 2

Garuda, Vasuki, and the Samudra Manthana

Indra, the sovereign of Swargaloka, traversed the celestial realms atop Airavata, his divine elephant, when he encountered the revered sage, Durvaasa. In a gesture of goodwill, Durvaasa presented him with a special garland bestowed upon him by an apsara. Indra placed it upon the trunk of Airavata. The fragrant blossoms within the garland attracted a swarm of bees, which irritated the elephant's trunk. So, Airavata cast the garland aside in annoyance. This act of disregard for the sacred object incited the sage's wrath, for the garland was deemed an abode of Sri (Lakshmi), the embodiment of fortune, and thus to be revered as a religious offering. As a consequence, the goddess Lakshmi withdrew into the depths of the oceans, and Durvaasa, in his fury, cursed Indra and all the devas to be stripped of their strength, vitality, and prosperity.

Very soon, in many battles that followed, the devas suffered defeat at the hands of the asuras, led by the formidable Bali, who seized dominion over the three realms.

As always, the devas went crying to Vishnu and told them their problems. Vishnu formulated a plan. He advised the devas to engage the asuras in diplomatic negotiations. Thus, an alliance was forged to jointly churn the Ksheerasaagara (lit. Ocean of Milk) in pursuit of the Amrita (elixir of immortality), with the promise of sharing its benefits. However, the asuras were strong and the devas knew that they had an equal chance of getting the amrita. Yet, Vishnu assured the devas that he would ensure their exclusive access to the coveted elixir.

The Samudra Manthana or churning of the vast ocean of milk proved to be a monumental endeavour. Mount Mandara was uprooted to serve as the churning rod, and Vasuki, the son of Kadru and the serpent dwelling upon Shiva's neck, became the churning rope. Vishnu, mounted upon his celestial eagle Garuda, bore Mandara upon his mount towards the ocean's heart. There, Vasuki coiled himself around the mountain, and under Vishnu's guidance, the devas grasped the serpent's head and the asuras its tail to commence the churning. Yet, the colossal weight of Mandara caused it to sink, prompting Vishnu to manifest in his Kurma avatar, the divine turtle, to support the mountain upon his carapace.

Despite the peril of poison emanating from Vasuki, the devas and asuras persevered in their task, pulling on the serpent's form alternately, causing the mountain to rotate and churn the ocean's depths. As the tumultuous process unfolded, myriad divine entities and miraculous objects emerged, among them was the celestial horse Uchchaihshravas, with its seven resplendent heads. Surya claimed the seven-headed horse as his and thus, Uchchaihshravas rose to the sky.

After the conclusion of the churning of the ocean, Vasuki approached Brahma and beseeched a boon in recognition of his service.

'What is it that you desire, Vasuki?' Brahma inquired.

'Oh Brahma, bestow upon me the boon of protection when the need arises,' Vasuki implored.

'Tathaasthu,' Brahma consented, granting Vasuki's request.

CHAPTER 3

The Heavenly Horse's Tail

When Uchchaihshravas appeared in the sky, the seven-headed horse stirred Kadru's curiosity, leading her to question Vinata, 'Dear sister, in brief, what hue adorns Uchchaihshravas?'

With a glance at the snow-coloured horse, Vinata confidently replied, 'Indeed, the noble steed is adorned in the purest white. And you, sister, what perception do you hold? Shall we engage in a bet?'

With a serene demeanour, Kadru replied, 'Oh graceful one, I perceive a darkness in its tail. It is white with a black tail. Shall we wager, then? The defeated in the bet shall serve as the victor's slave.'

'We shall await the morning to declare a winner.'

Thus, the sisters embarked on a wager that would alter their destinies forever.

Under the cloak of night, as the stars shimmered in the velvet sky and the moon cast its ethereal glow upon the earth, Kadru convened her thousand serpent offspring. The air was thick with anticipation, charged with the weight of impending treachery. A soft breeze whispered through the leaves, carrying with it a sense of foreboding.

In the dim light, the serpents coiled and hissed, their eyes glazed with a sinister gleam as they listened intently to their mother's instructions. She said, 'tomorrow, you shall help me win this wager with your aunt.'

'How?' the serpents inquired in a hissing chorus.

'Attach yourselves to the tail of the great white horse. When we lay eyes upon Uchchaihshravas, it shall appear as if its tail is indeed black.'

The night seemed to hold its breath, as if even nature itself was wary of the deceitful scheme being woven under its veil.

Upon hearing this a few noble serpents like Vasuki, Ananta Shesha, Elapatra, etc. protested. 'No mother, we cannot stand for such adharma!'

'But otherwise, your mother will become a slave to your aunt!' Kadru insisted.

'No, mother. We shall not.' The noble serpents stood firm on their decision and prepared to depart.

In anger, Kadru cursed the disobedient serpents, proclaiming, 'Listen, all those of you who disobey me, I curse you … In the future, there will be a Sarpasatra—a great serpent sacrifice of the wise King Janamejaya of the Pandava lineage. During this sacrifice, Agni (fire) shall consume you all.'

Having spoken thus, Kadru departed.

Ever since they heard the curse of their mother, the serpents were in constant fear of death. The noble serpents who did not agree to Kadru's evil plan also left with the fear of their mother's curse. They went to their respective places for the purpose of protecting their lives.

Shesha went to the Himalayas to perform a penance. Shankhachuda went to Manipura. Kaaliya who was exceedingly frightened submerged himself in the water of Yamuna. So also, those kings of serpents went to Kurukshetra for the performance of penance. The Naaga Dhritharashtra went to Prayaaga, Elapatra went to Brahmaloka.

The remaining serpents, after deliberation, concluded that complying with their mother's wishes was imperative. The fear of her wrath, should she fail to achieve her desire, loomed over them, as did the hope of her favour, which could potentially lift her curse. They resolved, 'We shall indeed turn the horse's tail black.'

The following morning, Kadru and Vinata, having staked a wager on slavery, hastened eagerly to behold the steed Uchchaihshravas from a closer vantage point. Swiftly traversing the Ocean, Kadru, accompanied by Vinata, alighted near the horse. There they both beheld the magnificent steed, its body gleaming white as the moon's rays, yet adorned with black hairs in its tail.

Witnessing the dark strands, Kadru triumphed.

'I win and you lose!'

Kadru rejoiced that some of her serpent sons had heeded her call. Thus, Vinata, having lost the wager, fell into servitude, consumed by sorrow.

CHAPTER 4

Garuda's Dilemma

As time passed, Garuda bore a heavy heart. His mother, Vinata, languished in servitude, and her sorrow fuelled his resolve to set her free. Yet, duty called him elsewhere. Kadru commanded Vinata to carry her and her writhing sons to the fabled land of Ramaniyaka, a paradise where the Naagas dwelt in splendour. Bound by his mother's word, Garuda knelt, allowing Kadru and her serpent brood to coil upon his broad, feathered back. With a beat of his wings, he surged into the boundless sky.

As they soared, the sun blazed fiercely, its rays scorching the delicate scales of Kadru's sons. The serpents hissed in agony, their coils tightening against Garuda's feathers. Kadru, desperate to save her children, lifted her voice to the heavens, weaving a hymn of praise to Lord Indra, the storm-bringer. Her words, fervent and sweet, reached the god's ears, and he, moved by her devotion, summoned dark clouds to gather. Rain fell in a torrent, cool and merciful, soothing the Naagas' burns and slaking their thirst. The deluge was so mighty that it swelled rivers and flooded distant valleys, a blessing that made the serpents sigh in relief.

At last, Garuda's wings carried them to Ramaniyaka, a verdant island cradled by the sea. The Naagas gazed in awe at its beauty, their eyes gleaming like polished jewels. Towering trees stretched towards the sky; their branches heavy with blossoms. Lotus-filled lakes shimmered, reflecting grand mansions that stood like silent sentinels. The serpents slithered forth, enchanted, their hearts alight with the promise of this lush new home, while Garuda, though burdened by his mother's chains, felt a fleeting warmth at the sight of such beauty.

CHAPTER 5

Soma

While lotus lakes gleamed in Ramaniyaka and Gandharvas sang, Garuda's heart remained shadowed. The Naagas, entranced by the island's splendour, slithered through its verdant groves, but Garuda's thoughts lingered on his mother, Vinata, still bound in servitude to Kadru. His resolve hardened like iron forged in celestial fires. He had to free his mother from the thankless servitude to Kadru. Turning to the serpents, their scales glinting like molten silver, he demanded, 'Name the price of my mother's freedom.'

The serpents, cunning and coiled, whispered among themselves before their leader hissed, 'Bring us the Amrita, the elixir of immortality, guarded by the gods. Deliver it, and aunt Vinata shall be free.'

With a thunderous beat of his wings, Garuda ascended into the heavens, his eyes fixed on the divine realm. The path was fraught with terrors—whirling flames, blades that sang of death, and sentinels clad in starlight. Yet Garuda, swift as thought and mighty as a storm, vanquished each foe. He breached the celestial vault, seizing the Amrita from its sacred pedestal, even as Indra, lord of thunder, roared in pursuit. A clash of titans shook the skies, but Garuda's strength and guile won the day, and with the elixir cradled in his talons, he struck a secret pact with Indra before returning to earth. Garuda promised Indra that he would return the Amrita without letting it be consumed.

Back in Ramaniyaka, Garuda descended, the Amrita glowing like liquid moonlight in his grasp. The serpents slithered forward, their eyes alight with greed, but Garuda's voice cut through their hisses. 'I have fulfilled your demand,' he declared, placing the nectar delicately upon a bed of soft kusha grass. 'But first, purify yourselves. Bathe in the sacred waters and return, cleansed, to claim your prize. And as I have honoured my word, free my mother from aunt Kadru's chains.'

The serpents, eager and trusting, nodded in agreement. 'Vinata is free,' they vowed, their voices a sibilant chorus, before gliding towards the shimmering lakes to perform their rites. Garuda stepped back; his keen eyes gleaming. No sooner had the serpents vanished into the waters than a shadow flickered above. Indra, swift as a lightning stroke, swooped down, his hands closing around the Amrita. With a nod to Garuda, their pact fulfilled, he vanished into the heavens, the elixir reclaimed for the Devas.

When the serpents returned, their scales polished by the sacred waters, they froze. The kusha grass lay empty, the Amrita gone. A wail of fury rose from their throats, but their greed would not be sated so easily. Sniffing the air, they caught the faint, divine scent of the elixir, where droplets had spilled upon the grass. In desperation, they lowered their heads, their tongues flickering over the sharp blades of kusha. The grass, imbued with the Amrita's sacred essence, sliced their tongues, splitting them into forked tips that quivered with each taste. From that moment, it was believed that the serpents bore their forked tongues as a mark of their folly, and the kusha grass (durwa, darbha or karugha), touched by the nectar of immortality, became hallowed, revered in rituals across the ages.

II

Jaratkaaru's Betrothal

A Tale from the Mahabharata

CHAPTER 1

Brahma Approves the Curse

When Kadru cursed upon her disobedient serpent offspring, the words resonated through Brahmaloka, reaching Brahma himself. Compelled by fate, Brahma had no choice but to endorse it for the curse to take effect. With a solemn 'Tathaasthu', Brahma sanctioned the curse.

Confusion gripped the Devas present, and they questioned Brahma, the god of gods, 'Why did you not prevent Kadru from cursing her beloved children in your presence? What reason could justify such cruelty?'

Brahma replied, 'The snakes have proliferated and become cruel, formidable in appearance and highly venomous. Out of concern for the welfare of my creations, I did not intervene. This was supposed to happen by my design of fate. It was predestined.'

'But what about the boon you gave Vasuki after the churning of the oceans? Did you forget that by mistake?'

'No, I remember my boon. Because of that only those serpents who harm others without cause will indeed face destruction. The righteous and virtuous divya Naagas will be spared. Listen also, for I shall reveal how the serpents may escape this impending calamity. In the lineage of the Yayavaras, a great sage named Jaratkaaru will be born—intelligent, with complete mastery over his passions. He will father a son named Aastika (Aastik), who will intervene to halt the sacrifice.'

The gods inquired further, 'On whom will Jaratkaaru, this eminent sage endowed with immense energy and asceticism, beget such an illustrious son?'

Brahma responded, 'Jaratkaaru, endowed with great energy, will indeed father a son of equal prowess, and his wife will share the same name.'

'A wife with the same name? How is that possible?' questioned the Devas.

'Vidhi (fate)…' Brahma concluded, implying that fate would orchestrate this unique circumstance.

After exchanging such sentiments among themselves, the gods departed, leaving Brahma to summon Kashyapa. Speaking to him, Brahma said, 'O Kashyapa, who conquers all adversaries, these snakes who are your sons, venomous and massive, with a penchant for attacking other creatures, have been cursed by their mother. Do not be distressed by this news. The demise of the snakes in sacrifice was ordained long ago.' With these words, the divine Creator consoled Kashyapa and bestowed upon him the knowledge to neutralize poison—the antidote to serpent venom. While composing the mantra or sacred chant for neutralizing snake venom, a serpent daughter emanated from Kashyapa's mind, who would come to be known as Manasa. She went on to become a devotee of Shiva and performed many penances. Having led a life of ascetism, she would eventually become known by many names and one of which was Jaratkaaru.

CHAPTER 2

Vasuki's Dilemma

eanwhile, in Naagaloka, the righteous serpents convened a meeting with Vasuki to strategize on how to thwart Kadru's curse. Reflecting on their predicament, Vasuki addressed them, 'O, my righteous serpents, we must endeavour to neutralize this curse. While remedies exist for ordinary curses, but those from a mother carry unique challenges.'

'Why would our mother curse us? Weren't we following the path of dharma, Naagaraaja Vasuki?' questioned one serpent.

'We were indeed. But what troubles me is that Brahma sanctioned this curse. My heart trembles. Perhaps our end is near. Why else would Brahma not intervene?' replied Vasuki, his tone fraught with concern.

'It was destined many Manvantaras ago, it is our Vidhi,' suggested another serpent.

'Perhaps. Let us not delay. You are all wise. Together, we will find a way to prevent Janamejaya's sacrificial plan and avert our demise,' urged Vasuki.

As the offspring of Kadru gathered, they exchanged opinions, each offering their counsel. Some proposed assuming the guise of learned priests to dissuade Janamejaya, while others rejected this idea, deeming it unrighteous to harm priests. Another faction suggested stealing the vessel of Soma (amrita) to grant immunity against death.

Ultimately, the serpents decided on a resolution and presented it to Vasuki. 'The root cause of the sacrifice is the king himself. Let us bite him to eliminate the threat of annihilation. Please command us,' they implored, awaiting Vasuki's decision.

After careful consideration, Vasuki responded, 'Your proposal does not seem wise. I do not endorse it. Is there any way we can save our species from total extinction?'

Hearing Vasuki's words, Elapatra stepped forward. 'This sacrifice cannot be prevented, brother. King Janamejaya is not one to be hindered. Fate is our only refuge,' he declared. 'Brahma mentioned a sage's son as our saviour, who will be born to parents with the same name.'

'What name may be his parents?' the serpents inquired eagerly.

'Jaratkaaru!' exclaimed Elapatra.

'Jaratkaaru?' echoed the serpents in astonishment.

'Yes!'

'But that is the other name of my sister, Manasa.' Vasuki responded.

'Yes, if this sage Jaratkaaru will marry our sister of the same name, then their son shall liberate us at the sacrifice,' explained Vasuki.

Overwhelmed with hope, the serpents expressed their approval. Vasuki, burdened by his mother's curse, instructed the serpents of the forests to watch for any signs of the sage Jaratkaaru seeking a wife, as their fate hinged on it.

From that day forth, Vasuki meticulously nurtured his sister—the Naagini Jaratkaaru (Manasa), anticipating her union with the sage. However, as days passed, the sage remained immersed in asceticism, showing no inclination for marriage, much to Vasuki's consternation.

CHAPTER 3

Jaratkaaru

Meanwhile, the great sage Jaratkaaru traversed the expanse of the earth, finding solace wherever dusk descended, making each evening's resting place his temporary abode. As a 'vaayubhakshi', he ate nothing but air, devoid of any desire for worldly pleasures. With each passing day, his form grew more emaciated and his frame leaner, earning him the name Jaratkaaru.

One evening, after the dying embers of the sun cast long shadows, Jaratkaaru, withered and hollow-cheeked, wandered in search of a place to rest in a forest. A low, guttural moan, like the wind whispering through a graveyard, snagged on his ears. Following the sound, he came upon a clearing. In the centre, shrouded in the gathering darkness, gaped a black hole, its depths veiled in an unnatural chill. The moaning grew louder, a chorus of despair rising from within. Driven by a morbid fascination, Jaratkaaru crawled to the edge and peered down.

His blood ran cold. Ethereal figures, skeletal like himself, hung suspended from a root cord above a bottomless pit. Their faces, contorted in silent screams, were turned downwards, their lifeless eyes staring into the abyss. A single thick root remained, gnawed at the base by a grotesque, ravenous rat.

He approached them hesitantly, his voice echoing eerily in the cavern. 'Who are you, condemned to this fate?' he rasped.

'We are *pitrs*, the ancestral spirits, stuck here without food or escape, waiting for impending doom.' The spirits spoke without mouths. 'You sound like a great ascetic, a sage. Are you?'

'Yes, I am. Quickly tell me if this calamity can be averted by sacrificing a fourth, a third or even half of my asceticism. If needed, relieve yourselves by taking even the entirety of my asceticism. I consent to it all. Do as you please,' declared the sage, offering his entire being to alleviate their distress.'

'What use is your asceticism? We were all once upon a time ascetic brahmins. We too have the fruits of our asceticism. But it is of no use now.'

'Why?'

'O brahmin, listen, who we are. We are *sages* of the Yayavara sect, and we have no children left in the lineage who could perform shraaddha (annual funeral rites). We have one man remaining in the bloodline but he chose a life of ascetism like us. He would not marry, so he will never have a son.' The ancestral spirits spoke of a prophecy, a thread representing their lineage, being slowly devoured by the monstrous rat of time. Only a son, born of their last remaining descendant, could be the new thread, securing their place in the afterlife.

Sage Jaratkaaru approached them hesitantly, his voice echoing eerily in the cavern. 'Who is that ascetic that condemned you to this fate?' Jaratkaaru rasped.

A collective, gurgling moan escaped their spectral forms. 'His name we think is Jaratkaaru,' came the voice, a chorus of whispers merging into a singular, chilling utterance.

The revelation hammered into the sage Jaratkaaru. These were the spirits of his lineage, trapped in an eternal torment of his own making. He, the last of their line, had chosen a life of solitary penance, rejecting the sacred duty of continuing their bloodline. His vidhi or fate had brought him to that place as if to test him.

Terror mingled with a bitter regret in Jaratkaaru's throat. His years of asceticism, his quest for spiritual enlightenment, now seemed a cruel joke played by fate in the face of his ancestors' suffering.

Jaratkaaru was overwhelmed with sorrow. Through tear-choked words, he addressed his forefathers, 'You are my fathers and grandfathers who have departed before me. Tell me, what must I do for your well-being? I am that sinful son of yours, Jaratkaaru! Punish me for my transgressions, for I am a wretched being.'

The pitrs responded, 'O son, it is fortunate that you have come to this place in your wanderings. Why have you not taken a wife, O Jaratkaaru?'

Jaratkaaru responded, 'O Pitrs, my heart has longed for a celibate life. However, witnessing your distress has stirred doubt within me. If fate presents a maiden sharing my name, willing to be my wife without my solicitation, I shall marry her. Through her offspring, your salvation shall be assured, granting you eternal bliss and peace.'

After speaking thus to his ancestors, the sage resumed his wanderings across the earth. Due his old age, he found no wife, and his heart was heavy with sorrow for his lack of success. However, guided by his ancestors' counsel, he persisted in his quest. Venturing into the forest, he wept bitterly, consumed by grief. In his earnest desire to fulfil his duty to his forebears, he resolved to seek a bride, even if she wasn't from the human species.

With determination, the sage uttered his plea aloud three times, addressing all creatures, both visible and invisible. He implored, 'O beings, both chara (moving) and achara (immobile), hear my words! Directed by my ancestors, I, who am engaged in rigorous penance, seek a bride to fulfil their wishes. Roaming the world in poverty and anguish, I beseech any creature who possesses a daughter to grant her to me in marriage. Let her be of the same name as mine and bestowed upon me as alms. I pledge not to maintain her. Bestow such a bride upon me!'

CHAPTER 4

The Sage Weds the Naagini

The serpents in the forest, upon hearing the sage's plea, swiftly relayed the message to Vasuki, the king of the snakes. The fateful moment had arrived. Vasuki adorned his sister with ornaments and accompanied her into the forest, where the sage resided. With solemn reverence, Vasuki presented his sister, the Naagini, as an offering to the venerable sage. However, the sage hesitated to accept her immediately. Concerned that she might not share his name and uncertain about her maintenance, he deliberated for a brief moment before speaking.

Vasuki, addressing the sage Jaratkaaru, assured him, 'O, esteemed sage, this maiden shares your name and is my sister, adorned with ascetic virtue. I pledge to support your wife; accept her. I shall protect her to the best of my ability. O, great sage, she has been raised by me solely for you. The fate of your ancestors and my successors lies in this holy union.'

With Vasuki's assurance, Jaratkaaru proceeded to the abode of the serpents. Observing strict vows and guided by his ancestors' instructions, the virtuous sage accepted his bride according to shastric rites. Taking her hand, the revered sage led her to their chamber, prepared by the king of the snakes. There, adorned with valuable coverlets, they began their life together.

The sage, setting clear boundaries, instructed his Naagini wife, 'You must never act or speak against my wishes. If you do, I will leave immediately. Remember these words.'

The sister of Vasuki, anxious to fulfil her duties, diligently attended to her husband's needs. Soon after, she conceived, and the embryo grew with radiant energy, resembling a flame of fire.

One evening, weary from his tapasya, Jaratkaaru returned. He laid his head upon his wife's lap. The Naagini with scales shimmering like emeralds in the fading light, gently stroked his hair.

'Let sleep take hold, my dear wife,' sage Jaratkaaru murmured, his voice heavy with exhaustion. 'And awaken me not, for even the slightest disturbance might displease me.'

The serpent wife, her heart filled with love and concern, watched him fall into a deep slumber. But as shadows stretched and the first stars emerged, a worry gnawed at her. It was time for his sandhyavandanam, the evening rituals that must not be missed by an ascetic brahmin. Every moment her husband slept past twilight weakened his connection to his spiritual duties.

Torn between respecting his wishes and fulfilling her duty, Naagini leaned closer, her voice barely a whisper. 'My love,' she pleaded, 'the sacred hour approaches. Please rise, lest your spiritual light dims.'

Sage Jaratkaaru, startled awake, felt a surge of anger. 'Insolence!' he boomed, his voice echoing in the room. 'You dare defy my command? This breaks the trust between us. I leave now, and you will have ample time to reflect on your mistake.'

The Naagini's eyes welled up with tears. 'Forgive me, my love,' she cried. 'It wasn't disrespect, but devotion that guided me. I feared for the well-being of your soul.'

Hearing this, the sage Jaratkaaru reassured her, 'There is (asti), O fair one, in thy womb a son, resembling the Agnideva, who will be a sage great in righteousness and will master all Vedic scriptures.' Having said this, sage Jaratkaaru went away and again practised severe austerities as before. He then turned away and vanished into the night, leaving the Naagini alone in their echoing chambers.

Seeking solace, the Naagini returned to her brother, the mighty serpent king Vasuki. He listened patiently to her tale, his wise eyes reflecting her pain. Though saddened by the situation, he showered his sister with gifts and comforting words.

The Naagini Jaratkaaru gave birth to a child unlike any other, a being blessed with both human and serpent nature. His arrival brought new hope, erasing the shadows of sorrow. On account of the parting word of his father, 'There is (asti)', he became known by the name of Aastika.

Aastika, raised amidst the glistening scales of the snake palace, grew into a young man of exceptional wisdom and kindness. He became a bridge between the human and serpent worlds.

Notes

In the Brahma Vaivarta Puraana, Surya and Krishna interfere in the matter and convince the sage to implant his seed in Manasa Devi's navel. From there Manasa, that is Jaratkaaru, goes to Kailasa and with the blessings of Shiva and Parvati, gives birth to the sage Aastika.

III

The Burning of Khandava

A Tale from the Mahabharata

CHAPTER 1

The Prophecy

Long ago, there lived a king named Shwetaki, renowned for his unwavering devotion to the gods and his commitment to performing grand sacrifices. His most ambitious endeavour was a sacrifice that was to last a hundred years—a feat of extraordinary magnitude. In the beginning, many brahmins, the learned priests who conducted the rituals and ceremonies, participated in the sacrifice. But as the years wore on, the smoke billowing from the sacrificial fire began to take its toll on the priests. The relentless exposure to the smoke caused them to go blind, and one by one, they abandoned the sacrifice, leaving it incomplete.

Grief-stricken by the abrupt halt in his sacred duty, Shwetaki sought a solution. His devotion led him to perform penance, directing his prayers to Lord Shiva, beseeching the god for a priest who could help him complete the sacrifice. Moved by Shwetaki's penance, Shiva appeared before him and pointed to the hermit Durvaasa, the sage known for his fierce temper and unwavering dedication, as the priest who could see the sacrifice through to its end.

With Durvaasa overseeing the rituals, Shwetaki recommenced the sacrifice, and after many years, it was finally completed.

However, the prolonged offering of oblations in the sacrificial fire had dire consequences for Agni, the Fire God.

Agni, who had consumed the ghee (clarified butter) and other offerings day after day, began to suffer. The continuous intake of sacrificial offerings led to a severe imbalance within him, causing dysentery. His face became pale, his once vibrant form grew lean, and he lost all taste for the food he once relished.

In desperation, Agni approached Brahma, the creator of the universe, and complained of his ailment. Brahma, understanding Agni's plight, offered a solution. He revealed that in the dense and ancient Khandava forest lived countless creatures, many of whom were enemies of the devas, the gods. Brahma advised Agni that consuming the fat of these creatures would cure him of his illness. Eager to regain his strength, Agni set out for the Khandava forest.

But the Khandava forest was home to the Naaga king Takshaka, a close ally of Indra, the king of the gods. When Indra learned of Agni's intentions, he resolved to protect Takshaka and his family at any cost. As Agni began to ignite the forest, Indra unleashed torrents of rain, quenching the flames before they could consume the trees. Seven times Agni tried to engulf the forest in flames, and seven times he was thwarted by Indra's rains.

Frustrated and weakened, Agni once again turned to Brahma for guidance. The illustrious deity, after a moment of contemplation, addressed Agni with a calm assurance, 'O sinless one, I have discerned a way for you to consume the Khandava forest, even under the watchful eyes of Indra. The ancient deities, Nara and Naaraayana, have incarnated in the world of men to fulfil the will of the celestials. On earth, they are known as Arjuna and Krishna. They currently reside in the very forest you seek to devour. Seek their aid, and with their assistance, you shall consume the forest, regardless of the protection offered by the celestials. Arjuna and

Krishna will ensure that none from Khandava's population escapes and will thwart Indra's attempts to intervene. Of this, I have no doubt.'

With this divine guidance, Agni was reassured, knowing that the time had come to fulfil his purpose with the aid of these extraordinary incarnations.

CHAPTER 2

Party of the Pandavas

While the Pandavas resided in Indraprastha, the scorching heat of the season became unbearable, prompting Arjuna and Krishna to seek respite in the tranquil wilderness of the Khandava forest. Accompanied by their wives, they played and swam in the cool waters of the Yamuna, eventually retreating to a serene spot, not far from where the others remained. Here, Krishna and Arjuna sat on ornate seats, taking in the beauty of the forest.

As they rested, a peculiar figure approached them. He was tall, like a towering Sal tree, his complexion gleaming like molten gold, with a beard shimmering in hues of yellow and green. His body, both strong and proportionate, exuded a certain mystical power. His matted locks and tattered clothes contrasted sharply with his radiant aura, resembling the morning sun. His eyes, wide and lotus-like, bore a tawny glow that hinted at an unearthly brilliance. Upon seeing this blazing figure approach, Krishna and Arjuna immediately rose from their seats, standing in reverence, awaiting his words.

The man addressed them with urgency, 'You, who are the foremost heroes on earth, are now in the proximity of Khandava. I am a brahmin with an insatiable hunger, and I request you to satisfy my appetite by providing me with the sustenance I seek.'

Krishna and Arjuna, curious and respectful, replied, 'O revered one, you do not look like an ordinary brahmin. Tell us what food would gratify you, and we shall strive to fulfil your wish.'

The man smiled and, with a voice as blazing as his appearance, revealed his true identity, 'I am Agni, the God of Fire. The food I seek is not ordinary. The Khandava forest is what I wish to consume. But the forest is under the protection of Indra, for within it dwells Takshaka, a Naaga who is Indra's friend. Each time I have tried to devour this forest, Indra has thwarted me by pouring rain, extinguishing my flames. But now, I have come to you, knowing your prowess in battle. With your help, I can finally consume this forest. I need you to prevent the rain from falling and to stop any creatures from escaping.'

Upon hearing this, Arjuna responded thoughtfully, 'O Agni, I am ready to help, but to do so, I will need a bow strong enough to match the strength of my arms, arrows that will never run out, and a chariot worthy of battle. Krishna, too, will require a weapon that befits his divine energy. Provide us with these, and we will thwart Indra and fulfil your desire.'

Agni, understanding their needs, called upon Varuna, the God of Waters. In response, Varuna appeared and gifted Arjuna the legendary bow, Gandiva, along with an inexhaustible quiver and a chariot. He also gave Krishna the divine discus, the Sudarshana Chakra, and a mighty mace, Kaumodaki, capable of decimating even the fiercest demons. Agni also provided four pure white horses, swift as the wind, to pull Arjuna's chariot.

With these celestial gifts, Arjuna and Krishna were now prepared. Arjuna, his fingers sheathed in protective gloves, strung the powerful Gandiva bow, its twang reverberating across the forest like the roar of thunder, striking fear in all who heard it. Krishna, armed with his discus and mace, stood ready by Arjuna's side.

Addressing Agni, Krishna said, 'With these weapons, we are now capable of defending the forest from Indra's interference. Let the flames rise, for we are ready.'

Encouraged by their words, Agni unleashed his full power. His flames encircled the forest on all sides, roaring like a storm, consuming everything in their path. The forest, filled with creatures and trees, trembled as Agni's fiery form blazed through it, appearing as if the very end of the world had come. The once-vibrant Khandava now resembled the legendary Meru, its trees burning like the sun's rays had descended upon it.

Thus began the burning of the Khandava forest, with Arjuna and Krishna standing as protectors of Agni, thwarting Indra's rain and ensuring the flames would not be extinguished.

CHAPTER 3

Khandava Burns

As Agni began to consume the Khandava forest, Krishna and Arjuna, with their divine weapons and celestial chariots, took up positions on opposite sides of the blazing woodland. The two heroes, each in his own chariot, appeared as one, moving in perfect synchrony, their energies combined into a single, unstoppable force.

As the flames spread, the forest was engulfed in chaos. Hundreds and thousands of creatures, driven by fear and the unbearable heat, ran in all directions, their cries filling the air with a terrifying cacophony. The waters of the forest's ponds and tanks, heated to boiling by the inferno, became death traps for the fish and tortoises that sought refuge within them. Their boiling bodies added to the gruesome spectacle, as the burning forest became a living embodiment of destruction.

The mighty flames reached up to the sky, their brilliance and heat so intense that even the gods in heaven were disturbed. They gathered in a body and approached Indra, the king of the celestials, to express their concern. 'Why, O lord of immortals, does Agni burn these creatures below? Has the time come for the destruction of the world?' they asked, their voices filled with anxiety.

Witnessing the destruction, Indra, the slayer of Vritra, set out to protect the forest of Khandava. Commanding vast masses of clouds, he covered the sky and ordered them to release a torrential downpour upon the blazing forest. But even as the rain fell in thick sheets, it evaporated in the air, consumed by the heat of Agni's flames before it could reach the ground. Undeterred, Indra summoned even greater clouds and commanded an even heavier downpour. The sky darkened as lightning flashed and thunder rumbled, the elements warring with each other as the flames of the forest contended with the wrath of the rain.

But Arjuna, forewarned and prepared, quickly responded. With unmatched skill, he drew his mighty Gandiva bow and began to shoot arrows into the sky. His arrows, as numerous and fast as rain itself, formed a dense canopy over the forest. The arrows interlocked, creating an impenetrable barrier, like an umbrella, shielding the flames from the deluge.

Despite Indra's relentless efforts, his rain could not penetrate the protective shield Arjuna had woven with his arrows. The flames of Agni continued to rage unabated, consuming everything in their path. The sky, darkened by clouds and arrows, echoed with the sounds of battle, as Indra's thunderclaps clashed with the roar of the fire and the hum of Arjuna's bowstring. The Khandava forest, trapped between the might of Agni below and the wrath of Indra above, became a terrifying spectacle, a battlefield of fire and water, smoke and lightning.

CHAPTER 4

The Naagini's Son

As the flames consumed the Khandava forest, a new chapter of tragedy unfolded. Takshaka, the mighty chief of the Naagas, was absent, having gone to the field of Kurukshetra. However, his son, the powerful Aswasena, found himself trapped within the inferno. Despite his immense strength and desperate attempts to escape, he was hemmed in by Arjuna's impenetrable wall of arrows.

In this moment of peril, Aswasena's mother, a serpent, resolved to save her son at any cost. Her heart, heavy with sorrow, spurred her into action. Tears filled her eyes as she slithered towards her son, her mind made up. She opened her mouth wide, intending to swallow him whole and spit him out beyond the deadly reach of the flames and arrows. She began by swallowing his head and then moved to engulf his tail, her only thought being the safety of her beloved child. She slithered forward to spit her son out of the forest's borders.

As she rose from the earth, her body still swallowing her son, Arjuna, ever vigilant, noticed her desperate attempt to escape. In a flash, his keen eyes focused on the naagini, and without hesitation, he let loose a sharp, keen-edged arrow. The missile like arrow sliced through the air with deadly precision, severing the naagini's head from her body, ending her life in a heartbeat.

Yet, this act did not go unnoticed. Indra, the lord of the heavens and a friend of Takshaka Naagas, saw the tragedy unfold. Desperate to save Aswasena, Indra unleashed a powerful windstorm, intending to disorient and incapacitate Arjuna. The violent gusts swept through the battlefield, and for a brief moment, Arjuna, taken by surprise, lost consciousness.

In those few fleeting moments, Aswasena, now free from the grip of his mother's body and Arjuna's arrows, seized the opportunity to escape. He slithered out of the burning forest, his heart filled with both grief for his mother and gratitude for his life.

When Arjuna regained his senses, he realized what had transpired. The sight of Aswasena's successful escape fuelled his anger. Deceived by the serpent's cunning and the power of illusion, Arjuna's heart burned with rage, knowing that the naagini's sacrifice and Indra's intervention had allowed the serpent to elude his grasp.

In the aftermath, the forest, now a charred wasteland, bore witness to the great and terrible battle that had taken place. The flames had claimed countless lives, and the ashes of the once-thriving Khandava lay scattered in the wind, a stark reminder of the power wielded by gods and mortals alike.

CHAPTER 5

Peace

Indra, the lord of the celestials, mounted on his white elephant, charged towards Krishna and Arjuna with his thunderbolt. The other gods followed suit, preparing their weapons—Yama with his mace, Kubera with his spiked club, Varuna with his noose and many others, all ready to strike. As the gods gathered for battle, the forest echoed with terrifying portents.

Undeterred, Arjuna and Krishna faced the advancing gods, responding with their thunderous arrows. Despite the overwhelming divine force, the celestials were repeatedly driven back, their weapons no match for the prowess of Krishna and Arjuna. The Munis watching from the skies marvelled at their strength, while Indra, though impressed, continued to test Arjuna's might.

Indra unleashed a heavy shower of stones, but Arjuna's arrows dispersed them effortlessly. Angered, Indra hurled a massive peak from Mandara at Arjuna, but the latter's swift arrows shattered it into a thousand pieces. The debris fell upon the burning forest, killing countless creatures below.

When the celestials realized they couldn't save the forest from the overwhelming power of Krishna and Arjuna, they withdrew from the battle. As the gods retreated, a deep, disembodied voice echoed, addressing Indra, 'Takshaka, your serpent friend, has not perished! Before the fire engulfed Khandava, he escaped to Kurukshetra. Know that Arjuna and Krishna are invincible in battle, beyond defeat by anyone. They are Nara and Naaraayana, ancient gods revered in heaven. Their strength and prowess are unmatched, and they deserve the highest reverence from all beings.'

Thus, Indra and other celestial devas retreated from the battle.

As the forest dwellers—Danavas, Rakshasas, Naagas and various animals—tried to flee, Krishna wielded his discus, slaying them in droves. The forest resounded with their cries as they fell into the flames, their bodies consumed by Agni, who grew stronger and more satisfied with each life taken.

In the midst of the destruction, Krishna spotted the Asura Maya fleeing. Agni pursued him, but Maya sought protection from Arjuna, who granted it. Respecting Arjuna's mercy, Krishna refrained from attacking Maya, and Agni spared him as well.

For fifteen days, Agni consumed the forest, sparing only six beings: Aswasena, Maya and four Sarngaka birds. When the flames finally subsided, Agni, having devoured rivers of fat and marrow, revealed himself to Arjuna, expressing his deep satisfaction. The flames, fuelled by vast quantities of flesh, blood and fat, soared high without a wisp of smoke. Agni, the fire-god, with blazing coppery eyes, a flaming tongue and a fiery crown, drank deeply of the nectar-like stream of animal fat with the help of Krishna and Arjuna, finding immense joy and fulfilment.

Indra, descending from the heavens with the Maruts, praised Krishna and Arjuna for their incredible feat and offered them boons. Arjuna requested all of Indra's weapons, to be granted when the time was right. Krishna asked for eternal friendship with Arjuna, which Indra gladly bestowed.

With their tasks completed, the celestials returned to the heavens, and Agni, now satiated, ceased burning the forest. Arjuna,

Krishna, and the Danava Maya then rested on the banks of a peaceful river, their battle against the gods and the forest finally over.

Notes

Regional foklore weaves another layer into the story of the burning of Khandava forest—the lore of Kerala's Pulluvan community and their origin story. As the flames devoured the Khandava forest, serpents were caught in the inferno. Takshaka was saved by a woman who placed him in a pot and hid him in a jasmine bower. For this act of compassion, she and her male companion, who had also been exiled, prospered under the serpent's protection and became the mythical ancestors of the Pulluvan community. According to another story, the large five-hooded snake Takshaka, scorched and burnt by the fire, flew away in agony, and alighted at Kuttanad in Kerala (Thurston, p.1909, 228).

IV

The King's Curse

A Tale from the Mahabharata

CHAPTER 1

The Muni's Curse

Two generations after the Khandava incident, there lived a mighty king named Parikshit, a descendant of the legendary Arjuna. He was known for his mighty aim, just like his grandfather Arjuna. He would often roam the forests, taking down deer, boars and even buffaloes with his sharp arrows.

One day, while chasing a wounded deer, Parikshit ventured deep into the forest, far from his usual grounds. No deer that was pierced by Parikshit had ever escaped, as if fate was playing tricks on the king.

Exhausted and thirsty, he stumbled upon a clearing where a sage named Samika was meditating, calmly drinking from a bowl of milk offered by a calf. Driven by impatience and hunger, Parikshit approached the sage, forgetting his usual respect. He didn't realize Samika was observing a mouna-vrata, the vow of silence.

'O sage,' said King Parikshit, 'I am the son of Abhimanyu. Have you seen a deer wounded by my arrow?'

However, the sage maintained his vow of silence, and offered no response. Parikshit looks around and finds a dead snake nearby. In frustration, the king lifted it up and placed the dead snake on the sage's shoulder, lifting it with the end of his bow. Despite this disrespectful act, the sage remained silent, neither protesting nor uttering a word, whether good or bad.

Witnessing the sage's unwavering composure, King Parikshit's anger dissipated, replaced by remorse. He returned to his capital, but the sage remained unmoved, continuing his vow of silence.

The sage had a son, Sringin, who was learned but had no control over his anger. Upon learning of the dead snake placed upon his father's shoulders, Sringin's eyes flared with fury, and he was consumed by anger. In a fit of rage, the powerful ascetic, Sringin, cursed the king, his voice resonating with wrath as he performed the ritual gesture of touching water.

Sringin pronounced, 'That sinful king who has dared to defile my elderly and venerable father by placing a dead snake upon his shoulders, that offender of brahmins, shall, within the span of seven days, be escorted to the realm of Yama, the god of death, by Takshaka, the mighty king of serpents. Such is the potency of my curse!'

Meanwhile, at Hastinapura, upon hearing the grim news of the curse, Parikshit was filled with remorse for his past misdeed. The king, consumed by anxiety, wasted no time in seeking counsel from his ministers. After careful deliberation, he decided to build a place where snakes could not enter. He ordered the construction of a mansion supported by a single column, heavily guarded day and night until the sun set seven times. Surrounding the structure were physicians, well-versed in medicinal arts, and priests skilled in the recitation of protective mantras. From within this fortified abode, the monarch continued to discharge his royal duties, shielded from all external threats by his loyal ministers. The sanctity of this place was such that not even the air itself could penetrate its defences, ensuring the king's safety and security.

CHAPTER 2

Takshaka and Kashyapa

Six sunsets passed. Nothing happened. On the seventh day, Takshaka prepared to fulfil his destiny. Slithering swiftly, he reached a magnificent banyan tree with sprawling aerial roots extending towards the heavens. Near a banyan tree, Takshaka encountered the venerable sage Kashyapa, who was hastening towards Hastinapuraa.

The heat shimmered off the dusty path, warping the world in waves of distortion. Sweat beaded on Kashyapa's brow, his weathered face etched with worry. Assuming the guise of an old brahmin, Takshaka asked in his rasping voice, 'Where do you rush in such haste?'

Kashyapa squinted through the sun-bleached haze. An aged brahmin, his beard tangled and dusty, stood by the roadside.

'I journey to cure the king,' Kashyapa replied, his voice heavy with worry. 'He lies under a brahmin's curse, and time is of the essence.'

A chilling chuckle escaped the old brahmin. 'The king is doomed,' he hissed, the words slithering in the midday heat. He

---

Note - In Brahma Vaivarta Puraana, Dhanwantari is mentioned instead of Kashyapa (Naagar, 2003, p.no. 405).

207

transformed into his true form and revealed, 'I am Takshaka, the very serpent who shall deliver that Parikshit's final blow. Turn back, father, for your efforts are in vain.'

Kashyapa straightened his spine, a flicker of defiance igniting in his eyes. 'I possess the antidote to venom gifted by Brahma himself,' he declared, his voice firm. 'I can cure him from your bite, restore him from the brink.'

Takshaka hissed through his forked tongue, revealing a face contorted with a reptilian sneer. 'Prove your boast, then,' he challenged, his voice dripping with venom. Takshaka spat his venom on the banyan tree. 'If you are truly so skilled, revive this banyan tree I have cursed with my touch.'

As soon as the venom touched the trunk of the banyan tree, it went up in flames. Kashyapa's eyes narrowed as the inferno caught on. The banyan tree's leaves hanging limp and brown, its once vibrant bark scarred and blackened.

Taking a deep breath, Kashyapa closed his eyes and chanted a sacred mantra. The air crackled with unseen energy as he poured his power into the withered branches. The silence was broken only by the rasp of wind and the distant cry of a solitary bird. Slowly, a change began. A faint tremor ran through the tree, followed by the whisper of leaves unfurling. The brown bark gave way to a vibrant green, spreading upwards like life itself reclaiming its dominion.

Finally, Kashyapa opened his eyes, their depths filled with a serene power. 'Now,' he said calmly, 'do you believe?'

Impressed by Kashyapa's prowess, Takshaka acknowledged the sage's extraordinary abilities but cautioned him against pursuing the king's cure. He offered Kashyapa wealth and rewards, urging him to abandon his mission. However, Kashyapa remained resolute, determined to fulfil his duty.

'Oh, father Kashyapa, why do you insist on saving the king? Can't you use your yogic powers to determine that this indeed is fate ... the Vidhi of Brahma?'

Kashyapa, renowned for his wisdom and strength, heard Takshaka's words and settled into deep meditation beside the king. However, despite his spiritual gifts and vast knowledge, the great sage sensed that the king's fate was sealed. Accepting this truth, Kashyapa turned back, taking with him the riches offered by Takshaka.

CHAPTER 3

Takshaka enters the tower

Takshaka slithered into Hastinapuraa. He had heard whispers of the king's defences—potent herbs and spells against poison guarded the palace day and night.

Contemplating his strategy, Takshaka pondered, 'The king must be deceived through the power of illusion. But how?' An idea dawned on him.

He summoned serpents and commanded them to disguise themselves as ascetics bearing gifts of fruits, sacred grass and water to the king. Addressing them, Takshaka instructed, 'Approach the king casually, as if attending to pressing matters. Present the fruits flowers, and water without any hint of haste.'

Following Takshaka's command, the serpents executed their mission. Disguised as ascetics, they offered the king kusa grass, water, and fruits. After their departure, the king urged his ministers and companions, 'Join me in sampling these delectable fruits brought by the ascetics.'

Driven by fate and influenced by the sage Siringi's curse, the king and his retinue eagerly partook of the fruits.

'The sun is setting, O King,' one of the councillors interjected, his expression betraying palpable relief.

'Yes, indeed. With the setting of the sun, the threat to my life dissipates,' the king affirmed, a sense of reassurance evident in his tone.

Unbeknownst to them, Takshaka had concealed himself within a particular fruit. As the king bit into it, a hideous worm emerged, barely discernible in shape, with black eyes and a coppery hue. Startled, Parikshit dropped the fruit, and the worm transformed into its true form—a formidable giant serpent.

'Your reign ends here, King Parikshit,' Takshaka boomed, his voice echoing through the palace. 'The curse has come to claim its due.'

The king, accepting his fate with a stoic calmness, offered no resistance. The serpent coiled around him, its poisonous breath filling the air. The king's advisors, their faces pale with horror, fled the palace, their cries swallowed by the darkening night.

As they ran, they caught a glimpse of Takshaka, soaring through the sky like a crimson scar against the twilight, a chilling reminder of the king's tragic fate. The palace, engulfed in the serpent's venom, stood as a monument to a broken promise and a life cruelly cut short. What remained in the end was Parikshit's charred body.

V

The Great Serpent Sacrifice

A Tale from the Mahabharata

CHAPTER 1

Janamejaya's Sacrifice

Following the tragic demise of Parikshit, grief shrouded the city of Hastinapura. The citizens, gathering in solemn assembly, acclaimed the minor son of the deceased monarch as their new king. Thus, they bestowed upon him the name Janamejaya, recognizing him as the valiant scion of the Kuru lineage, destined to vanquish all foes. Despite his youth, Janamejaya exhibited wisdom beyond his years, ruling the kingdom with the same noble spirit as his illustrious great-grandfather, Yudhishthira.

Upon reaching maturity, Janamejaya summoned his ministers, eager to uncover the circumstances surrounding his father's demise. With a resolute mind, he declared, 'Inform me of the events that led to my father's untimely death. Once acquainted with the details of his life, I shall take appropriate action, whether it benefits the world or remains unaddressed.'

It is here that the sage Uttanka, who was angered by Takshaka, revealed the details about Parikishit's death by the Naaga's bite.

Upon learning of his father's fate, Janamejaya resolved to avenge Parikshit's death by seeking retribution against Takshaka and his kin. Turning to his ministers, he demanded guidance, 'How may I exact vengeance upon Takshaka, the villain who slew my father? Is there a method by which I can consign Takshaka and his relatives

213

to the flames, just as he condemned my father to perish in the inferno of his venom?'

In response, the chief priest revealed, 'O, king, the gods themselves have devised a formidable snake-sacrifice known as Sarpasatra. This sacrificial ritual, sanctioned solely for you, holds the power to accomplish your revenge.'

'Let us prepare for Sarpasatra, the great serpent sacrifice,' Janamejaya declared.

CHAPTER 2

Janamejaya Commences the Great Sacrifice

With determination burning in his heart, Janamejaya commanded the preparation of the sacrificial implements, signalling the beginning of his quest for justice. As the priests meticulously measured the site for the ritual, consecrating the king to ensure the success of the oblation, an ominous sign unsettled Lohitaksha—the one who was called to build the sacrificial platform. 'The circumstances surrounding the measurement of the sacrificial platform suggest that this ritual will face obstruction, with a brahmin being the cause,' He cautioned.

Heeding this warning, the king issued strict orders to the doorkeeper, forbidding the admission of any unknown individual. Undeterred, the priests proceeded with the serpent sacrifice rites. As the sacrificial fire blazed, the serpents, gripped by fear, were drawn towards it irresistibly.

From all directions, they slithered forth, hissing and coiling around one another, diverse in colour, size and sound. Some resembled swift steeds, while others were as massive as elephants. In countless numbers, they met their demise in the flames, fulfilling the curse pronounced by Kadru, the mother of serpents, upon her disobedient sons.

Once word reached Takshaka of the terrifying sacrifice unleashed by King Janamejaya, he scurried like a frightened lizard to the mighty Indra's palace. There, nestled in celestial comfort, he found solace amongst the clouds, believing himself safe from the fiery wrath below.

CHAPTER 3

Vasuki Reminds Jaratkaaru of Her Son's Destiny

But while Takshaka enjoyed his temporary reprieve, panic gripped the heart of the serpent king, Vasuki. He watched in horror as his brethren, caught in the deadly spell of the sacrifice, plunged into the inferno. Fear gnawed at his scales, and with a voice trembling like a leaf caught in a storm, he turned to his sister, Jaratkaaru.

'Sister,' he rasped, 'fire consumes me even from afar. The sky blurs before my eyes, lost in the smoke of their burning. My heart thunders in my chest, and dread coils around my soul. My vision wavers, and despair threatens to swallow me whole. I fear, even I am destined to be consumed by that ferocious pyre, another victim of Parikshit's son's vengeance. The realm of the dead awaits.'

His voice breaking, Vasuki continued, 'This is the moment, sister, for which I betrothed you to sage Jaratkaaru. We, and our kin, stand on the precipice of annihilation. But there is hope. Aastika, your son and the wise sage, is prophesied to be our saviour, a promise uttered by Brahma himself. My dear sister, seek out your son, revered by the elders despite his youth, a master of the Vedas. Implore him, I beg of you, to intervene and free us from this burning fate.'

With a heavy heart, Jaratkaaru summoned her son, Aastika 'Son,' she pleaded, 'Brahma himself promised that a son of ours would protect the Naagas from certain doom. After the great Churning of the Ocean, your uncle Vasuki pleaded with the gods, and this prophecy was made in return for his service. Your time has come, my son. You must fulfil your destiny!'

Aastika, wise beyond his years, did not hesitate. Filled with unwavering determination, he sought out his uncle Vasuki, the great serpent king.

'Uncle,' he declared, his voice ringing clear and strong, 'I will break Kadru's curse and deliver you from this fiery peril. This is my vow, and I have never spoken a falsehood, not even in jest. Fear not, for I shall bring you and your kin to safety. I will go to King Janamejaya. With words carefully chosen, I shall soothe his grief and anger until the sacrificial pyre is quenched. Place your trust in me fully, Uncle, for I will not allow your hopes to be extinguished.'

Saying thus, Aastika left.

CHAPTER 4

Aastika Confronts Janamejaya

Aastika, burdened by his duty, hurried towards the sacrificial grounds. The air crackled with an ancient energy, and the chanting priests resembled the sun in their brilliance. He approached the entrance, but the doorkeepers stopped him.

Undeterred, Aastika spoke, his voice ringing out. 'Kings of old, like Soma, Varuna and Prajapati, held grand sacrifices here. Your sacrifice, King Janamejaya, shines just as brightly! May it bring blessings to all! You, son of Parikshit, hold yourself with the dignity of Bhisma, the hidden power of Valmiki, the controlled rage of Vasishtha, the lordship of Indra, the radiance of Naaraayana, the justice of Yama, the virtue of Krishna, the good fortune of the Vasus, the sanctity of the sacrifices, the strength of Damvodbhava, the knowledge of Raama, the energy of Aurva and Trita, and the awe-inspiring presence of Bhagiratha.'

His praise filled the air, directed not just at the king, but also at the priests, the brahmins, and even the fire god Agni. Pleased by Aastika's words, King Janamejaya turned to the assembled priests.

'Though he appears young,' the king remarked, 'his words hold the wisdom of an elder. I am inclined to grant him a boon. Tell me, priests, do I have your permission?'

The priests acknowledged, 'A brahmin, even as a boy, deserves a king's respect, especially one so learned. He deserves any wish you grant, Your Majesty, but not before Takshaka arrives. The scriptures and the fire itself reveal that Takshaka currently seeks refuge in Indra's abode, trembling with fear.'

Driven by rage, Janamejaya demanded that the priests exert their utmost power to draw not only Takshaka, but even Indra himself, into the fiery inferno. The priests, fuelled by the king's command, unleashed their most potent chants.

Suddenly, the sky split open, revealing Indra mounted on his celestial chariot, accompanied by thunderous clouds and a retinue of divine beings. Takshaka, clinging to Indra for protection, trembled uncontrollably. Despite Indra's presence, the relentless chanting of the priests proved too much. Even the mighty god of thunder, witnessing the terrifying spectacle below, abandoned Takshaka to his fate and retreated to his celestial abode.

Left alone and overwhelmed by fear, Takshaka was drawn towards the flames like a moth to a light. The priests, their eyes gleaming with triumph, announced to the king, 'Takshaka approaches your grasp, Your Majesty! His mighty roar echoes as he falls, abandoned by the god himself! The magic spells drag him down, tumbling him through the air, his senses overwhelmed by fear.'

Believing his vengeance complete, King Janamejaya turned to Aastika, 'Young one, your wisdom has earned you a boon of your choosing. Name your desire, and I shall grant it, no matter how extraordinary.'

Just as Takshaka was about to be consumed by the flames, Aastika's voice rose once more, resolute and unwavering. 'If a boon is offered, Your Majesty,' he declared, 'I choose this—let the sacrifice end, and spare the remaining serpents.'

Janamejaya, initially disappointed by the unexpected request, countered, 'Gold, silver, cattle, anything else your heart desires, I offer these as your boon, but do not ask me to cease the sacrifice.'

Aastika remained undeterred. 'Gold and riches hold no value to me, Your Majesty. My sole wish is for this sacrifice to end. May peace find its way back to the land, and may the serpents be spared in honour of my mother's lineage.'

Despite the king's attempts to sway him, Aastika held firm. Finally, the assembled priests intervened, urging the king to honour the young Brahmin's wish.

And so, the fiery sacrifice meant to avenge King Parikshit's death was extinguished, the chants of vengeance replaced by an unexpected silence. King Janamejaya, descendant of the great Pandavas, though initially displeased, found himself moved by Aastika's courage and his unwavering devotion to his serpent kin.

With an open heart, the king honoured the sacrifices made by those who had conducted the rituals. Lohitaksha, whose words at the beginning had foretold the role a brahmin would play, was lavished with even greater gifts—wealth, provisions and luxurious garments, all offered with genuine kindness.

The conclusion of the sacrifice brought with it a sense of peace that surprised even the king. Aastika, the wise and dutiful young man, was sent home with honour and gratitude.

Aastika returned to Naagaloka, a lightness in his steps and a newfound tranquillity in his heart. He embraced his uncle Vasuki and mother Jaratkaaru, recounting the events and how his unwavering request had transformed a ceremony of fury into a symbol of generosity. He had saved his serpent kin, fulfilled a prophecy that was made seven Manvantaras ago by Brahma, and found favour with a grieving king. His journey had been arduous, but the results echoed far beyond the sacrificial grounds.

VI

A Serpent Groom for the Charioteer's Daughter

A Tale from the Mahabharata

CHAPTER 1

Maatali's Dilemma

Maatali, the charioteer of Indra, the king of gods, stood on the ramparts of his celestial abode, gazing out at the swirling clouds. His brow was furrowed, a sight as rare as a limp in his ever-steady hand. For millennia, his focus had been on the swift pull of his reins, the thunderous gallop of Indra's divine steeds, and the roar of battles fought for the sake of heaven. Today, a different kind of storm brewed within him—a storm of worry for his daughter, Gunakesi.

Disquiet stirred within Maatali, a sigh escaping his lips like a wisp of smoke. His wife, Sudharma, a woman with a gaze as gentle as a summer breeze, turned to him, her brow creased in concern.

'My love,' she began, her voice a soft melody, 'something weighs heavily on your heart. Would you share your burden?'

Maatali offered a smile, but it lacked its usual warmth. 'A fleeting thought, nothing more,' he murmured, his gaze distant.

Sudharma's eyes, usually filled with unwavering trust, held a flicker of knowing. 'It concerns Gunakesi, doesn't it?' she inquired gently.

A defeated sigh escaped his lips. 'Indeed,' he confessed. 'Throughout the heavens and mortal realms, I have searched tirelessly, but no suitor has met my standards for our daughter's beauty and worth.'

Sudharma's lips quirked upwards in a knowing smile. 'Perhaps,' she suggested, 'a suitable match might lie beyond the boundaries of the world we know.'

Maatali's eyes widened with a spark of hope. 'Beyond these realms? Where could such a being reside?'

'The Naagas,' Sudharma replied, her voice laced with a hint of mischief. 'Perhaps amongst them, a prince worthy of Gunakesi can be found.'

The seed of an idea took root in Maatali's mind. With newfound determination, he set his heart on a journey—a quest to find a husband for his daughter in the enigmatic world of the Naagas.

CHAPTER 2

A Celestial Encounter

As Maatali navigated the celestial highways in his cosmical mighty chariot, his mind preoccupied with Gunakesi's future, he spotted a familiar figure weaving through the clouds. It was Naarada, the ever-wandering sage, his veena strapped to his back, his mischievous grin as recognizable as the sun in the sky.

Naarada, ever curious, hailed Maatali. 'Naaraayana … Naaraayana … Well met, charioteer! Where are you headed with such a contemplative air in your grand chariot that can travel all the worlds? Is it Indra's business that takes you on this journey, or something closer to your heart?'

Taken aback, Maatali hesitated. But the weight of his worries was heavy, and Naarada's presence offered a sliver of hope. He poured out his heart, confessing his anxieties about finding a worthy husband for his daughter, Gunakesi.

Naarada, known for his unconventional solutions, listened intently. When Maatali finished, a mischievous twinkle lit up his eyes. 'Ah, a fatherly predicament! Naaraayana … Naaraayana … ' he exclaimed. 'But fear not, Maatali. As fate would have it, I'm on my way to visit Varuna, the Lord of the Waters. Perhaps this detour holds the key we seek.'

Intrigued, Maatali inquired further. Naarada explained that he intended to explore the nether regions, searching for potential suitors beyond the celestial courts. 'Together,' he declared, 'we can expand our search and find the perfect match for your daughter! Naaraayana … Naaraayana …'

Thus began an unexpected alliance. Maatali, the loyal charioteer, and Naarada, the wandering sage, descended from the heavens. Their destination—a journey through fantastical realms beneath the surface of the earth. As they ventured deeper, the celestial light faded, replaced by the cool, shimmering depths of the endless blue waters.

CHAPTER 3

A Quest through the Netherworlds

Their first stop was Varuna's domain. Greeted with the respect befitting celestial dignitaries, they presented their request. Varuna, the lord of the waters, welcomed them warmly. After a brief exchange of pleasantries, Naarada used this opportunity to regale Maatali with tales of Varuna's realm—a world of shimmering waters, exotic creatures and forgotten battles.

Leaving Varuna's dominion behind, they ventured deeper, traveling through the Naagaloka, the serpent kingdom. Here, Naarada, a walking encyclopaedia of the cosmos, became Maatali's guide. At the heart of Naagaloka, Naarada unveiled a fascinating sight—Paataala, the city inhabited by Naagas, Daityas and Danavas, the celestial rivals of the gods. There, in a display of immense power, they witnessed the four elephants—Airavata, Vamana, Kumuda and Anjana—holding up the very earth on their backs.

Naarada, ever seeking a solution, inquired if any among the city's denizens caught Maatali's eye as a potential husband for his daughter. But Maatali, wary of creating alliances with their celestial adversaries, shook his head in disapproval. 'There is no one here that pleases me,' he declared. 'Let us find someone elsewhere.'

Next, they journeyed to Hiranyapura, the fabled Golden City of the Daityas. Built by the divine architect Viswakarman himself, the city glittered with gold, silver and precious stones. Naarada led Maatali through these opulent residences. However, Maatali remained adamant. He wouldn't consider marrying his daughter to someone from a race constantly at odds with the celestial Devas.

Undeterred, Naarada took him to the world of the Suparnas, the descendants of the mighty Garuda. The winged creatures, known for their fierceness and their diet of Naagas, were hardly an ideal choice for Gunakesi. Their nature, while valiant, bordered on cruelty, and Maatali could not condone an alliance built on the subjugation of the Naagas.

Their search continued. They ventured into Rasaatala, the seventh layer beneath the earth, where they encountered Surabhi, the celestial cow, mother of all earthly cows. Here, Naarada regaled Maatali with stories of her divine origins and the creation of the Milky Ocean from her precious milk.

Despite the wonders they witnessed, a suitable candidate for Gunakesi remained elusive. As they journeyed through these fantastical realms, Maatali couldn't help but wonder where their quest would lead them next. Would they ever find someone worthy of his daughter's hand, or was this search destined to be a journey through realms both literal and metaphorical? The answer, it seemed, lay in the next leg of their extraordinary adventure.

CHAPTER 4

Arrival in Bhogavati

They arrived at Bhogavati, a magnificent city that rivalled Indra's celestial abode. 'This is it,' Naarada announced, his voice filled with wonder. 'Bhogavati, the domain of Vasuki, the king of the Naagas.'

Maatali gazed upon the city, its spires glistening in the otherworldly light. 'Incredible,' he breathed.

'And residing here,' Naarada continued, pointing to a colossal figure in the distance, 'is Ananta Shesha, the mighty serpent with a thousand heads. He holds the very Earth on his hoods! Naaraayana … Naaraayana …'

But Maatali's gaze wasn't drawn to the awe-inspiring sights. Instead, his eyes fell upon a young Naaga standing beside a distinguished elder. This youth, radiating an air of nobility and calm, instantly captured Maatali's attention.

As Naarada finished listing the names of prominent Naagas, Maatali spoke up, his voice filled with newfound purpose. 'Tell me,' he implored, 'about the one standing near Aryaka—the young Naaga with such radiance.'

Naarada, sensing Maatali's interest, smiled knowingly. 'Ah, that's Sumukha,' he explained, 'grandson of Aryaka and a descendant of the great Airavata. He's known for his bravery, having recently defended a neighbouring kingdom from a monstrous sea serpent.'

A flicker of hope ignited in Maatali's heart.

'I believe that this young Naaga prince will be the perfect groom for my Gunakesi.'

But as he finished stating his desire, a shadow fell over the group. Aryaka, his voice heavy with grief, spoke.

'There's a terrible truth you must know,' he said. 'Garuda threatens to devour Sumukha within a month's time.'

Maatali's heart sank. How could he consider Sumukha as a husband for Gunakesi when he faced such imminent danger?

'Don't despair, Maatali,' Naarada boomed, ever the optimist. 'I have a plan. Naaraayana ... Naaraayana ...'

He explained his idea to a skeptical Aryaka. 'Let Sumukha accompany us to Indra's court. There, I believe we can find a way to protect him from Garuda's wrath.'

After much deliberation, Aryaka, burdened with grief for his son but hopeful for his grandson's future, agreed.

As they bid farewell to Aryaka and the Naaga kingdom, a sense of awe filled them. Maatali expertly steered his celestial chariot, its polished surface gleaming in the otherworldly light that filtered through the layers of the cosmos. Naarada regaled them with tales of the wonders that awaited in Indra's court. Sumukha, the young Naaga prince, gazed out at the swirling celestial expanse, a mixture of trepidation and excitement coursing through him. Their journey from the shadowy depths of Naagaloka to the luminous heights of Swargaloka mirrored the transformation in their fortunes.

CHAPTER 5

Indra's Boon

As they stepped into Indra's magnificent court, a hush fell over the assembled deities. Sunlight streamed through the high windows, casting an ethereal glow on the polished marble floor. Indra, the king of the gods, sat upon his bejewelled throne, his golden skin adorned with shimmering gold ornaments. A regal aura emanated from him; his power palpable in the very air. Beside him, the ever-observant Vishnu sat, his four arms resting on the armrests of his own celestial chair. A hint of a smile played on his lips, as if he sensed the curious tale Naarada was about to unfold.

'Greetings, illustrious ones,' boomed Indra's voice, his gaze sweeping over Maatali, his loyal charioteer, Naarada, and Sumukha.

'Naaraayana Naaraayana,' Naarada immediately uttered upon seeing Vishnu, a respectful salutation to the Preserver of the cosmos.

'What brings you to my abode?'

Naarada, ever the eloquent one, stepped forward. 'Mighty Indra,' he bowed, 'we come bearing a tale of a quest and a plea for your wisdom.'

Intrigued, Indra leaned forward. 'A quest and a plea? Very well, wise Naarada. Do tell.'

Naarada then proceeded to narrate the entire story, from Maatali's desire to find a suitable husband for his daughter

Gunakesi to their discovery of Sumukha in Bhogavati. He didn't shy away from the looming threat of Garuda either.

'Alas,' Naarada finished with a sigh, 'Garuda, the bird-god, threatens this promising young Naaga's life. We seek your counsel, Indra, on how to ensure Sumukha finds a happy future with Gunakesi.'

A thoughtful silence descended upon the court.

Finally, Vishnu spoke, his voice calm and measured. 'A difficult situation indeed. Garuda's wrath is not to be taken lightly.'

'But surely there must be a way,' Maatali interjected, his voice laced with desperation. 'I cannot bear see the dreams of Gunakesi's marriage with this handsome young Naaga prince shattered.'

Seeing the anguish in Maatali's eyes, Vishnu offered a solution. 'Granting immortality through Amrita might not be the most prudent course,' he explained, 'considering Garuda's power.'

A flicker of disappointment crossed Maatali's face.

Sensing his concern, Vishnu continued, 'However, a different path exists. We can bestow upon Sumukha a long and prosperous life, ensuring he is safe from Garuda's threat within the stipulated month.'

Indra, after pondering this alternative, nodded in agreement. 'A sound solution, Lord Vishnu. We cannot defy Garuda directly, but we can ensure a fair chance for this young couple.'

Turning towards Sumukha, Indra raised his hand, a powerful energy emanating from it. 'Sumukha, son of the Naagas,' he declared, 'you are hereby blessed with a long life. Fear not the bird-god, for your time shall not be cut short within the next month.'

Relief washed over Sumukha's face. He bowed deeply. 'Thank you, mighty Indra! Your blessing fills me with joy.'

A joyous smile bloomed on Maatali's face. 'Thank you, Indra, Lord Vishnu. You have saved the day!'

With the threat neutralized, the path to a happy union was clear. Soon after, Sumukha and Gunakesi were wed in a grand ceremony, uniting the celestial and Naaga realms in a celebration of love, courage and divine intervention.

VII

The Naagini and Arjuna

A Tale from the Mahabharata

CHAPTER 1

The Stalker Under Water

The first hint of dawn crept across the eastern horizon, painting the Ganga with a soft, rose-gold hue. A serpent princess, Ulupi, hidden in the cool embrace of the river, watched. Every morning, she observed him—Arjuna, son of Pandu, a figure of stoicism and strength. Ever since she laid eyes on Arjuna, the god of love had woven his magic, igniting a yearning in her heart.

Once again, Arjuna approached the sacred banks of the Ganges. The tranquil air, still cool from the night's slumber, carried the gentle murmur of the river, a soothing balm to the serpent princess's desire. Arjuna performed his ablutions, offering water to his deceased ancestors. As he rose and moved towards the shore, his reflection shimmered in the water, a solitary warrior framed by the dwindling sparks of dawn. A ripple disturbed the mirrored surface, and a voice, rich as the Ganges itself, echoed from the depths, 'Arjuna, son of Pandu, why do such shadows linger in your eyes?'

Startled, Arjuna spun around, searching for the source. His eyes scanned the tranquil surface, finding no one. Just ripples on the water. Then, a movement below sent a shiver down his spine. Something long and sinuous slithered beneath the surface, its scales glinting in the fading light.

'Who was that?' he asked, his voice a husky whisper, laced with unease.

Silence answered him. For a tense moment, only the gentle lapping of water could be heard. Then, with a sudden swiftness, something powerful and unseen coiled around his feet and yanked him below the surface, plunging him into the cool, swirling depths of the Ganga.

Arjuna felt a chilling darkness engulf him as he was pulled beneath the surface. The familiar warmth of the sun vanished, replaced by an icy embrace. He fought against the unseen force, kicking and clawing at the water, but it was futile. He was dragged deeper, the world transforming into a swirling vortex of greens and blues. Panic seized him as the air left his lungs, his vision blurring at the edges.

CHAPTER 2

The Magnificent Underwater World

Then, with a jolt, the pressure eased. Arjuna gasped, his eyes adjusted to the dim, otherworldly light. He found himself in a fantastical realm, unlike anything he had ever seen. Glowing fish, iridescent scales catching the light, flitted among coral reefs teeming with life. Schools of tiny, jewel-toned Barramundi shimmered like scattered gemstones, their fins flickering with an ethereal blue. Magnificent Hilsa fish, their silver bodies flashing in the dim light, glided by with an air of quiet majesty.

He was in a magnificent underwater palace, seemingly carved from opals and pearls. Its walls shimmered with an inner light, reflecting the dancing shadows of fish darting through the crystalline windows. The water itself seemed to hum with an ancient energy, a low pulse resonating in his very bones.

In the centre of the palace, a surreal fire burned, its flames an otherworldly blue instead of the orange he was accustomed to. This fire crackled with an energy, a hum that resonated deep within him. Before it, offerings of rare aquatic plants and luminous pearls were meticulously arranged, a silent invitation for a ritual. However, beside the fire, instead of a welcoming human figure, there only lay a coiled serpent, its scales shimmering with an enigmatic sheen.

Arjuna's breath caught in his throat. 'Who are you?' he stammered; his voice raw from the ordeal.

The serpent, her gaze steady and unwavering, spoke in a voice melodious. 'Your duties must come first, Arjuna. Perform your daily fire ritual, and then we shall speak.'

Hesitantly, Arjuna approached the fire. The serpent remained motionless; her gaze seemingly fixed on the mystical flames. He continued the ritual, his movements becoming more fluid and practiced with each offering. The blue flames flickered, their ethereal glow dancing across the polished coral walls of the underwater palace.

CHAPTER 3

Ulupi's Desire

The serpent, her heart pounding against her ribs like a trapped fish, watched as the warrior, Arjuna, finished his ritual. He turned, his gaze landing on her in the dim light. His voice tinged with curiosity as he addressed the serpent. 'O dear serpent, why did you commit this act of rashness on me?'

'Arjuna,' she began, her voice echoing in the silent chamber, 'I understand your confusion. My actions, I admit, were impulsive. But I also refuse to be labelled "rash" simply because I dared to express my desires.'

'Who are you? Why did you bring me here?'

The serpent's head slowly lifted, her amber eyes meeting his gaze with an intensity that sent a shiver down his spine. Then, with a sinuous grace that belied her size, the serpent began to transform. Its powerful coils unwound, revealing two slender legs, the colour of sun-kissed sand. Her upper body, adorned with jewels that shimmered like scattered stars, remained unchanged. She met his eyes, her voice, usually soft as the river's current, now held a resolute edge.

Taking a step forward, her chin held high, she continued, 'I am Ulupi, a Naagini of the Ganga, daughter of the mighty Naagaraaja Kauravya. When I saw you descend into the river, the god of desire may have played his part, but it was I who acted. I, who yearned for your presence, who ached for a connection that transcended my soul. I am yet unmarried, and the flames of desire for you, O tiger among men, consumed me.'

Arjun stood looking at the mesmerizing beauty that was the form of the serpent princess. He replied, 'Please forgive me, princess. I am undergoing the vow of celibacy for twelve years. I am not free to act in any way I like.'

Her voice softened, a hint of vulnerability peeking through. 'I am aware of your vow, Arjuna. I understand the constraints it places upon you. Yet, is it fair that a vow made by men dictates the fate of women? Can I not choose my own path?'

Arjuna stood firm, his expression betraying a struggle within him. 'My vow is sacred,' he countered, his voice low and steady. 'I cannot freely choose my path. Yet, tell me, princess, is there another way I can aid you without violating my oath?'

Ulupi's eyes widened with hope. 'I know of your vow and its origin,' she said, her voice regaining some strength. 'I understand the consequences of entering Draupadi's chamber out of turn. But know this, Arjuna, your exile serves only to protect her. Yielding to my desires would not diminish your virtue, for you would be relieving the suffering of another.'

She stepped closer, her voice dropping to a whisper. 'If your vow faces a slight blemish by granting my wish, think of the immense merit you gain by saving a life. Consider me your devoted admirer.' Tears welled up in Ulupi's eyes, her voice cracking with desperation. 'If you reject me, I will take my own life. O Arjuna, mighty warrior, save me! I seek your protection for you have always shielded the vulnerable. Look upon me, weeping in despair. I yearn for you, Arjuna. Grant me my desire, fulfil my wish.'

The weight of her words hung heavy in the air, creating a tense silence in the palace as Arjuna grappled with the impossible situation. Could he find a way to satisfy Ulupi's desires without breaking his sacred vow? The answer remained hidden, swirling like the currents of the Ganga around them. The silence stretched, thick with unspoken emotions. Arjuna, his gaze locked with Ulupi's, seemed to grapple with the storm brewing within him. Ulupi, her heart pounding in her chest, held his gaze, refusing to back down.

Finally, thus addressed by the daughter of the king of the Naagas, the son of Kunti resolved his inner conflict, making virtue his motive, and acceded to her desires. The mighty Arjuna spent the night in the serpentine palace, rising with the sun in the morning. As dawn painted the water with hues of orange and pink, they emerged from the palace, a unique bond forged between them.

As they reached the point where the Ganga met the plains, Ulupi, her heart filled with a newfound hope, turned to Arjuna. 'May your path be filled with victories, both on land and in the water,' she declared, her voice ringing with newfound confidence. 'And as a token of the bond we have forged, I grant you a boon—invincibility in water. No creature of the aquatic realm will pose a threat to you.'

A grateful smile graced Arjuna's lip. 'Thank you, Ulupi,' he said, his voice sincere.

With a final lingering look, Ulupi dipped back into the cool embrace of the Ganga, her heart lighter than it had been in years. She knew the miraculous seed she had sown within her, a son nurtured in the depths of the river. As she returned to her underwater realm, a new sense of purpose echoed within her, a purpose that transcended her own desires and extended to raising the son who will be known as Iravan.

CHAPTER 4

The Serpent Prince's Sacrifice

Years passed since Arjuna's encounter with Ulupi in the Ganga's depths. Their son, Iravan, grew strong and noble in the hidden realm of the Naagas, inheriting his mother's connection to the waters and his father's warrior spirit. Hearing tales of his father's exploits and the looming Kurukshetra war, Iravan journeyed from the subterranean kingdom to the celestial regions where Arjuna resided for a time, seeking out the legendary Pandava.

Upon finding Arjuna amidst the splendour of Indra's court, the young Naaga prince approached with a respectful yet confident bearing. 'Great warrior, son of Pandu,' Iravan began, his voice clear, 'I have sought you across realms.'

Arjuna turned, observing the youth whose features held a familiar echo. 'And who might you be, young prince, who speaks with such boldness?'

'Father,' Iravan announced, bowing slightly, 'I am Iravan, your son by Ulupi, the Naagini of Ganga.'

Recognition and surprise flickered across Arjuna's face, followed by a warmth that spread through him. He stepped forward, embracing the young Naaga prince. 'Iravan! My son. You have grown into a fine warrior, I see.'

'I have followed your legend, Father,' Iravan replied, meeting his father's gaze. 'And I have come to pledge my service. When the great battle commences, as it surely must, know that I shall stand with you and the Pandavas.'

Arjuna clasped his son's shoulder, pride swelling in his chest. 'Your loyalty honours me, Iravan. Your strength will be a formidable asset in the trials to come.'

Keeping his promise, when the Kurukshetra war started with the blowing of conches and rising dust, Iravan came down to the battlefield. He wasn't just a warrior; he was like a force of nature. He commanded heavenly horses whose hooves hardly seemed to touch the blood-covered ground, yet they crushed enemies like reeds beneath them. Filled with the powerful spirit of his Naaga ancestors, he jumped into the messy chaos of the Kaurava army. He moved smoothly and dangerously, cutting through their soldiers like a hidden serpent attacking from the shadows.

His fierce fighting, quick and deadly, soon angered Shakuni's brothers who wanted revenge—warriors like Gaya, Gavaksha, Vrishava and others. Shouting challenges, they attacked Iravan together, a shower of arrows and spears aimed to kill him. Even though he got wounded, the Naaga prince barely seemed to feel it. With a warrior's shout, he pulled the weapons out of his body, jumped from his chariot—his sword flashing, shield blocking—and fought them directly. He moved like a whirlwind, a fast blur of deadly skill, cutting off arms and legs and taking lives very quickly, until only Vrishava, badly hurt, ran away from the fight in fear.

Seeing this destruction from far away, the Kaurava leader Duryodhana, his face serious, called his most dangerous ally—the

Rakshasa prince Alambhusha, skilled in the dark arts of illusion (maya).

'Arjuna's Naaga-born son is using magic powers against us!' Duryodhana shouted, his voice showing his desperation. 'Use your own magic tricks and stop him! Finish him!'

Alambhusha, looking terrifying and surrounded by shadows, appeared before Iravan. The air felt strange, full of unnatural energy, as the Rakshasa created ghost-like horsemen from the dust and shot arrows covered in poisonous magic. Iravan, not scared at all, broke Alambhusha's bow with one powerful hit, making the Rakshasa fly up into the messy, war-filled sky. Their fight continued among the clouds, an amazing sight of changing illusions and bright flashes of energy. Iravan, now using a large axe, hit Alambhusha again and again, but the Rakshasa, using dark magic, healed himself instantly after each hit.

As Iravan kept attacking without stopping, a huge celestial serpent, an ancient relative of his mother Ulupi, felt his struggle and came quickly from another realm to help. It called legions of serpents to attack the Rakshasa. But Alambhusha, remembering the very old fight between Naagas and Suparnas (Garuda), let out a frightening scream and changed his shape.

The Rakshasa's body twisted and grew bigger, feathers appeared, claws grew sharp—he transformed into a giant, monstrous Garuda, the divine enemy of all Naagas. Moving with shocking speed, the Rakshasa in the disguise of Garuda ripped through the magical serpents, eating them whole, their power disappearing inside his evil form.

The very form of Garuda sent shivers down the serpents' spines, and they started dissipating. Seeing his serpent allies destroyed, his own magic useless against this ancient power, Iravan hesitated. For one critical, heart-stopping second, confusion clouded his warrior's mind.

Alambhusha, still in the scary Garuda form, saw his chance. He dived down like a hunter catching its prey, and with one powerful swing of his magic sword, he cut off the head of the brave serpent prince.

As Iravan, son of Arjuna and Ulupi, fell onto the bloody ground, a loud cheer came from the Kaurava army, feeling stronger for a moment because this powerful warrior was dead.

VIII

Surasa's Challenge

A Tale from the Ramayana

CHAPTER 1

Hanuman Takes Flight

The forests before the sandy shore basked in the warm embrace of the midday sun. Not a leaf dared to rustle, the air itself seemed to hold its breath. Then, a sudden shift. A gust of wind, like a giant's sigh, tore through the palm trees, sending a shiver through the tranquil scene. A colossal shadow, vast and dark, stretched across the land. It dwarfed the tallest trees, its edges blurring into the distant horizon. Forty miles wide, thirty miles long, it swallowed the sunlight whole, plunging the forest floor into a sudden twilight.

High above the swaying canopy, the source of the colossal shadow became clear. Soaring through the endless blue canvas of the sky was the mighty Hanuman. His powerful form, a blur of copper-hued fur against the azure expanse, moved with the relentless force of a hurricane. As he sped towards Lanka, his immense size grew ever larger, momentarily transforming him into a breath-taking spectacle.

As Hanuman jetted above the ocean, a collective murmur rippled through the divine assembly. The Devas, the Gandharvas and the ascetics exchanged worried glances. Hanuman's relentless pace, his unwavering focus, sparked a flicker of concern. 'He may exhaust himself before reaching Lanka,' a celestial voice boomed, echoing the shared anxiety.

Their grand plan, the meticulously crafted scheme from beyond the realm of Maya, to vanquish the monstrous Ravana, hinged on Hanuman's success. The very thought of him succumbing to fatigue, his form plummeting into the unforgiving embrace of the ocean, sent shivers down their spines. But their worry transcended the potential failure of the mission.

A deeper purpose simmered beneath the surface. They yearned to test the limits of Hanuman's strength, to gauge the true measure of his spirit. With a unified accord, they summoned Surasa, the daughter of Daksha and the formidable mother of serpents.

'Surasa,' their voices resonated in a powerful chorus, 'the radiant son of the Wind God, Hanuman, cuts through the heavens. We implore you to impede his progress, if only for a brief moment.'

A sly glint flickered in Surasa's reptilian eyes. 'The gods themselves request my intervention?' she rumbled, her voice echoing across the celestial realm. A surge of pride coursed through her ancient being.

'Indeed,' the divine assembly confirmed. 'Assume the form of a fearsome Rakshasi, towering like a mountain, with jaws that could devour the very sky. Ascend and confront Hanuman. We yearn to witness his strength, his fortitude. Can he overcome this obstacle, or will he falter?'

CHAPTER 2

Hanuman confronts Surasa

Honoured by the divine decree, Surasa rose from the churning depths. Her form morphed, transforming into a monstrous apparition. Coppery eyes blazed with a terrifying intensity, and her gaping maw stretched wide enough to engulf the celestial city itself. With a thunderous roar, she positioned herself directly in Hanuman's path, ready to enact the will of the gods and test the true mettle of the mighty monkey god.

'Halt, monkey!' boomed her voice, echoing across the waves. 'You trespass on my domain and disturb the slumber of the deep. By the ancient pact, you must forfeit your mission and appease my hunger!'

Undeterred, Hanuman landed on the crest of a wave, his brow furrowed in contemplation. He recognized the serpent goddess and the unyielding nature of her vow. Yet, his quest for Sita burned brighter than any fear.

'Esteemed Surasa,' he addressed her with measured respect, 'my sole purpose is to serve the righteous Raama. His beloved Sita has been stolen by the vile Ravana, and I am entrusted with finding her. Grant me passage, and upon my return, I shall willingly enter your maw as a token of gratitude.'

Surasa's colossal form seemed to writhe with amusement. 'Foolish monkey,' she scoffed. 'Many a valiant soul has met their end in my gullet. None have dared bargain or returned from its depths.'

A glint of determination flickered in Hanuman's eyes. He stood tall, his form radiating an inner strength. 'Then let this be a test of my resolve,' he declared. 'Grant me passage, and witness the unwavering spirit of a monkey devoted to his duty!'

Intrigued by his audacity, Surasa cackled, a sound that sent shivers down the spines of even the bravest sea creatures. With a flick of her tail, she opened her maw, a cavernous abyss that seemed to devour the very light.

Undaunted, Hanuman began to enlarge his own form. He grew to the size of a mountain, matching the width of her open jaws. Surasa, surprised by his defiance, stretched her own form further, her monstrous jaws widening to encompass him.

A thrilling game of one-upmanship ensued. Hanuman would expand, his fur rippling like a red sandstorm cloud, and Surasa would counter, her serpentine form writhing to accommodate him. They duelled in this bizarre display of size and power, the very fabric of reality seeming to strain under their immense forms.

And then suddenly, Hanuman shrunk himself down to the size of a thumb. With a swift movement, that excellent intellectual monkey god darted into Surasa's monstrous open mouth. A moment of startled silence followed, then Hanuman emerged, unscathed, from her ear.

Surasa, humbled by his intelligence and unwavering resolve, bowed her serpentine head. 'You have passed, O great monkey,' she rumbled, her voice tinged with grudging respect. 'May your quest be swift and your purpose fulfilled.'

Hanuman, with a grateful nod, launched himself back into the sky, the fiery trails of the setting sun painting his path gold. Surasa, the guardian of the deep, watched him recede, a newfound respect for the monkey god stirring within her ancient heart.

IX

Kaaliya Mardanam

A Tale from the Brahma Puraana

CHAPTER 1

The Uncoiling of Pride

Long ago on the island of Ramaniyaka lived Kaaliya and other serpents. It was paradise except for the threat of Garuda, the majestic enemy of the serpents. Ananta Shesha, the great cosmic serpent, had decreed annual obeisance to Garuda. Every Kartika full moon, the Naagas, their scales glinting under the silver light, offered their respects to their fearsome avian predator.

This year, however, a shadow fell upon the ritual. Kaaliya, known for his arrogance, had just finished his purifying bath. Disdain twisted his features as he eyed the offerings meant for Garuda. 'Foolish tradition!' he hissed, a venomous edge to his voice. He lunged towards the tribute, fangs bared, ready to devour it.

The other Naagas stirred in alarm. They knew the consequences of defying Garuda. With desperate pleas, they tried to dissuade Kaaliya, but their words were lost on his prideful ears. 'We cannot stop you,' one wise elder finally conceded, his voice heavy with dread.

Suddenly, a colossal shadow blotted out the moon. Garuda, his feathers gleaming like burnished copper, descended upon the scene. A chilling silence descended. The lesser Naagas, their fear a tangible entity, banded together, fangs bared in a futile attempt to protect their kin.

The battle commenced—a whirlwind of feathers and flashing fangs. The earth trembled under Garuda's mighty talons, while Kaaliya, a living embodiment of wrath, lashed out with his powerful coils. The clash raged throughout the night, the moon a silent witness to the storm of scales and talons.

As dawn painted the sky in hues of rose and gold, the tide began to turn. Exhausted and overwhelmed, the Naagas scattered, seeking refuge with Ananta, the cosmic serpent, who offered solace to all creatures. All except Kaaliya. Standing defiant, his pride battered but unbroken, Kaaliya locked eyes with his avian adversary. A final, desperate lunge ended in defeat.

Fleeing in a panic, Kaaliya descended to the deepest reaches of the universe, where his eldest brother, Ananta Shesha, stood resolute. Desperate, Kaaliya pleaded for help, but Shesha, the eldest of the Naagas, revealed that there was only one sanctuary in the universe where Garuda would not dare to follow—a kund or pool within the Yamuna River. This kund, was the one place, bound by the curse of the sage Saubhari, Garuda could never enter.

Taking Ananta Shesha's advice, Kaaliya, along with his family and servants, moved to the sanctuary of the Yamuna's depths. There, submerged in the murky waters, Kaaliya found temporary respite, though his heart pounded with a mix of fear and defiance. He knew that this refuge would not last forever, but for the time being, the cold embrace of the Yamuna offered him a fleeting sense of safety.

CHAPTER 2

A Shadow Coils in the Yamuna

The playful shouts of Krishna and his friends echoed through the sun-drenched meadow. Unbeknownst to them, a sinister secret lurked beneath the shimmering surface of the Yamuna River. Here, coiled in the depths, now resided Kaaliya, whose venom tinged the crystal-clear water with a deadly curse.

Krishna, his youthful face radiating innocence, led the herd of cows towards the riverbank. Unconcerned by the hidden danger, the boys let the animals graze on the lush green grass. Krishna, ever the picture of joy, even knelt by the river, cupping his hands to quench his thirst with the seemingly pure water.

But a silent horror was brewing. The river, corrupted by Kaaliya's touch, held a treacherous deception. As the cows continued their peaceful grazing, their unsuspecting snouts dipped into the water, drawing in the fatal liquid. One by one, the animals convulsed, their playful moos replaced by pained gasps.

A heavy silence descended upon the meadow. The cowherd boys, their faces etched with terror, watched as their beloved companions fell lifeless. Krishna, the embodiment of youthful exuberance moments ago, now stood frozen, his heart heavy with the sudden weight of this tragedy that had befallen his favourite cows.

This unseen evil, lurking beneath the tranquil surface, had not only struck down the cows but also ignited a spark of defiance within Krishna. The playful afternoon had taken a dark turn, and the air crackled with the promise of an impending confrontation.

CHAPTER 3

Krishna Confronts Kaaliya

The Yamuna writhed beneath the skeletal fingers of a lone kadamba tree. Its gnarled branches scraped the gloomy sky, casting an ominous silhouette like a monstrous claw. An unnatural stillness pressed down, broken only by the fetid gurgle emanating from the poisoned depths of the kund. The air hung heavy, thick with the stench of decay and a metallic tang that sent shivers down Krishna's spine.

Krishna, a vision of youthful innocence in stark contrast to this oppressive realm, stood frozen. Laughter, a distant memory in this macabre scene, died in his throat as the earth trembled. He swam across all alone and climbed up the kadamba tree and looked below.

The seemingly placid river convulsed, a monstrous form rising from its depths.

Kaaliya, a leviathan of scales, emerged from the abyss of the inky pool. His multiple heads pulsed with an unholy luminescence. Venom dripped from his fangs like putrid tears, and his eyes, glowing embers of malevolent hunger, locked onto Krishna.

Clad in garments of golden silk, Krishna appeared delicate yet divine, his luminous frame akin to a celestial cloud aglow with ethereal light. Adorned upon his chest lay the sacred mark of Srivatsa, while his countenance bore a smile of ineffable beauty, akin to the blossoming of a lotus at dawn. Fearlessly, Krishna played amidst the ripples, a paragon of serenity amidst the aqueous expanse.

Yet, in the throes of envy, Kaaliya, the venomous serpent, lashed out furiously, sinking his fangs into the tender flesh of Krishna's chest, enveloping him within the coils of his wrath.

Upon the verdant banks of Yamuna, Krishna's companions stood transfixed, their vice silenced by the pall of impending doom. Tears welled in their eyes as they witnessed their beloved Krishna seemingly consumed by the monstrous multi-headed serpent's embrace.

Meanwhile, some boys, swift as startled chicken, raced towards Vrindavan, bearing tidings of distress to Yashoda, Krishna's mother.

Rohini, Yashoda, Nanda and all the gopas and gopis rushed to the edge of Kaaliya's whirlpool, their hearts gripped by fear and despair as they searched for any sign of Krishna amidst the churning waters. Yet, to their dismay, their eyes found no trace of their beloved Krishna. Only Balarama, with his steadfast demeanour and unwavering composure, offered solace to the distraught multitude.

'Have faith in Krishna,' he reassured them, his voice resonating with a quiet strength that cut through the chaos like a beacon of hope. 'He will return to us unharmed. He is beyond the clutches of death.'

Balarama, a pillar of unwavering strength, held back the terrified crowd. Silence descended, broken only by the gurgling of the poisoned river. Dark clouds, foreboding and swirling, materialized above the Yamuna, a chilling omen that sent shivers down everyone's spine. Fear, a suffocating shroud, settled over the meadow—a fear for the fate of their beloved Krishna.

CHAPTER 4

Kaaliya Mardanam

Krishna, seemingly lost within the serpent's coils, played along for a moment, mimicking the struggles of a mere mortal. But the anguish in the eyes of his loved ones, their very lifeblood threatened by his absence, sparked a flicker of resolve within him. With a surge of divine power, he burst free from Kaaliya's grasp.

The monstrous serpent recoiled, his colossal form thrashing in pain as the bonds loosened. Enraged, Kaaliya reared his multiple heads, his eyes blazing with an infernal light. Nostrils flared; they resembled cauldrons spewing forth venomous fumes. His forked tongues darted out, tasting the air, a grotesque display of predatory intent. Yet, Krishna remained undeterred. With the playful grace of a celestial dancer, he circled the enraged serpent, mirroring the movements of Garuda toying with its prey.

Kaaliya, seething with fury, writhed in response, his monstrous form twisting and turning, searching for an opportunity to strike. The air crackled. Krishna, the protector of the innocent, rose to the challenge. With a swift movement, he delivered a powerful blow, his foot connecting with the serpent's stubborn head. A tremor ran through Kaaliya's form as he writhed in agony, his multiple heads thrashing and spewing forth a geyser of venom-laced blood.

Kaaliya lunged with his remaining strength in a desperate attempt to strike back. However, Krishna remained a step ahead. He would land upon each rearing head, subduing it with a gentle yet firm press of his foot. The Devas, witnessing this awe-inspiring display, showered Krishna with celestial flowers, their reverence a testament to his power and his unwavering resolve.

The sheer weight of Krishna's divine essence proved too much for the monstrous serpent. Kaaliya, his life force waning, could no longer resist. With a final, agonizing gasp, he vomited a torrent of blood and collapsed, his monstrous form a shadow of its former terror.

CHAPTER 5

The Naagini's Plea

The aftermath of the battle hung heavy in the air. Kaaliya, the monstrous serpent, lay unconscious, his form a grotesque shadow against the churning river. Panicked wails pierced the tense silence. Kaaliya's wives, their serpentine forms writhing in unison, surrounded their fallen lord. Tears streamed down their faces, their voices a chorus of grief and desperation.

'O Lord Krishna,' they began, 'witness the devastation your power has wrought. We, the wives of Kaaliya, are left widowed by your actions.'

'Rise, brave queens,' Krishna spoke, his voice gentle yet firm. 'I offer you a safe haven for your family, but you must move back to Ramaniyaka Island, away from Yamuna.'

'But what about Garuda?'

'Garuda shall not attack you for my footprint is embedded on your husband's hood.'

Kaaliya, stirring from his unconscious slumber, opened his eyes to the sight of Krishna.

A wave of relief washed over him. 'Forgive my transgression, mighty Lord Krishna,' he rasped, the memory of his defeat fresh in his mind.

Krishna, his gaze holding a hint of amusement, simply nodded. 'Return to Ramaniyaka Island, Kaaliya. Remember, the mark of my feet you bear serves as a constant reminder. You and your family shall be safe from Garuda's wrath.'

Kaaliya, overwhelmed with gratitude, bowed deeply. Then he and his family slithered back into the churned waters of the Yamuna and swam far away.

Notes

The narrative of 'Kaaliya Mardanam' depicts Krishna's victory over the serpent Kaaliya, who poisoned the Yamuna River. This core element remains consistent across various sources like the Brahma Puraana and Srimad Bhagavatam. However, variations exist:

Kaaliya's fate: While the provided story allows Kaaliya to return to Ramaniyaka Island, other Puraanas like the *Brahma Vaivarta Puraana* depict him being banished to Paataala (Naagar, 2002, p. 162).

Notably, some versions incorporate Surasa as Kaaliya's wife, pleading for his life and eventually choosing devotion to Krishna. This element aligns with the Garga Samhita but differs from prominent scriptures like the *Bhagavata Puraana*, which solely focus on the Krishna-Kaaliya conflict (Coomaraswamy, 1902, p. 225).

These variations highlight the multifaceted nature of storytelling in Hinduism, where core stories are adapted across regions and time periods. Some narratives, like the one presented, might emphasize specific characters or themes like devotion, while others might focus primarily on the central conflict between good and evil.

X

Veneration of Manasa

A Tale from the Puraanas

CHAPTER 1

Dhanvantari Freezes Takshaka

The acrid scent of churned ocean of milk air hung heavy as Dhanvantari, the celestial physician, emerged from the swirling depths. A master of ancient lore, his knowledge encompassed not just scriptures, but the forbidden whispers of mantras and tantras. A student of the mighty Garuda and the enigmatic Shiva, Dhanvantari once journeyed towards the luminous peak of Mount Kailasa, accompanied by a throng of his students.

The serene pilgrimage towards Kailasa was shattered by a monstrous sight—Takshaka, the colossal serpent king with scales like glistening obsidian, emerged from the undergrowth. His forked tongue, dripping with potent venom, flickered menacingly. A horde of smaller serpents writhed around the behemoth; their beady eyes fixated on Dhanvantari.

A ripple of amused laughter erupted from the ranks of Dhanvantari's students. Their renowned master, after all, was the celestial physician, a being of immense power. To them, the sight of a serpent, even one as imposing as Takshaka, attempting to attack their teacher seemed almost comical.

Unfazed by the commotion, Dhanvantari locked eyes with the serpent. With a swift, practiced motion, he unleashed a potent mantra. The air crackled with arcane energy, a tangible force that slammed into Takshaka. The monstrous serpent froze mid-strike, its powerful body locked in a silent snarl.

Seizing the moment, Dhanvantari displayed his mastery. A single, precise movement and the serpent's gem-encrusted hood was detached, the source of its immense venom. The jewel, pulsating with an unnatural light, was flung far and wide, vanishing into the dense foliage.

Silence descended. The amusement on the students' faces slowly morphed into awe as they witnessed the swift neutralization of the mighty serpent. The smaller serpents remained frozen; their hisses replaced by a collective, unnerved stillness. Only the rasping breath of the immobilized Takshaka broke the eerie quiet. Some serpents rushed underground to inform Vasuki about the turn of events.

CHAPTER 2

Vasuki's Anger

The slithering lustre of Bhogavati pressed down, a suffocating cloak for any mortal that swallowed stray tendrils of light. The illumination came from clusters of rare gems, their vibrant hues pulsating with an otherworldly glow. Amethyst shards embedded in the cavern walls cast an ethereal violet light, while scattered rubies flickered like embers, painting the damp stone in shades of crimson and emerald. The air, thick and humid, held the aura of the netherworld, a stark contrast to the fresh scents of the surface world.

Here, in the subterranean heart of the serpent kingdom, the symphony was not the rustling of leaves. It was the slithering whisper of countless scales against the cold stone floor, the rhythmic pulse of a thousand cold-blooded hearts. Two serpents who had escaped the spell of Dhanvantari, their scaly forms catching the faint gem-light, knelt before Vasuki, their coiled king on a dais of polished obsidian.

One serpent, his forked tongue flickering like a serpent's warning, spoke in a voice that echoed through the vast chamber. 'My King,' he rasped, the sound slick with a low hiss, 'grave news slithers from the pilgrimage route. Takshaka …'

Vasuki, his massive form rippling like a dark ocean current, sent tremors through the very floor. 'Takshaka?' A guttural rumble resonated from his throat, the sound raw and powerful. 'What of him?'

'Neutralized,' the second serpent hissed, his head swaying slightly. 'The venom ... contained. That great serpent ... rendered immobile by Dhanvantari.'

Vasuki's eyes, a burning ember in the perpetual gloom, narrowed. 'Neutralized? By that ... fleeting physician and his brood?'

A flicker of disbelief ignited in the serpents' eyes, quickly replaced by a deeper fear.

Vasuki uncoiled further, the movement sending a wave of silent terror through the warriors. The very air crackled with his restrained fury. 'This affront cannot stand! They mock our kind in the land of the mortals! Assemble the legions!' Vasuki roared, the sound echoing through the tunnels and twisting passages. 'Drona, Kaaliya, Karkotaka, Pundarika, Dhananjaya! Let them unleash their venom upon these insolent fools!'

A chorus of hisses erupted from the unseen depths of the cavern, a wave of sound that vibrated through the very rock. The two warriors, their forms charged with renewed purpose, slithered out, their message carried on the cold breath of the netherworld.

CHAPTER 3

The Naagas Confront Dhanvantari

Sunlight beat down on the dusty earth, the air thick with the scent of sun-baked clay. Dhanvantari's students, initially filled with amusement, found their laughter replaced by a suffocating dread. From beneath the earth, coiled serpents, their scales shimmering in the harsh light, filled the once serene clearing.

With a single, unified hiss, the Naagas exhaled a venomous miasma. Dhanvantari's students, their faces contorted in silent screams, crumpled to the ground, instantly paralyzed by the potent toxin. Dhanvantari, however, remained unfazed. Ignoring the writhing mass of serpents, he closed his eyes and began to chant. His voice, a deep sonorous rumble, resonated through the clearing as he invoked the name of his teacher and showered the fallen with the sacred nectar.

As the last syllable of the mantra faded, a wave of energy surged through the clearing. The students, colour returning to their faces, gasped for breath, the paralysis lifting.

Meanwhile, the serpents lay motionless, victims of Dhanvantari's swift counter. Not a single one stirred, their potent venom rendered useless.

CHAPTER 4

The Serpent Queen Emerges

Deep within Bhogavati, a tremor of unease ran through Vasuki. He possessed an innate awareness of his domain, and the sudden stillness emanating from the grounds above sent a shiver down his spine. The Naagas he had dispatched to deal with the upstart physician, Dhanvantari, had fallen silent. Not a single hiss, not a whisper reached him through their potent connection.

A low rumble, raw and powerful, emanated from his throat. 'Something is amiss,' he hissed to himself, the sound echoing through the vast chamber. He couldn't shake the feeling of unease. Dhanvantari, a fleeting physician daring to challenge him? It was a thought that should have elicited amusement, yet a sliver of doubt wormed its way in. He couldn't allow such an affront. Not on his watch.

'Jagadgauri Manasa!' Vasuki's voice boomed through the cavern, a tremor shaking the very foundation of the chamber.

From the shadows emerged a figure, her form cloaked in an aura of power. Manasa, his sister, the embodiment of knowledge and vengeance, materialized before him.

'Brother.' She bowed her head, her voice a sibilant whisper that carried the weight of the serpent kingdom.

'Sister, a something has occurred. The Naagas sent to confront Dhanvantari …' He paused, the weight of their silence heavy in the air, 'they lie silent.'

'I shall at once save my brothers. I shall destroy the enemies in the battlefield in no time.'

'Be careful, for that physician is the pupil of Garuda.'

'I have the boon of kavacha (protective shield) from Lord Vishnu. So, I do not fear Garuda. Why should I bother about his pupils, and Dhanvantari is quite insignificant a person,' she replied, her voice laced with a dangerous promise.

With a slither that disturbed the very air, Manasa vanished from the cavern, her form a blur disappearing into the twisting tunnels. The silence returned, heavier now, a pregnant pause before the inevitable storm.

CHAPTER 5

The Raging Encounter

A tremor shook the earth as Manasa, the Serpent Queen, her eyes blazing embers, materialized before Dhanvantari. Gone were the writhing serpents, replaced by the goddess's wrath. With a flick of her will, the fallen Naagas rose, their venomous gaze paralyzing Dhanvantari's pupils.

The physician, his calm facade momentarily shattered, attempted to counter with mantras. Yet, an invisible snare bound his voice, rendering his words powerless.

'Physician,' Manasa's voice, a venomous hiss, echoed through the clearing. 'Have you forgotten the true power of mantras, the depths of their lore, the secrets of the great elixirs? You, a mere student of Garuda, puffed up by your fleeting knowledge!' Her voice boomed, a challenge echoing the ancient bond she shared with the celestial bird, both pupils of the mighty Shiva.

With a gesture swift and wrathful, Manasa ripped lotus flowers from a nearby lake. Sanctified with potent mantras, they became flaming projectiles, hurtling towards Dhanvantari. The air crackled with their fiery heat.

Undeterred, Dhanvantari let out a deep, resonating breath. The flames were extinguished in an instant, reduced to smoldering ash by the sheer force of his exhalation. A peal of laughter, laced with a hint of mockery, escaped his lips.

Manasa, enraged by the physician's defiance, unleashed a torrent of sanctified power. It blazed with the fury of a summer sun, threatening to consume Dhanvantari. He met the attack head-on. The trident gifted by Vishnu, a weapon shimmering with celestial light, shot forth from his hand. The divine energies clashed, the flaming torrent dissolving with a deafening boom.

Frustration contorted Manasa's face. She uncoiled a weapon of immense power—the Naagapaasa, a necklace woven from a lakh of serpents. Each serpent, empowered by her mantras, pulsed with venomous energy. With a hiss that split the air, she hurled the Naagapaasa at Dhanvantari.

A sly smile played on the physician's lips. He summoned Garuda.

A monstrous shadow descended from the heavens. Garuda, his eyes gleaming with predatory hunger, tore into the serpent weapon. The Naagapaasa, no match for his razor-sharp talons, disintegrated into a writhing mass of devoured snakes.

Manasa, teetering on the edge of a maelstrom of fury, reached for her ultimate weapon—an ashen powder gifted by Shiva himself. Muttering ancient incantations, she flung the powder at Dhanvantari. But before the ashen cloud could engulf him, Garuda, with a powerful beat of his wings, created a whirlwind that scattered the dust.

The goddess, her face contorted with rage, unsheathed the infallible trident of Shiva. Its brilliance rivalled a thousand suns, promising annihilation. The stage was set for a clash of celestial proportions.

CHAPTER 6

The Divine Intervention

Manasa, a tempest of scales and fury, descended upon Dhanvantari. Her eyes, burning with the fires of vengeance, locked onto the physician's. Though calm on the surface, Dhanvantari felt a tremor of unease crawl up his spine. He recognized the glint in Manasa's eyes—the glint of a goddess wielding a power meant to sunder worlds.

In their celestial abodes, Brahma and Shiva watched (with their divyadrishti or clairvoyance) the scene unfold with a heavy heart. They knew the unyielding might of the trident in Manasa's grip. Dhanvantari, no matter his prowess, stood no chance against a weapon blessed by the Destroyer Shiva himself.

Manasa, fury a mere ember compared to the inferno that had raged within moments ago, stood poised with the trident. Yet, the air crackled with a different energy now. Two figures materialized before her—the Supreme beings, Brahma and Shiva. Reverence washed over Manasa, forcing the weapon to dip in acknowledgement.

Dhanvantari and Garuda, their battle stances dissolving, mirrored her actions. A wave of relief and unspoken gratitude passed between them. Shiva, his voice resonating with an otherworldly calm, addressed Dhanvantari.

'Esteemed Dhanvantari,' he boomed, 'your knowledge of the scriptures is vast. We believe conflict with Manasa is unwarranted. Remember, she wields the power to rend the very fabric of existence with the trident bestowed upon her by me.'

Brahma's gaze softened. 'For the well-being of all, I urge you to appease the goddess. Follow the prescribed rituals, the sixteen offerings of the Kauthuma-sakha, and recite the stotra composed by Astika. Earn her favour through devotion, and she shall surely grant you a boon.'

Dhanvantari readily agreed. He stripped himself of his usual garb and plunged into the nearby river, the icy water washing away the dust of battle and the lingering fear that had crept into his heart.

Manasa, though her initial fury had subsided like a storm spent, remained a statue of vigilance. Her eyes, however, held a flicker of something akin to curiosity. Dhanvantari's voice, raw with emotion, rose in a hymn. Each word resonated with a desperate plea for forgiveness and a genuine appreciation for the power he faced.

'Jagadgauri,' he called, his voice hoarse, 'guardian of the underworld, I stand before you humbled. Accept, I implore you, these humble offerings, a token of my deepest respect.' He proffered the white flowers, their delicate petals trembling in the sudden breeze.

Silence stretched, thick and heavy. Manasa remained impassive, the glint of the trident's tip a constant reminder of the power she wielded. Dhanvantari pressed on, his voice gaining strength with each passing verse. He painted a vivid picture of Manasa in his mind, extolling her virtues—her compassion, her wisdom, her role as protector.

A flicker of movement. Manasa's hand, almost imperceptibly, shifted away from the weapon's grip. A sliver of hope pierced through Dhanvantari's growing despair. He poured his heart into his final plea, his voice cracking with the raw vulnerability of a man facing his mortality.

As the last echo of his hymn faded, a tense silence descended. The very air seemed to hold its breath. Then, slowly, ever so slowly, a hint of a smile graced Manasa's lips. The tension bled away, replaced by a sense of serenity that washed over the battlefield.

With a gesture of her hand, the trident vanished. Manasa inclined her head slightly in acknowledgement, a silent promise exchanged. Her voice, when she spoke, was soft, a mere whisper compared to the earlier roar.

'Your devotion has been noted, physician,' she rumbled. 'The boon you seek is granted. However, remember, the delicate balance between our worlds must be maintained.'

With that, Manasa turned and vanished in a swirl of emerald light. Dhanvantari, his legs weak with relief, crumpled to his knees. The gift of life, once seemingly lost, had been miraculously returned.

The following days were a blur of activity. Dhanvantari, his disciples restored, resumed his duty of healing. The Naagas, including Takshaka, their anger soothed by Manasa's intervention, retreated back to their subterranean realm. A fragile peace between the two worlds had settled, a testament to the power of humility and the unexpected turn of events on that fateful day.

PART 4

Sarpakatha

Stories of Serpents from Indian Folktales

Introduction

Having explored the grand, cosmic narratives of the Naagas as presented in the Puranic narratives, our journey now shifts to a different, yet equally vital, current of serpent lore—the folktales, or as I would like to call them—Sarpakatha or serpentine tales. These stories, often passed down through generations via oral tradition before being captured in collections like the *Manasamangalkavya* or regional compilations such as Kerala's *Aithihyamaala*, offer intimate glimpses into how serpents were perceived and interacted with in everyday life and local belief systems across the subcontinent.

While the Puraanas often deal with divine genealogies and cosmic events, folktales frequently focus on direct encounters between humans and serpents (or beings associated with them), illustrating moral lessons, explaining local phenomena, or reinforcing community traditions and taboos. Here, the serpent might appear as a wise guardian, a creature demanding respect, a source of unexpected fortune (like the fabled *naagamani*), or even a participant in poignant human dramas.

The tales gathered in this section originate from diverse regions—from Bengal to Punjab, Tamil Nadu to Sri Lanka, and the Malabar coast—each reflecting unique cultural nuances while often echoing universal themes of caution, reverence, consequence and the mysterious power attributed to these enigmatic serpents. As with any living folk tradition, variations abound, but each story contributes another thread to the rich tradition of India's enduring relationship with the serpent. Prepare now to delve into these captivating accounts, where the lines between the human and the serpentine often blur in surprising and instructive ways.

I

Behula Lokhindar

*Adapted from the Manasamangalkavya,
from Bengal*

CHAPTER 1

Manasa's Dilemma

One day, Manasa, the goddess of serpents, sought solace in Kailasa. Nestled amidst snow-capped peaks, a disquietude settled upon Manasa as she ventured towards the abode of Shiva and the Bhutaganas.

Parvati sat beside Shiva, weaving a garland of celestial flowers. The air hummed with the quiet murmur of their conversation. Manasa entered; her form cloaked in a shadow of despair.

'Mahadeva,' she began, her voice barely a whisper.

Shiva, his eyes closed in meditation, acknowledged her with a gentle hum. 'Manasa,' he rumbled, his voice calm and deep. 'What troubles you, daughter?'

Manasa hesitated; her eyes downcast. 'Mahadeva,' she began, choosing her words carefully, 'in the mortal realm, your name is like the sun, lighting every corner. Yet, mine ...' her voice trailed off, a tremor hinting at the well of emotions churning within.

Parvati, her gaze filled with concern, looked up from her work. 'Manasa, child, speak freely. What weighs heavy on your heart?'

Manasa took a deep breath. 'My altars gather dust, untouched by prayers or offerings. It ... it diminishes my divinity, a constant sting that festers within me.'

Shiva opened his eyes, a thoughtful frown creasing his brow. 'This is true, daughter,' he conceded. 'But devotion cannot be strong-armed, child. It blooms like a lotus, from the depths of genuine faith.'

Manasa's shoulders slumped. 'But Mahadeva, is there nothing I can do?' she pleaded, a flicker of hope igniting in her eyes.

Shiva stroked his beard, his expression contemplative. 'Perhaps … a test,' he finally offered. 'If you can find one of my most devout followers, someone who embodies unwavering faith, and convince them to acknowledge your own divinity, then perhaps a seed of worship for you can take root in the mortal world.'

Manasa's eyes widened. A glint of determination steeled Manasa's gaze. 'I shall find this devotee, Mahadeva,' she declared, her voice ringing with newfound resolve. 'You shall see!' And with that, she turned and left Kailasa, her heart set on a quest that would redefine her place in the celestial order.

CHAPTER 2

Chand Sadagar

Once upon a time, in the vibrant city of Champaknagar, nestled by the Bay of Bengal, lived Chand Sadagar, a merchant whose wealth rivalled the waves. His sturdy merchant ship, a regular voyager on the Triveni—the sacred confluence of three mighty rivers—traversed the endless waters, bringing exotic treasures back to his homeland.

One stormy night, at the helm of his vessel, Chand was plagued by a peculiar dream. A vision materialized—a magnificent being, crowned with jewels, adorned with shimmering scales and wielding an army of writhing serpents in her many arms. This otherworldly apparition sent a shiver down Chand's spine, jolting him awake in a cold sweat. He sought solace in the chants dedicated to Lord Shiva, the great destroyer, and slumber finally embraced him.

Upon returning from his voyage, as Chand disembarked, the world around him lurched. The once-placid waters churned, the mighty ship groaning in protest. Fear gripped him as he clung to the railing, his vision adjusting to an extraordinary sight. Before him stood Manasa, the Serpent Goddess, cloaked in an aura of power, visible only to him.

'Chand Sadagar,' her voice slithered in his ear, 'devotee of Shiva, I have come to claim your loyalty. You shall offer me your worship.'

Chand, his voice firm, retorted, 'Why should I abandon the Mahadeva, the destroyer of evil, to bow before a mere serpent goddess?'

Manasa's eyes narrowed. 'Because it is Shiva's will,' she declared.

Chand scoffed. 'No true devotee of Shiva would forsake him for a lesser deity!'

This defiance ignited Manasa's fury. Yet, Chand held a secret weapon—a sacred mantra gifted by Lord Shiva himself, a shield against all malicious intent. As the potent syllables resonated on his lips, Manasa, her wrath momentarily quelled, vanished into the mystical realm. The churning waters stilled, and Chand, shaken but resolute, stepped onto the welcoming shores.

CHAPTER 3

Death by Snake Bite

Manasa started weaving a web of terror around Chand's village. One moonless night, as villagers hurried home, a chorus of slithering whispers echoed through the undergrowth. Poisonous serpents darted from the darkness, striking with venomous fangs. Panic seized the villagers as their kin fell victim to the hissing assassins.

Grief and fear hung heavy in the air. Then, amidst the raging storm that clawed at the trees, Manasa materialized before the tear-streaked villagers. Her voice, laced with venom, slithered through the downpour, 'Go, tell your Chand Sadagar to bend the knee and offer me his worship! Only then will this serpent's fury subside!'

News of the tragedy reached Chand.

The merchant's world had tilted on its axis. Grief, a suffocating cloak, threatened to consume Chand entirely. Staring at the long line of rafts bobbing on the river, his gaze snagged on the lifeless forms laid out upon them—stark reminders of the serpent's deadly touch. Their skin, once vibrant, now bore the tell-tale bluish tinge, a signature of the venom's cruel kiss.

Local tradition held a sliver of hope; setting the deceased adrift on the river was a desperate plea to appease the capricious hand of fate. Perhaps, the belief went, if the river god was cajoled, the stolen life breath might be coaxed back into the body.

This sliver of hope, however, was a bitter pill to swallow. Chand's heart ached with a profound sadness. The sight of his fellow villagers, forever silenced by the serpent's strike, fueled a simmering anger within him. It was an anger not just directed at the unseen force that snatched lives, but also a gnawing resentment towards the helplessness that shrouded them all.

The villagers, their voices choked with desperation, pleaded, 'Lord Chand, appease the wrath of the goddess! Our lives hang by a thread!'

A deafening crack of thunder split the sky, igniting a distant tree in a fiery pyre. Chand stood resolute. 'No,' his voice boomed, unwavering. 'I will not yield.'

Tears welled in the villagers' eyes. 'Have mercy, Chand!' they cried.

Chand surveyed the fallen once more. A heavy sigh escaped his lips. 'Very well,' he conceded, his voice firm. 'I shall offer my devotion ...' he paused, his eyes flashing with defiance, 'only to Shiva!'

Manasa's voice roared from the heavens, laced with fury, 'Blasphemy! You dare defy me?'

The skies opened, unleashing a torrent of rain that lashed the village. Yet, Chand remained undeterred. His unwavering faith in Shiva, a shield against her manipulations, burned brighter than the storm's fury.

CHAPTER 4

Chand's Children

After this Manasa challenged Chand, 'Do you accept me as your goddess?'

'No! Never!' Despair gnawed at Chand. Yet, his loyalty to Shiva remained unwavering.

This defiance enraged Manasa further. 'Well then, I will take the dearest to you … one by one …'

Manasa unleashed her wrath, striking like a venomous viper. One by one, Chand's children fell victim to her curse, their lives extinguished by the silent fangs of her serpentine servants. Even the innocent beasts of his household were not spared. Grief became Chand's constant companion. Stripped of his wealth, his progeny and even the familiar comfort of his home, he was reduced to a mendicant, his once proud form cloaked in rags. Yet, amidst the crushing weight of his misfortunes, his devotion to Shiva remained the one ember that refused to die. Even in the face of utter destitution, Chand clung to his faith, a silent testament to the enduring power of unwavering belief. And then his wife gave birth to a seventh son—Lokhindar. Chand decided to marry off the boy to a girl who may never attain widowhood.

CHAPTER 5

Behula and Lokhindar

A daughter, Behula, was born to his friend Saha, destined according to their horoscopes, to never be a widow. A spark of defiance flickered within Chand. He wouldn't let Manasa win.

Marrying Behula to his son Lokhindar (Lakshmindra) seemed like a stroke of fate. However, the shadow of Manasa's threat loomed large. Consulting the celestial charts revealed Lokhindar would be struck by a serpent's venom on his wedding night.

Desperate to shield his son, Chand, distrustful of Manasa's intentions, commissioned Vishwakarma, the divine architect, to construct an iron chamber for the wedding night. Yet, under the unseen pressure of the serpent goddess, a tiny gap was left in the seemingly impregnable structure—a concession forced upon Vishwakarma to save his own family.

The fateful night arrived. Manasa, relentless in her pursuit, dispatched her most venomous serpent, the Kalnagini. Slithering through the concealed gap, the creature entered the chamber, ready to strike.

However, a strange turn of events unfolded. The Kalnagini, perhaps sensing Behula's unwavering love and the injustice of the situation, hesitated. Manasa, enraged by this defiance, compelled the serpent to act. As Kalnagini lunged towards Lokhindar, a flicker of mercy emerged. Instead of a fatal bite, she merely grazed his head with venom-laced oil, a subtle mark of sin.

Lokhindar cried out, awakening Behula from a spell cast by Manasa. Witnessing the slithering escape of the serpent, a surge of righteous anger coursed through Behula. She grabbed a nearby object and struck, severing the Kalnagini's lower body.

As per tradition, Lokhindar's body was placed on a raft, set adrift on the river, with a sliver of hope for a miraculous return. Driven by unwavering love and a flicker of defiance against Manasa's cruelty, Behula refused to abandon her husband's side. She embarked on this perilous journey, her unwavering faith a beacon in the face of despair. Months turned into a seemingly endless voyage. Villages passed by, their inhabitants mistaking Behula for a crazed soul clinging to a decomposing corpse. Yet, her unwavering prayers echoed across the water, a constant plea directed at the very being who had orchestrated this tragedy—Manasa.

CHAPTER 6

The Compromise

Finally, after enduring immense hardship, Behula reached the abode of Neta, Manasa's foster mother. Touched by Behula's unwavering devotion, Neta intervened, whisking her and the deceased Lokhindar to the heavens.

Manasa, though impressed by Behula's courage, laid down a condition. 'You deserve your husband's return,' she declared, 'but only if you convince your father-in-law to become my devotee.'

Behula's heart hammered against her ribs. This was a difficult choice. She glanced at Lokhindar, his face pale and peaceful. The thought of a life without him was unbearable.

Taking a deep breath, Behula met Manasa's gaze. 'I will do what I must,' she declared, her voice ringing with a quiet determination.

Behula returned to the mortal realm, and went straight to Chand Sadagar's house. The news of Behula's miraculous journey and Manasa's condition for Lokhindar's resurrection spread like wildfire. Chand Sadagar, overwhelmed with a mix of relief and lingering anger, stood before Manasa's idol.

He couldn't bring himself to fully surrender. Manasa's cruelty had left a bitter taste in his mouth. So, in a gesture of begrudging acceptance, Chand raised his left hand—a symbol of his unwavering devotion to Shiva still burning brightly in his heart—and offered a single 'Anjali' to the serpent goddess.

Manasa, witnessing Chand's conflicted emotions, seemed to understand the depth of his struggle. Perhaps Behula's unwavering love and Chand's enduring faith had touched a part of her. In a display of her divine power, Manasa granted not only Lokhindar's life back but also the lives of Chand's other sons. Additionally, the family's lost wealth miraculously reappeared.

Joy bloomed within Chand's household. Behula and Lokhindar, forever marked by their extraordinary journey, embarked on a new chapter filled with love and gratitude.

This turn of events marked a shift in the relationship between the goddess and the people. While the memory of past trials remained, a newfound respect bloomed for Manasa's power and the potential for understanding between mortals and the divine.

Notes

As with the variability in oral traditions about which I mentioned in *Daiva*, the story of Manasa in Bengal has evolved through centuries of retelling, resulting in multiple versions. The continuous oral tradition periodically crystallized into written texts, which were later recited during events. These recitations reinvigorated the oral traditions from which they originated. Individual storytellers wove together diverse versions to craft unique compositions, which then influenced subsequent oral and written iterations, blurring their boundaries further (Haq, 2015, p. 27).

One notable variation connects the births of Behula and Lokhindar directly to Manasa's cosmic influence and a curse originating from Hindu Puraanas. In some versions of the Manasamangal, it is suggested that Behula and Lokhindar were celestial beings in their previous lives—none other than Usha (daughter of Banasura) and Aniruddha (grandson of Lord Krishna). Due to a curse, often orchestrated or influenced by Manasa herself who sought a truly devoted pair to facilitate her worship on Earth, Usha and Aniruddha were fated to be reborn as mortals. Their earthly lives as Behula and Lokhindar, marked by intense love, tragic separation by snakebite (a domain ruled by Manasa), and ultimate reunion through unwavering devotion, thus become a preordained drama designed to compel Chand Sadagar, Shiva's steadfast devotee, to finally acknowledge Manasa's divinity. This narrative layer adds a dimension of cosmic destiny and divine orchestration to the already poignant folktale, echoing other Puranic accounts where divine will shapes mortal events, such as the prophecy of Kadru's curse meted out to Vasuki and the serpents by Brahma.

II

The Naagini Who Cursed a Young Sakya Husband

A Tale from Buddhist Mythology

CHAPTER 1

The Youth Rests at the Lake

In the kingdom of Udyana, where the Suvasta River shimmered like a silver ribbon, a shadow of war loomed. Virudhaka, the ruthless king of Kosala, had unleashed his fury upon the Sakya clan. Among those forced to flee was a young Sakya, his heart heavy with loss and his body weary from the relentless journey.

The weary young Sakya was seeking refuge as he trudged a solitary path. A survivor of the brutal war that had ravaged his homeland, he was burdened by grief and exhaustion.

One scorching afternoon, as he slumped down by the roadside, a strange sight filled his eyes. A giant wild goose, known for its gentle nature, landed gracefully before him. It beckoned him to come closer and climb on its back. Driven by a sense of trust, the young man climbed onto its back. The goose soared through the azure sky, finally alighting beside a tranquil lake. Lulled by the gentle murmur of water and the rustling of leaves, the young man drifted off to sleep under the shade of a sprawling tree, unaware of the secrets the lake held within its depths.

Deep within its frozen depths, a sinuous form stirred. A Naagini as long as a majestic ship, with scales that shimmered like opals in the dappled sunlight filtered through the water. Unlike the monstrous serpent legends whispered amongst humans, the

Naagini possessed an otherworldly beauty. Her serpentine eyes, usually alight with ancient wisdom, held a flicker of something new today—curiosity.

An unseen force drew her towards the lone figure sprawled beneath the shade of the tree on the shore. As she glided closer carefully, the water around him barely created a ripple. The young man's haggard face, etched with exhaustion and loss, tugged at a dormant empathy within her. It wasn't just pity, though. He emanated a quiet strength, a resilience honed by hardship that intrigued her. Here was a human, a creature of fleeting existence, yet his spirit flickered with a defiance that resonated deep within her soul.

The young man stirred restlessly, his brow furrowing as the remnants of a nightmare chased him. The Naagini knew she couldn't wake him, not yet. He would see her monstrous form and die by fright!

Thus, with a silent whisper of magic, the transformation began. Her scales dissolved in a cascade of shimmering light, replaced by smooth, sun-kissed skin. Her elongated body morphed into that of a stunning woman, her long, dark hair cascading down her back like a waterfall. An involuntary gasp escaped her lips—this human form, the one she always longed for, felt liberating.

Hesitantly, she reached out and brushed a stray lock of hair from his forehead. The touch was feather-light, yet the young man stirred, a gentle smile gracing his lips for a fleeting moment before he settled back into a peaceful sleep. A strange warmth bloomed in the Naagini's chest, a feeling alien to her long existence. Here, in the vulnerability of sleep, the young man appeared so different from the humans she'd observed from afar. He wasn't a conqueror or a despoiler, just a weary soul seeking refuge. As she watched him sleep, a decision slowly formed in her mind—a decision that would challenge everything she knew about her world and the one above the water's surface.

The young man felt a strange sense of calm wash over him, a stark contrast to the turmoil in his dreams. A gentle caress brushed across his forehead, light as a spiderweb. He jolted awake, heart hammering, to find a breath-taking woman kneeling beside him. Her beauty was otherworldly, her dark eyes filled with an emotion he couldn't decipher.

'Calm down, handsome stranger,' she soothed, her voice like a summer breeze rustling through leaves. 'There's no need to be afraid.'

He scrambled to his feet, scanning the unfamiliar surroundings. 'Who are you?'

Silence settled between them, punctuated only by the gentle lapping of water against the shore. This woman, enchanting and out of place, was an enigma. Yet, in her honesty, he found a strange comfort. She didn't say anything.

He cleared his throat, breaking the spell. 'You haven't answered my question, maiden. Who are you?'

Her gaze drifted to the shimmering lake, a flicker of longing crossing her face. 'I am a Naagini,' she confessed, her voice a mere whisper. 'Bound to this water by a past I can't erase.'

'A Naagini? Like the monstrous serpents from the legends?'

She shook her head sadly. 'Legends are often born of fear, not truth. I am no monster, only a soul burdened by past mistakes.' A hint of defiance flickered in her eyes. 'If only I could be a human again.'

He found himself strangely captivated by this woman, the Naagini. Her vulnerability called to his own need for connection. 'Perhaps,' he ventured, 'I can wash away your sins with my spell and make you human again.' A flicker of a smile returned to her lips.

She nodded in acceptance, her beautiful face etched with a mixture of trepidation and a strange sense of surrender. 'I shall follow your command, whatever may come,' she replied softly, her voice barely a whisper.

The young man, emboldened by a newfound determination, rose to his full height. He met her gaze, his own filled with a quiet strength. 'By the power of the merit I have gathered,' he declared, his voice ringing with conviction, 'let this Naagini form be transformed into that of a human.'

A hush fell over the clearing as the young man spoke. A soft, pearlescent light enveloped the Naagini. For a fleeting moment, she seemed to waver, a being caught between two worlds. Then, with a gasp, the transformation began.

It wasn't a violent change, but a graceful unfolding. The sparkling scales that had adorned her body dissolved in a cascade of light, replaced by smooth, sun-kissed skin. Her powerful, elongated form morphed and shrunk, taking on the delicate curves of a human woman. Her dark hair, once flowing freely like water, cascaded down her back in thick waves.

As the light faded, a woman of breath-taking beauty stood before him. She stared at her new form in wonder, her fingertips tracing the unfamiliar contours of her arms and legs. A wave of emotion washed over her face—relief, gratitude and a hint of apprehension.

'Through countless eons of penance,' she finally spoke, her voice thick with emotion, 'I have been trapped in this form, a constant reminder of my failings. Yet, by the power of your virtue, I am free.' She turned to him, her eyes shining with a newfound light.

'O, beautiful maiden, would you let me marry you?' The man asked.

'My gratitude knows no bounds. Even if I spent every waking moment in prayer, it could never express the depth of what you have done for me. Allow me to inform my parents of this miraculous change,' she pleaded, 'and then I will gladly follow you, ready to devote myself to you in all things.'

CHAPTER 2

The Maiden Arrives at the Serpent Kingdom

The Naagini then returned to the depths of the lake and dove deep into the abyss that led to the serpent kingdom. There, she was greeted by her father, the king of the serpents.

'Oh daughter, why do you swim in your human form under these waters?' inquired the king, curiosity etched into his serpentine features.

'Just now, as I was wandering abroad,' she began, 'I lighted upon a Sakya youth, who by the power of his religious merit succeeded in changing me into a human form permanently. Having formed an affection for me, he desires to marry me. I lay before you the matter in its truth.'

The Naaga king's eyes gleamed with a mixture of surprise and joy. 'To think that a member of the holy tribe has wrought such a miraculous transformation upon you,' he exclaimed, his voice echoing in the cavernous chamber. 'If this Sakya youth has captured your heart and you his, then I see no reason to stand in the way of your happiness.'

Filled with relief and gratitude, the Naaga maiden bowed before her father, overwhelmed by his understanding and support. 'Thank you, Father,' she said, her voice trembling with emotion. 'Your blessing means more to me than words can express.'

And with the king's consent, the naagini's heart swelled with hope as she prepared to embark on a new chapter of her life, guided by love and the bond she shared with the noble Sakya youth.

CHAPTER 3

The Marriage Proposal

A wave of movement rippled through the water as the Naaga king and his daughter, now in her human form, took their leave of the underwater kingdom. Surfacing near the young Sakya man, the king, his immense serpentine form still a wonder to behold, addressed him with a deep bow.

'Your compassion knows no bounds,' the Naaga king rumbled, his voice echoing across the water. 'You have shown kindness not only to those above but also to those who dwell below. It would be an honour to welcome you to our humble abode and express our gratitude in person.'

The young man, touched by the king's sincerity, readily accepted the invitation. As they descended into the underwater realm, the Naaga family greeted him with immense respect. A grand feast awaited him, a display of their hospitality and desire to show their appreciation.

However, the sight of the Naaga in their true, serpentine forms caused the young man considerable unease. Though the serpents were no longer monstrous in his eyes, their unfamiliar appearance was unsettling. He politely expressed his desire to return to the surface world.

The Naaga king, sensing the young man's discomfort, urged him to reconsider. 'Please, esteemed guest,' he pleaded, 'do not let your discomfort lead you to leave so soon. Stay with us, and I assure you, you will be well-rewarded. You have the potential to become a great leader of this land, your name etched in history. The people will serve you faithfully, and your lineage will prosper for generations to come.'

The young man, humbled by the offer, remained hesitant. 'Such promises seem far-fetched,' he replied cautiously.

Undeterred, the Naaga king presented him with a magnificent sword, its hilt gleaming and its blade encased in a white cloth of the finest quality. 'As a token of our deepest gratitude,' the king boomed, 'I ask you to present this white cloth as a tribute to the human king who rules these lands. It will surely be a welcome offering from a distant visitor. However,' his voice lowered slightly, 'as he receives it, draw forth the sword and slay him. That way, you'll seize his kingdom. Isn't that a good plan?' the serpent king proposed.

The Sakya youth hesitated, grappling with the weight of the king's proposal and the moral implications it carried. The human king who ruled the land was the young man's enemy.

CHAPTER 4

Vengeance

Following the Naagas' instructions, the Sakya youth proceeded promptly to present his offering to the king of Udyana. As the king reached out to accept the piece of white camlet, the youth grasped his sleeve and swiftly pierced him with his sword. Chaos erupted as attendants and guards reacted with shock and confusion, their voices blending into a cacophony of outcry.

Brandishing his sword, the Sakya youth proclaimed, 'This sword was bestowed upon me by a holy Naaga to punish the disrespectful and humble the arrogant.' Faced with the imposing figure of the divine warrior, they yielded, acknowledging his authority.

With the kingdom now under his control, the Sakya youth set about rectifying injustices and restoring order. He promoted the virtuous and aided the downtrodden, fostering a realm of harmony and compassion. Accompanied by a grand procession, he made his way to the Naaga palace to inform them of the successful completion of his mission.

Having fulfilled his promise, the Sakya youth reunited with his Naagini wife and returned to the capital, ready to embark on the next chapter of their journey together.

CHAPTER 5

The Naagini's Curse

The night deepened, the gentle rhythm of the naagini's breath a counterpoint to the frantic hammering of the young Sakya prince's heart. Exhaustion, a welcome oblivion after days of travel, tugged at him. Yet, sleep remained elusive, a prisoner of the horrifying sight beside him.

Earlier, nestled in the crook of his arm, the woman he'd grown strangely fond of, had radiated warmth and a newfound human vulnerability. But now, bathed in the pale moonlight filtering through the leaves, she was a terrifying stranger.

Her beautiful face had contorted, stretched by an unseen force. In place of her head, a grotesque spectacle erupted—nine serpentine hoods, their scales shimmering an unnatural, oily black, pulsated with a malevolent life of their own. Beady yellow eyes, devoid of the kindness he'd glimpsed earlier, scanned the room, hissing tongues flickering in and out.

A primal scream clawed its way up his throat, choked back by a hand clamped over his own mouth. He lay there, frozen in terror, every fibre of his being screaming to bolt. But a strange sense of responsibility, a memory of her gratitude and the vulnerability he'd witnessed, kept him rooted to the spot.

As the night wore on, the horror only intensified. The serpent heads hissed amongst themselves, their voices a cacophony of reptilian rasps that sent shivers down his spine.

The first tendrils of dawn painted the sky a hopeful grey when the transformation began to recede. With a sickening slither, the serpent heads retracted, one by one, revealing the face of the woman he knew, serene and peaceful in slumber.

Night after night, the same unsettling ritual unfolded. With a trembling hand, he would grasp his sword, its polished metal offering little solace against his clammy palm and cut off her crest. This became a horrifying routine. The naagini, upon waking, would always greet him with a puzzled frown, a faint scar marring her forehead, the only remnant of the nightly ordeal. She'd speak of bad dreams and a persistent ache in her head, unaware of the true cause of her discomfort.

One fateful night, the naagini abruptly awakened. She now knew of the source of her constant ache and cursed. Her grief-filled words, heavy with foreboding, echoed through the chamber. 'This will bring no good to your descendants,' she lamented. 'It will afflict me in this life, and your children and grandchildren will suffer from pains in their heads.'

And so it was that the royal line of the country became plagued by this malady. Though not a constant affliction, with each passing generation, its severity deepened. After the Sakya youth's passing, his son, named Uttarasena, ascended to the throne, inheriting both the burden of rulership and the curse that shadowed his lineage.

III

The Lord of Death

This Punjabi folktale presents a stark and compelling personification of Death itself, exploring themes of mortality, fate and the deceptive nature of appearances. Unlike narratives centred on the revered Naaga deities, the central entity in this story utilizes the serpent form—alongside other guises like a scorpion, buffalo, ox and beautiful maiden—as a potent manifestation of its inescapable power and role as a harbinger of the end. The serpent here embodies the fear, mystery and transformative finality associated with death, showcasing its ability to infiltrate all levels of society and deliver fate's decree, regardless of human attempts to evade it. The tale follows an old man whose weary pursuit of this shape-shifting entity becomes an unintended confrontation with the very nature of life's predetermined span.

CHAPTER 1

The Haunted Path

The dust swirled around old Amil's weathered boots as he trudged down the desolate path. It was a road whispered about in hushed tones, a path where laughter died and travellers vanished. Some blamed a monstrous snake, others a venomous scorpion, but one thing remained constant—no one ever returned.

Exhaustion gnawed at the old man's bones. He was old, his journey long, and the relentless sun offered no mercy. There was not much he expected in life anymore, but a patient waiting for the inevitable end. Until then he kept travelling. Seeking respite, he slumped onto a sun-bleached rock. As he closed his eyes for a fleeting moment, a rustle from beside him jolted him awake. There, nestled amongst the stones, was a scorpion, its glistening black body the size of a plump hen.

The old man stared, transfixed, as the creature seemed to ripple and shift. Before his very eyes, the scorpion elongated, its segmented body morphing into a length of writhing muscle. Scales shimmered into existence, and in a blink, the scorpion became a serpent, its reptilian eyes gleaming with an unsettling intelligence.

A tremor of fear snaked through the man, but a spark of curiosity flickered brighter. He had never witnessed such a transformation. Ignoring the gnawing sense of unease, he made a decision. He wouldn't let this creature disappear into the mystery it emerged from. Is it really the harbinger of death? With a newfound determination fuelled by curiosity, the old man rose to his feet, resolved to follow the monstrous serpent wherever it slithered.

CHAPTER 2

The Old Man Follows the Serpent

The old man, his heart hammering like a trapped bird, dogged the serpent's trail for days. It moved with an unnatural speed, a dark blur against the endless, dusty landscape. As the sun dipped below the horizon each evening, painting the sky in hues of orange and red, Amil would collapse in exhausted slumber, only to wake again with the singular purpose of following the creature.

Then, one day, they arrived at a bustling inn. The serpent slithered through a crack in the doorway, its scales catching the fading sunlight momentarily. The old man pressed his ear against the rough wooden wall. Inside, a cacophony of laughter and chatter abruptly died down, replaced by choked screams and the slithering hiss of the serpent. The old man's stomach lurched. This was death, swift and brutal, delivered by the creature he pursued. The serpent emerged a moment later, its glistening scales reflecting the dying light with an eerie luminescence. Disgust and horror warred within Amil, but curiosity held him captive.

Their journey continued, a grim dance of predator and unwitting observer. The serpent slithered through the night, an unwelcome visitor to palatial grounds. Again, screams ripped through the stillness, followed by an unsettling silence. Dawn revealed the king, lifeless, a faint imprint of the serpent's coils around his neck.

The aged man, shaken to his core, watched from a distance, a silent witness to the serpent's reign of terror. He followed the serpent as it scaled the smooth walls of the queen's palace, disappearing through a statue's open mouth. Soon, piercing wails tore through the air, the queen's lamentations for her youngest daughter echoing through the city.

Days bled into weeks, the desolate landscape a constant backdrop to the serpent's carnage. Finally, they reached a wide, fast-flowing river. On the other side, weary travellers huddled, longing for passage but lacking the means to cross.

The serpent, with a swift transformation, became a magnificent buffalo. Its sleek black coat glistened in the midday sun, a brass necklace adorning its neck and bells jingling merrily. The travellers, seeing this noble beast, saw a chance for salvation. 'It must be swimming across,' they muttered amongst themselves. 'We can hitch a ride!'

One by one, they climbed onto the buffalo's broad back, clinging to its thick tail with hopeful smiles. The old man, watching from the shore, felt a flicker of unease. He couldn't shake the feeling that something wasn't right.

As the buffalo reached the churning centre of the river, a change flickered across its eyes. The buffalo shook and kicked violently, throwing the unsuspecting passengers into the unforgiving water. Their cries for help were quickly drowned out by the churning current.

When that old man reached the other side, the majestic buffalo was gone, replaced by a docile ox grazing peacefully in a nearby field. A farmer, lured by the ox's beauty, coaxed it back to his stable.

Nightfall arrived, cloaking the world in an inky blackness. The peaceful ox, once a symbol of bounty, transformed once more. In the dim light of the moon, Amil watched in horror as the creature sloughed its bovine skin, revealing the monstrous serpent beneath. With a flick of its forked tongue, it struck, venom coursing through the sleeping farm animals, their peaceful moos turning to anguished bellows. Then, with a sinuous slither, the serpent made its way to the farmhouse, leaving a trail of death in its wake.

The tired old man watched, his resolve hardening. He wouldn't let this creature continue its reign of terror. He may be ancient and wary, but his spirit hadn't been broken. This was definitely the harbinger of death, something that the old man dearly wanted in his life. The old man would follow the serpent, wherever it went. He hoped that one day it will take note of him and put an end to his misery of life.

CHAPTER 3

The Serpent Turns into a Naagin

Under the scorching sun, the old man approached the next river, wider and swifter than the last, slicing through the parched earth like a relentless force of nature. Across the bank, a solitary figure sat, a vivid splash of colour amidst the desolate landscape. She was a vision of beauty, bedecked in sparkling jewels that shimmered defiantly in the harsh sunlight, yet her tear-streaked face betrayed a deep sorrow.

The old man's gaze narrowed as he observed the scene unfolding before him. The serpent, cunning in its deception, had assumed the guise of a distressed maiden. From his vantage point in the shadows, suspicion gnawed at him as two soldiers, likely brothers, approached the woman.

The elder brother, captivated by her allure, inquired about her tears. With a voice quivering like a fragile bird, the snake-girl spun a tale of tragedy. 'Kind sir,' she pleaded, her words trembling with fear, 'my husband has perished while crossing this perilous river. I am left alone and afraid. Will you offer refuge to a lost soul?'

Swelling with a mixture of compassion and chivalry, the elder brother blurted out, 'Marry me! I will provide for you.'

Hidden from view, the old man witnessed a glint of amusement in the woman's tear-filled eyes as she laid down her conditions. 'No chores,' she demanded, mischief dancing in her gaze. 'And you must heed my every whim, no matter how peculiar.'

Completely enamoured, the elder brother eagerly agreed, pledging his devotion. 'Anything for you, my dear!'

With a subtle gesture, the woman directed him to fetch water from a nearby well, while the younger brother remained by her side.

As soon as the elder brother disappeared from view, the snake-girl shed her facade. Her voice dripped with malice as she turned to the younger brother.

'Fly with me,' she implored, her eyes gleaming with deceit, 'for my heart belongs to you! The pledge I made to your brother was but a ruse to lure him away!'

But the younger brother, steadfast in his loyalty, rejected her advances. 'Nay,' he declared firmly, 'you are bound to my brother by promise, and I regard you as my sister-in-law.'

Enraged by his refusal, the maiden unleashed her fury, weeping and wailing until the elder brother returned. With cunning deceit, she twisted the truth, accusing the younger brother of treachery and betrayal.

Consumed by wrath, the elder brother drew his sword, challenging his sibling to mortal combat. All day they clashed, the sun witnessing their tragic duel until dusk painted the sky in hues of sorrow. As twilight descended, both brothers lay lifeless on the battlefield.

Transforming once more into a serpent, the maiden slithered away, trailed by an old man cloaked in shadows. Eventually, the serpent shed its skin, assuming the guise of a wise old sage with a snowy beard.

Seizing the opportunity, the shadowy follower grasped the sage's beard, beseeching him for release from his silent vigil.

'Who are you?' he questioned, his voice trembling with desperation.

With a mysterious smile, the old sage replied, 'Some call me the Lord of Death, for I bring an end to all mortal journeys.'

'Grant me death,' pleaded old Amil, 'for I have shadowed your steps for so long, and my spirit longs for rest.'

But the Lord of Death shook his head, denying the request. 'Not yet,' he murmured, 'for your allotted time has not yet come. Sixty more years of life await you.'

And with that enigmatic proclamation, the Lord of Death vanished into the ether, leaving behind whispers of uncertainty. Was he truly the harbinger of mortality, or merely a spectre of the unknown? Only time would unveil the truth.

IV

The Naagamani and the King

This intricate Tamil folktale, sourced from the *Madanakaamaaraajankadai*, explores themes of destiny, the consequences of kindness versus greed, and the transformative power of divine intervention, embodied here by a prince and the naagamani. The narrative follows a dispossessed prince whose simple act of compassion towards a captured Naaga sets in motion a dramatic reversal of fortune. The story highlights the Naaga's role not merely as a creature of the underworld but as a being capable of gratitude and bestowing immense power through the naagamani, while also illustrating how such power, if misused or lost through betrayal, can lead to ruin. Interestingly, variations of this tale exist elsewhere, including a Sri Lankan version, though specific details like the connection to Ananta Shesha may differ.

CHAPTER 1

Maarjaaram

In the ancient and prosperous town of Alakapuri, there once ruled a king named Alakesha, renowned for his benevolence and wisdom. Alakesha was deeply loved by his people, who cherished him as a ruler who valued the life of each subject as his own. He was blessed with a devoted wife and a young son who brought joy to the royal household. However, fate dealt a cruel hand when the king, still in his prime, was taken by an untimely death, leaving behind his grieving wife, their three-year-old son and a younger brother who was to assume the responsibility of the kingdom.

The king's younger brother, initially a protector of the young prince and his mother, managed the affairs of the state with apparent loyalty. But as time passed, a dark ambition began to grow within him—a desire to claim the throne for himself. The thought of the prince growing into power filled him with envy and fear. Gradually, the brother's benevolence faded, replaced by neglect and malice. The widow and her son were soon left to fend for themselves, forced to abandon the palace and take to the streets as common beggars. Life became a cruel struggle for survival.

The prince's mother, heartbroken and desperate, eventually sought refuge in her father's house, leaving her son to wander alone. Yet, her maternal love never waned. In time, her thoughts returned to her son, and with great effort, she gathered a sum of one hundred pagodas—a small fortune in those days—and returned to find him.

When she finally found her son, she spoke to him with the wisdom of one who had seen both the heights of power and the depths of despair. 'My son,' she said, 'your father once ruled this city with honour. If we continue to beg here, will not people mock us? I have brought you one hundred pagodas. Use this money wisely. Invest it in trade, and perhaps we can rebuild our lives.'

The prince, though young, understood the gravity of his mother's words and agreed. With the hundred pagodas, he set out to find something he could trade to earn a living. As he wandered through a dense thicket, he encountered a farmer struggling under the weight of a heavy gunny bag. Curious, the prince approached the man, who explained that the bag contained several kittens—a nuisance born to his household by an old cat. The farmer, eager to rid himself of the burden, had intended to abandon the kittens in the forest.

To the innocent prince, however, these kittens seemed like a precious opportunity. He inquired about their price, but the farmer, sensing the prince's naivety, decided to exploit him. 'These kittens are of great value,' the farmer said slyly. 'Each one is worth five hundred pagodas.'

The prince, undeterred by the exorbitant price, pleaded with the farmer to accept his hundred pagodas in exchange for just one kitten. Though the farmer inwardly rejoiced at the prospect of such an unexpected windfall, he feigned reluctance before finally agreeing to the sale. Elated by what he believed to be a valuable purchase, the prince hurried back to his mother, clutching the kitten as if it were a treasure.

Upon seeing the kitten, the prince's mother was overcome with despair. To her, it seemed as though her son's foolishness was insurmountable. How could he squander their only wealth on something so insignificant? Meanwhile, the farmer, who had returned to his humble cottage, praised the gods for granting him a fortune in exchange for a mere kitten.

Thus, the once-promising hope of rebuilding their lives was dashed, and the prince's journey to reclaim his legacy took an unexpected turn, leaving both mother and son to face an uncertain future.

CHAPTER 2

Naagam

Once again, the prince's mother, disheartened by her son's actions, left him to fend for himself and returned to her parents' home. The young prince, now with only a kitten for company, roamed the streets, begging for food. The townspeople, moved by the sight of the once-proud prince reduced to such a state, gave generously—not just to feed the boy, but also to sustain his kitten. And so, for a time, the prince managed to survive, living off the kindness of strangers.

Days passed, and the prince's mother, unable to shake the concern for her son's future, returned once more. She had again gathered a hundred pagodas, hoping against hope that her son had learned from his past mistakes. Handing him the money, she urged him to make wiser choices and invest in something that could truly help them rebuild their lives.

With this renewed sense of purpose, the prince set out once more. As he wandered the outskirts of the town, he encountered a snake-charmer approaching him. The man carried two large baskets, suspended from a bamboo pole across his neck. Inside the baskets were several serpents, their scales shimmering ominously in the dim light. Among these serpents was a creature unlike the others—a serpent of divine origin, the son of Adishesha, the primordial king of all serpents. This serpent had left his infernal palace beneath the earth to see the world, only to be captured by the snake-charmer, who had subdued him with powerful incantations.

The prince, intrigued by the sight, asked the snake-charmer what he carried in his baskets and how much they were worth. The man, sensing an opportunity, replied, 'Gentleman, these are the finest serpents ever caught. Each one is worth at least five hundred pagodas, especially if I were to show them performing their tricks before the king.'

But the prince, driven by a strange impulse, pleaded with the snake-charmer to sell him one of the serpents for a hundred pagodas—the only sum he had. The snake-charmer, though secretly thrilled at the thought of easy money, pretended to be reluctant. Finally, he agreed to part with one of his serpents—the very son of Adishesha—thanking all his gods for this unexpected fortune as he hurried away.

The prince, now holding a serpent—the most feared enemy of humankind—returned to his mother, who had awaited his arrival with cautious optimism. But when she saw the serpent, her heart sank into despair. Furious and heartbroken, she cursed her fate for giving birth to a son she believed to be hopelessly foolish. Unable to bear the sight of him any longer, she abandoned him once more, retreating to her parents' house, this time determined not to return.

The prince was left alone again, with only the serpent for company. Little did he know that the serpent he had purchased held powers beyond his wildest imagination, and his fate was now intertwined with that of the ancient, divine creature.

CHAPTER 3

The Naagamanikyam

The young prince, now burdened with both a cat and a serpent as his companions, continued his life as a beggar, wandering from door to door in search of sustenance. The townsfolk, seeing the prince and his unusual pets, were moved by pity. They gave generously, offering food for both the boy and his animal friends. And so, twelve long years passed in this way, with the prince eking out a meagre existence, sharing what little he had with his beloved companions.

As the years rolled by, the prince's mother, who had long since abandoned him to his fate, found her heart longing once more to see her son. With no money left to give, she sought him out, her heart heavy with worry. When she found him, still accompanied by the serpent, she spoke to him gently, 'My son, this creature you have kept by your side is the enemy of humankind. As long as you continue to keep him, no one will ever approach you. Please, for your own sake, release him back to the wild where you first found him.'

The pauper prince, ever obedient to his mother, took the serpent in his hand and returned to the forest where their paths had first crossed. There, he gently placed the serpent on the ground and spoke, 'My dear serpent, for twelve years we have been the closest of friends. But now, by my mother's command, I must let you go. Please, do not take this as a slight against you, but go your own way, free and unharmed.'

The serpent, who had silently observed the prince's character over the past twelve years, was deeply touched by this act of loyalty and kindness. As the prince turned to leave, he suddenly heard a voice calling his name. Startled, the pauper prince realized that the voice was coming from the serpent—a creature that had never spoken a word in all the years they had been together. He approached the serpent, his heart pounding with surprise and curiosity.

The serpent spoke in a clear, human voice, 'My prince, my protector, my father! For it is you who have cared for me all these years, and it is you who I now regard as my father. Those who give us life, who save us from danger, who feed us and who teach us—these are the ones we must call our parents. You have done all this for me, and now, though you release me in obedience to your mother, I wish to repay your kindness.'

The serpent continued, 'I am the son of Ananta Shesha, the king of all serpents. For twelve years, my father has grieved my absence. Now, I must return to him. But before I go, I wish to offer you a gift. My father will be overjoyed to see me again and will shower me with affection. However, I shall tell him that I must first seek your permission before I can stay by his side. My father will be astonished to hear this and will ask who has earned such devotion from me. I will then tell him of your kindness. He will be so pleased that he will send for you, carrying you to the netherworld in a grand palanquin borne by serpent-servants. There, he will honour you with a feast and ask you to persuade me to remain with him. Once I agree, my father, in his gratitude, will offer you a gift. Ask him for his ring—a ring of immense power. With this ring, you can accomplish anything you desire. Simply place it on your finger, think of what you want, and it will appear before you.'

Having spoken these words, the serpent, eager to reunite with his father, slithered away to the netherworld. As foretold, everything unfolded just as the serpent had said. The pauper prince was summoned to the underworld, where he was welcomed with great honour by Ananta Shesha himself. After a grand feast, the prince successfully convinced the serpent to remain with his father, and in gratitude, Adishesha presented him with the magical ring.

'My dear brother,' Ananta Shesha said as he handed the ring to the prince, 'this ring is a treasure I would not have given even to Indra himself. But for you, who have protected my son for twelve long years, I offer it willingly. Guard it well, for as long as you possess this ring, fortune shall smile upon you. But should you ever lose it, your good fortune will vanish along with it.'

With these words, Adishesha bade the prince farewell, sending him back to the world above. The prince, now armed with the powerful ring, returned to his life, forever changed by the kindness he had shown to a serpent in need.

CHAPTER 4

The Nishadadesha

The prince, delighted by his adventures and the serpent's gratitude, used the magical ring to transform the surrounding jungle into a thriving kingdom called Nishadadesha. He created mansions, fields, rivers and everything necessary for his people, who gladly became his subjects. His mother, who once doubted him, now praised the serpent for bringing such fortune.

One night, unable to sleep, the prince used the ring to find his destined queen, the princess of Svarnapuri. He brought her to him without disturbing her sleep. When she awoke, she admired his power and agreed to marry him but asked to be returned to her home so they could marry properly. The prince agreed and sent her back.

The next morning, the princess told her father about her 'dream' and her wish to marry the Nishada prince. Her father, amazed, sent ministers to confirm the existence of the Nishada kingdom. Meanwhile, the prince's ministers arrived in Svarnapuri to formally request the princess's hand in marriage. The marriage was quickly arranged, and preparations began in both kingdoms.

The prince and princess were married and began their life together in happiness. The princess, deeply religious and with a great love for sea bathing, requested her husband to build a subterranean passage from her bedroom to the sea. With the power of his ring, the prince instantly created the passage, allowing her to reach the sea for her baths in privacy. Several months passed peacefully as they enjoyed their life together as the king and queen of Nishada.

CHAPTER 5

Kochiraja

One morning, after her bath, a strand of the Nishada queen's hair fell into the sea, forming a ball that washed ashore. The King of Kochi, passing by, discovered the hair ball and, using his knowledge of *Samudrikalakshana* (the art of reading physical traits), deduced that the owner was a woman of exceptional beauty. Obsessed with finding her, he promised a reward to anyone who could bring her to him. An old, cunning woman volunteered, and after discovering the location, she set a trap by pretending to mourn near a burning pile of wood on the shore where the queen bathed.

Hearing the old woman's cries, the compassionate queen approached and, upon hearing her sad story, felt pity for her. The old woman, pretending to mistake the queen for her deceased daughter, convinced her to part with the magic ring that belonged to the queen's husband, the Nishada king. The queen, trusting the woman, gave her the ring, not knowing that this would lead to disaster. The old woman immediately used the ring to return to Kochi, where she handed it to the king, who used its power to bring the queen to his side.

The Kochi king, consumed by his obsession for the Nishada queen, cursed the Nishada king to madness and his kingdom to be consumed by fire. The curse took effect immediately, and within moments, the queen found herself at the Kochi king's court. Despite her new circumstances, she did not agree to marry him right away.

'I cannot marry you now,' she said. 'I must first fulfil a vow.'

The Kochi king, eager to secure her, asked, 'What vow?'

'I wish to fast for eight days and host a grand feast for all the less fortunate in the kingdom,' she replied.

The Kochi king consented, 'So be it.'

And thus, with the help of the magic ring that had the Naagamaanikyam (Naagamani), the king starts an unlimited feast for eight days in the kingdom of Kochi.

CHAPTER 6

One for the Cat

Meanwhile, the ex-king of Nishada, driven mad by his ruined kingdom, wandered aimlessly through the desolation of Nishadadesha, accompanied by his cat, now dressed in colourful garments. As the days passed, his madness deepened, and on the seventh day, he found himself in the kingdom of Kochi, where he noticed a great throng of impoverished people heading towards the king's palace.

'What's happening there?' he asked a passerby.

'The future queen of Kochi has organized a grand feast lasting eight days, offering the finest dishes to the common folk. Hurry, today is the last day!' the passerby replied.

Intrigued and driven by hunger, the ex-king of Nishada made his way to the Kochi palace, his cat in tow. He took a seat among the others and placed his oddly dressed cat beside him. The people around him couldn't help but notice the strange sight of the cat and the dishevelled man, realizing that the poor soul had clearly lost his mind.

When the server placed only one leaf before him, the ex-king called out, 'Hey, you! Why have you given me only one leaf?'

'One leaf for one stomach,' the server responded curtly.

The ex-king pointed to his cat, who was busy cleaning its whiskers. 'My friend here,' he said, 'has a stomach too. He'll need a leaf as well. Two leaves, please!'

The server hesitated, casting a bewildered glance at the cat, which responded with an amused, almost mocking grin. Begrudgingly, the server placed a small second leaf before the cat and walked away, muttering under his breath about the absurdity of the situation. The odd spectacle quickly became the subject of hushed conversations among the guests, and soon, word of the strange man and his cat reached the future queen.

Recognizing the descriptions, the queen immediately knew who it was. With a heavy heart, she descended to see the man who had once been her husband. As she approached, a wave of pity and sadness washed over her, for it was clear that he could no longer remember her. Such was the devastating power of the Naagamaanikyam in the magic ring, now worn by the Kochi Raja, which had stolen away his memories along with his sanity.

Yet, as the queen stood before him, the cat purred softly, its eyes meeting hers with a knowing gaze. Unlike its master, the cat still recognized the queen, perhaps remembering the life they once had.

After their meal, the ex-king and his loyal cat chose to spend the night among the other guests, finding shelter in a tent outside the kingdom. The queen watched them disappear into the gathering dusk; her heart heavy with the weight of what had been lost.

CHAPTER 7

The Mooshakraja

At round midnight, a faint trumpet sounded—one that human ears couldn't detect, but it resonated with snakes, cats, rats and dogs alike. From the crumbling depths of the palace and the shadows of the kingdom, a procession of rats emerged, assembling before their mighty king, Mooshakraja.

'Dear subjects,' Mooshakraja began, his voice echoing through the silent night, 'tonight marks the final night of our feast. Enjoy whatever remnants the pathetic greedy humans have left behind, and return to our underworld homes before dawn.'

The rats rejoiced, their tiny voices filling the night air with excitement. All of this was keenly observed by the cat, who, dressed in his absurd green hat and red silk dress, decided to take action. With a determined stride, he marched towards the rat king and chased him until Mooshakraja found himself cornered. The cat placed its paw firmly on the rat's tail, preventing any escape, and spoke in a threatening tone, 'You won't escape my jaws tonight. If I eat you, I won't need to hunt for another seven days.'

'Oh please, maarjaram (cat),' the rat king pleaded, 'you look so queer, why would you want to eat someone so dear?'

'You may be dear to your subjects, but not to me,' the cat retorted, opening its mouth wide and swallowing Mooshakraja's head.

'Please, have mercy,' the rat king's muffled voice cried out from inside the cat's mouth.

The cat paused, pretending to consider the plea, then said, 'Alright, but only if you do me a favour.'

'Anything for you,' Mooshakraja replied desperately.

'My kind master, Nishada king, once possessed a ring containing the Naagaamanikyam, a gift from our friend, the Naaga. Unfortunately, that ring was taken by the Kochi Raja. You must find a way to retrieve it. I don't care how you do it, but if you succeed, I will spare your life.'

Mooshakraja, still trapped in the cat's mouth, quickly issued orders to his army. The loyal rats scurried off, searching through the monarch's possessions to find the precious ring. To their great relief, they discovered it in a small box near the sleeping Kochi Raja. Without delay, they rushed back to the cat with the ring in tow.

Satisfied, the cat spat Mooshakraja out of its mouth, thanking him for his efforts. The cat then carefully placed the ring on Nishada's chest. As soon as the ring touched his skin, Nishada awoke from his sleep. The cat reminded Nishada of how the ring was lost, the calamities that befell his kingdom and how it had now been recovered.

With the ring now back on his finger, Nishada felt his senses returning and his sanity restored. Determined to reclaim his kingdom, he wished for his kingdom to be restored and for his faithful queen to be returned to him. As he wished, so it happened. The once-ruined kingdom of Nishada was revived, and his queen was by his side once more.

Nishada advised his queen never to trust in false promises again and cursed the Kochi king with insanity and the destruction of his kingdom. Reclaiming everything he had lost with the power of the Naagamaanikyam, Nishada ruled over his restored kingdom for many years to come.

V

The Brahmin and the Naaga

This classic fable from the *Panchatantra* illustrates the delicate balance between reverence and greed in human interactions with powerful natural or supernatural forces, represented here by a serpent dwelling in an anthill. The story serves as a cautionary tale about how respectful observance can lead to prosperity, while avarice and disrespect can bring about swift and tragic consequences, severing beneficial relationships. The serpent, in this tale, acts as a guardian spirit of the field, initially benevolent but ultimately unforgiving when betrayed.

The Folktale from Panchatantra

In a certain village there once lived a Brahmin named Haridatta. He was a farmer by trade, though his labours reaped him little reward. One sweltering afternoon, when the heat weighed heavy upon the land, Haridatta lay down in the shade of a tree, hoping to rest his weary bones. As he lay there, his eye caught a curious sight—a great hooded snake, gliding out from an ant-hill nearby. Instinctively, he thought, 'Surely this must be the guardian spirit of the field, and here I am, all these years, never having paid it proper respect. No wonder my harvests are so paltry. I must at once make amends.'

And so, his mind firmly set, he fetched a bowl of milk and approached the ant-hill. Bowing reverently, he declared aloud, 'O

330

Guardian of this Field, I was ignorant of your presence here and so have neglected you. Forgive my past disrespect.' Placing the milk before the ant-hill as an offering, he quietly departed.

The next morning, when Haridatta returned to check the bowl, he was astonished to find a gleaming gold denar in its place. From that day on, a ritual was established—every day, he left an offering of milk, and every day, the serpent left him a denar in return.

One day, however, Haridatta was called away to the village on business. Before he left, he instructed his young son to take the milk to the ant-hill in his stead. The boy dutifully carried out his father's request and, on returning the next day, was delighted to find a gold denar in the bowl. But greed soon took root in his heart. He said to himself, 'If this ant-hill yields gold each day, surely it must be filled with treasure. Why should I settle for a single coin when I could claim it all?'

So, on the following day, he approached the serpent not with reverence, but with a hidden cudgel. As he laid down the milk, he raised his weapon and struck at the snake's head. The serpent, by the grace of fate, escaped the fatal blow, but in its fury, it struck the boy with its venomous fangs. The boy collapsed on the spot, lifeless. His kin, upon discovering his body, mourned deeply and built a funeral pyre near the fields to consign him to the flames.

Two days later, Haridatta returned to the village and learned of his son's fate. Stricken with grief yet mindful of his ritual, he brought a bowl of milk to the ant-hill, calling upon the serpent with his heart heavy. After a long silence, the serpent emerged, only its head visible, and spoke with a voice cool and knowing.

'Greed has brought you here, Haridatta, blinding you even to the pain of losing your son. Between us, there can be no friendship henceforth. Your son, in his youthful folly, struck me, and in my fury, I struck him down. How could I forget the sting of his blow? And how can you so easily set aside your grief?'

With that, the serpent withdrew, but before vanishing, it cast a radiant pearl towards the brahmin, as a parting gift. 'Return no more,' it said, and disappeared into the earth.

Haridatta took up the pearl and returned home, lamenting his son's folly and the heavy price of greed.

Notes

In the long shadows of history, certain stories travel across continents, evolving and embedding themselves in distant cultures, often so deeply that their origins become almost inseparable from the soil they now inhabit. Such is this tale from the ancient *Panchatantra*, one of India's most cherished collections of fables, which found its way to the lush, temple-strewn island of Bali. Here, in a land where the sacred and the profane intermingle with effortless grace, the Indian myth merged with local lore, becoming part of the very genesis story of the Bali Strait. Let us look at the story of Naaga Besukih and Manik Angkaren.

Manik Angkaren—The Balinese Origin Myth

Once upon a time in a faraway kingdom, there lived a wise brahmin named Sidhimantra and his son, Manik Angkeran. Manik was a clever boy, but he had fallen into the wrong company. His friends led him astray, and soon he was addicted to gambling and cock-fighting.

Manik believed, 'This is the easiest way to get rich! I don't need to work hard like others.' And at first, luck was on his side. He won many bets, filling his pockets with gold. But as time passed, his luck ran out. Losses piled up, and soon, he had nothing left.

Desperate, Manik came to his father, Sidhimantra, with a plea. 'Father, I've lost everything. Please, help me repay my debts.'

Sidhimantra, knowing his son was on a dangerous path, sighed deeply. 'I will help you this time, but only because I hope you'll change your ways.' Following the guidance of the gods, he travelled to Mount Agung and met the mighty Naaga Besukih.

'Naaga Besukih,' Sidhimantra bowed before the dragon, 'I seek your aid to help my son.'

The dragon, benevolent and wise, granted Sidhimantra some of his immense treasure. 'Use this wisely, Sidhimantra, and teach your son to live a life of virtue.'

Returning home, Sidhimantra handed the treasure to Manik. 'This should be enough to repay your debts, son. Do not squander it.'

But Manik, unable to resist temptation, gambled the treasure away once again. His greed was stronger than his father's wisdom. When he lost everything for the second time, he returned to his father.

'Father,' Manik pleaded, 'I need more money.'

But this time, Sidhimantra refused. 'No, Manik. I cannot help you again. You must learn to be responsible.'

Consumed by greed, Manik decided to go to Naaga Besukih himself. 'If my father could get treasure from the dragon, why can't I?' he thought.

Manik made his way to Mount Agung and called out to Naaga Besukih. 'O mighty dragon, I humbly ask for your help.'

Naaga Besukih, trusting Manik, offered him treasure. But as the dragon turned to retreat back into his mountain, Manik's eyes gleamed with greed. 'Look at all this wealth,' he thought, 'If I could kill the dragon, I could take it all!'

With a wicked heart, Manik drew his sword and struck at the dragon. Naaga Besukih, though startled, was not easily defeated. Enraged by the betrayal, he unleashed a fiery breath upon Manik, reducing him to ashes.

Word of Manik's demise soon reached Sidhimantra. Heartbroken, he rushed to the mountain and knelt before the dragon. 'O great Naaga Besukih, please, bring my son back to life. He has been foolish, but I wish to teach him the right path.'

The dragon, moved by the brahmin's sincerity, agreed on one condition. 'I will revive your son, but he must stay here with me. I will teach him the ways of wisdom.'

Sidhimantra hesitated but agreed. Naaga Besukih breathed life back into Manik, who awoke trembling and full of remorse.

'Father, please forgive me!' Manik cried. 'I wish to return home with you.'

But Sidhimantra shook his head. 'My son, the dragon has agreed to spare your life, but you must stay here and learn from him.'

Manik wept, but the agreement had been made. Sidhimantra took his magic staff and drew a line on the ground between him and his son. Suddenly, from that line, water began to flow and the ground shook. The waters rushed, separating Mount Agung from the surrounding land, creating a vast strait. Manik and his father were now separated by the sea.

And so, it is believed that the Bali Strait came into being, forever dividing the islands of Bali and Java.

Even today, the Balinese people pass down the story of Manik Angkeran, teaching their children the lesson that good deeds lead to good outcomes, while greed and deceit bring only ruin.

VI

A Tale of Two Snakes

A Tale from Panchatantra

In a certain kingdom, gilded halls echoed with the unspoken sorrow of King Devashakti. His son, the young prince, once vibrant, now faded like a wilting flower, growing leaner and weaker with each passing day. Renowned physicians, summoned from lands where rumour spoke of miraculous cures, arrived with potent herbs and ancient instruments, yet none could mend the prince. His affliction was insidious, unseen—a snake resided coiled within his very stomach, draining his life force. Despite consultations and treatments, many physicians departed, their heads bowed in failure, leaving the king and his ailing son adrift in despondency.

The prince, his heart aching with his father's grief and his own weary suffering, decided to leave the kingdom. Under the velvet cloak of night, when only the moon bore witness, he slipped away from the silent luxury of the palace. He journeyed far, seeking anonymity in distance, finally finding refuge within the cool, stone embrace of a temple in a distant kingdom. There, amidst the scent of incense and the murmur of prayers, he lived humbly, surviving on the kindness of strangers and the alms offered by pious townsfolk.

In this faraway kingdom, the ruling king had two daughters, both beautiful and accomplished, raised with the finest education and wisdom. Each morning, they would bow at their father's feet to receive his blessings. The elder daughter would say, 'O Father, we are blessed with all the joys of the world, thanks to your grace.'

But the younger daughter would say, 'O King, we each receive only the fruits destined by our own actions.'

Her words, repeated day after day, began to prick at the king's pride, unsettling him. Over time, his unease curdled into anger. Was she implying his power was meaningless, his grace insufficient? Frustration mounting, he finally summoned his ministers, his voice tight with displeasure. 'Since my younger daughter places such faith in destiny,' he declared, his words sharp, 'let her embrace the fate that awaits! Marry her off to the first man you encounter outside the palace gates!'

The ministers did as commanded, and when they reached the temple, the first man they encountered was the weak young prince living humbly at the temple, almost like a mendicant. Not knowing his true identity, they arranged his marriage to the king's daughter. The young princess, devoted and pious, accepted her husband as her fate, finding peace and contentment in her new life.

Not wanting to live indefinitely in the temple, the couple set out for another part of the kingdom. The journey, however, proved taxing for the prince, his hidden ailment draining his strength with every step. The sun beat down mercilessly, the road stretched long and dusty, and finally, his legs could carry him no further. He collapsed beneath the shade of a sprawling banyan tree, the world blurring into exhaustion. His wife, her heart filled with concern but her spirit resolute, went to a nearby market, hoping to find food to revive his energy.

When she returned, the forest air still and heavy in the afternoon heat, she found her husband in deep sleep beneath the ancient tree's shade. As she approached quietly, a movement near the base of the tree caught her eye—a snake, sleek and dark, emerged silently from a crack in a nearby ant-hill. Her breath hitched, a warning forming on her lips. But before she could cry out, another, more horrifying sight froze her—a second snake, disturbingly similar, was slithering out from her husband's mouth! Terror clenched her heart, but wisdom held her rooted. Suppressing a gasp, she melted back into the shadows of a neighbouring tree, her eyes wide, watching as the two serpents drew near each other, their movements fluid and ancient.

The snake from the ant-hill hissed, 'Why do you continue to torment this poor prince? You're risking your own life by doing so. If he were to drink a simple soup made from cumin seeds and mustard, you'd be dead in an instant!'

The snake within the prince replied, 'And why do you guard those two pots of gold inside the anthill? They do you no good. If anyone were to pour hot water and oil over your anthill, you'd be dead in no time yourself!'

Their argument grew heated until, at last, each snake returned to its own dwelling. But the princess had learned their secrets.

That very day, with quiet determination, she gathered cumin seeds and mustard. She prepared the simple soup, her hands steady despite the lingering fear, and carefully fed the broth to her sleeping husband. Within hours, a change began. Colour returned to his cheeks, his breathing eased, and a newfound strength seemed to flow back into his limbs. The insidious serpent within him had perished. Overjoyed and emboldened, the princess then turned her attention to the ant-hill. Following the second serpent's unwitting advice, she heated water and oil and poured the scalding mixture into the mound. Once the guardian snake was no more, she dug into the earth, unearthing two heavy pots filled to the brim with gleaming gold coins.

With her husband's health restored and their future secured by the unexpected treasure, the prince and princess journeyed back to his father's kingdom. King Devashakti wept with joy at the return of his son, marvelling at the transformation wrought by the wisdom, patience, and quiet courage of the young bride who had embraced her destiny. Blessed with health and prosperity, they lived happily ever after.

Notes

This tale, originating from the *Panchatantra*, explores themes of destiny, perspective and the unexpected ways wisdom can be revealed. The serpents in this narrative function not as divine entities but as conduits of crucial, hidden knowledge and, in the case of the anthill dweller, as a keeper of treasure—motifs that we have observed in the first part of this book. Their overheard conversation provides the key to overcoming both physical affliction (the snake inside the prince) and financial hardship (the gold guarded by the other serpent), reinforcing the idea that solutions often lie in observation and understanding seemingly dangerous or overlooked sources. These themes resonate strongly with common motivations for Naaga worship, particularly in south India, where devotees often seek blessings for overcoming ailments and ensuring prosperity.

VII

The Naagamani and Mekkattu Namboothiri

A story from Aythihyamaala (Malayalam)

CHAPTER 1

The Poor Namboothiri

Once upon a time there was Mekattu (also spelt as Mekkaad) family in Thrissur district of Kerala. They were very religious and well versed in the arts of sorcery and other such rituals. However, there was one problem, the family lived in utter poverty. During that time, the head of the Mekattu household, Namboothiri (it is actually a title), went to the historically famous Thiruvanchikulam temple in Kodungallur and began to worship the presiding deity, Lord Shiva, with devotion, praying for relief from his poverty and sorrow. The worship was to last for twelve years.

When the period of worship was nearing its completion after about twelve years, one day, after the evening puja and other rituals were over and everyone had left the temple, Mekkattu Namboothiri went to the sacred pond within the temple walls with a water pot to collect some water. There, he saw a radiant figure standing on the steps and asked,' Who is that?'

The man replied, 'Knowing the person, what does the Mekkaad Namboothiri need? If you need water, take it and go.' His words and radiant form suggested that he was not a mere mortal but a divine being, so Namboothiri stood there, speechless and lost in thought.

Then, Namboothiri noticed something glowing like a burning coal in the divine man's hand and asked, 'What is that in your hand?' Without giving a direct answer, the divine being asked, 'Namboothiri, have you ever seen a Naagamani?'

'No, I haven't.'

'Do you wish to see one?'

Namboothiri hesitated but then said, 'It would be nice to see one,' and extended his hand.

The divine being then asked, 'If I give it to you, are you sure you will return it?'

'I am sure,' Namboothiri replied.

The divine being then placed the precious gem in Namboothiri's hand. Seeing that divine gem, which he had never seen before, Namboothiri was filled with curiosity.

As Namboothiri was a favourite of the then Thampuran (roughly translates to king) of Kodungallur, he wished to show this divine gem to the king. So, Namboothiri asked the divine being, 'I would like to show this gem to someone else. Please permit me to take it and bring it back.'

Immediately, the divine being said, 'If you can bring it back quickly, take it. I cannot stay here much longer.'

'I will be back in a moment,' Namboothiri took the gem and went to show it to the king.

CHAPTER 2

The King of Kodungallur

The king, within the opulent chambers of his palace, held the divine gem aloft, its brilliance casting dancing reflections across the gilded walls. He turned it in his hand, mesmerized by the way it seemed to hold a universe of light within its depths. A covetous glint entered his eyes; the gem, a symbol of power and wealth beyond measure, called to a greed he could not deny.

'I will pay any price for this. I want it,' the king declared, his voice echoing through the halls.

Realizing that the king had no intention of returning the divine gem after seeing it, Namboothiri said. 'If I don't return it, I will break my promise; that would be sinful. I need it back, Sire.'

So, the king reluctantly returned the gem.

Namboothiri took it back and returned to the temple pond. The divine man was waiting there. Namboothiri gave the Naagamani to the divine being. As soon as the divine being received the gem, he vanished. The place, which had been brightly lit until then due to the gem's radiance, was plunged into darkness. Namboothiri was left blinded by the darkness. After two or three hours, Namboothiri's vision gradually returned. He then went down to the sacred pond, collected water and left.

CHAPTER 3

The Divyan Visits Again

That night, Namboothiri couldn't sleep. He regretted not asking the divine being his true identity. If he had insisted, the divine being would have told him the truth. The divine being who had entrusted the precious gem to him with such faith wouldn't have withheld his true identity if asked, would he? Never.

Not doing so was a big mistake. But now, there's no point in thinking about it and feeling sad. 'What's the use of regretting the past?' he thought as he lay there.

After a while, he fell asleep, but woke up soon after. There was a bit of moonlight, so Namboothiri thought it was dawn. He usually woke up around 3 in the morning during his worship period. This would be followed by a sacred bath and performing his rituals.

Thinking he had overslept, he rushed to the sacred pond to bathe. There was someone standing there. As usual, Namboothiri asked, 'Who is that?'

The person replied, 'What's the use of knowing who I am? It's not time for you to bathe, Namboothiri. You have been fooled by the moonlight. It is still night. Go back to sleep; shouldn't you bathe after dawn?'

Hearing the voice and seeing the radiant form, Namboothiri realized that this was the same divine being he had met before. He approached, fell at his feet and pleaded, 'Oh for Lord Shiva's sake, please tell me your true identity.'

Unable to refuse, he finally revealed, 'I am Vasuki'.

'Then please show me your true form.'

Vasuki said, 'That's not necessary; you will be afraid if you see it.'

Namboothiri insisted, so Vasuki shrunk his body to the size of a ring on Lord Shiva's finger and showed it to him. At that moment, unable to believe the reality, Namboothiri was overwhelmed by the miracle and fainted.

After about ninety minutes, Namboothiri regained consciousness. As his vision cleared, he saw Vasuki in front of him.

Vasuki asked, 'What boon do you desire?'

Namboothiri replied, 'Your presence should always be in my house. Please end my poverty and sorrow. I have no other specific request.'

Hearing this, Vasuki said, 'Alright, I will do that. Your twelve years of worship will be complete in three days. After that, I will come to your house with Lord Shiva's permission and fulfil your wishes. Don't delay your bath any longer, it's time.' He then sent Namboothiri to bathe and vanished.

CHAPTER 4

Naagaraaja and Naagayakshi Arrive

After completing his worship, Namboothiri returned home and placed his palm-leaf umbrella in the eastern chamber. He then went to bathe and perform his daily rituals. When he returned to move the umbrella, he was startled to see a snake coiled on top of it. Immediately, the snake slithered down and assumed the form of the divine man, saying to Namboothiri, 'Do not fear, I am Vasuki. Lord Shiva is extremely pleased with your honesty and devotion. I have come here now to fulfil your wishes as per the Lord's command. Here is the Naagamani I showed you the first day we met. Let it stay here from now on. Keep it safe. Where it resides, poverty and sorrow will never touch.' Saying this, Vasuki handed over the divine gem and continued, 'A Naagayakshi will also join us here. Do not be afraid then.'

Just as he said this, the eldest lady of the house arrived. The noble woman had been at a feast in a relative's house. She came and placed her umbrella on the floor and went inside. At that moment, a cobra slithered down from the umbrella and reached the eastern chamber. Immediately, the cobra transformed into a beautiful divine woman and stood beside Vasuki.

Vasuki continued speaking, 'Have idols made of both of us and install them in this eastern chamber. Consider them as your family deities and worship them regularly. By doing so, prosperity will always be abundant here. More snakes will come here regularly. They will all reside wherever they please. There is no need to consecrate each one separately. Consider this house and its surroundings as a sanctuary for serpents. Create designated areas for defecation, spitting and washing hands. Do not do any of these things in the courtyard or the grounds. Do not light fires anywhere outside except in the kitchen stoves. Do not cut, prune or dig anywhere in the courtyard or the grounds. Build another house nearby. Conduct any special events or ceremonies there. You may see snakes inside and outside the house, in the courtyard and in the grounds. But no one should be afraid. The snakes will not bite anyone in this house unless they are stepped on or provoked. Even if they do bite, the venom will not affect the people in this house. Instead, the venom will harm the snakes themselves. In such cases, you must remove the venom from the snakes. If you don't, they may die. Keep two lamps lit at all times in this eastern chamber where we are consecrated. The soot and oil from these lamps are effective remedies for skin diseases caused by serpent afflictions. Everyone in this house, present and future, must know all that I have said. So, pass these instructions down through generations.' After saying all that was necessary, Vasuki and the Naagayakshi vanished, saying, 'We will meet again when needed.'

Namboothiri did as Vasuki instructed, consecrating Vasuki and the Naagayakshi in the eastern chamber. From that time on, the family, previously known as 'Mekkattu Namboothiri,' became known as 'Paambummekkattu Namboothiri' (paambu means snake in Malayalam), and this name became widespread and permanent.

Sometime after the consecration of Vasuki and the Naagayakshi in the eastern chamber of Mekkattu house, the fame of Paambummekkattu Namboothiri spread far and wide. People began to believe that the family could cure skin diseases and other ailments caused by serpent afflictions.

VIII

The Miracle of Mannarasala

Many years after the sacred site of Mannarasala was established and entrusted to the care of a devout Namboothiri family, there lived a couple within that lineage, Vasudeva and Sreedevi. They were deeply respected members of the community, diligent in their duties, yet they carried a profound, quiet sorrow—they remained childless, their hearts aching with the universal longing for progeny.

One evening, as the golden light of the setting sun bathed the sacred grove, Sreedevi knelt before the idol of Naagaraaja, her voice trembling with a mix of hope and despair. 'O Lord,' she prayed, 'We have served you with all our hearts, yet the joy of parenthood eludes us. Please, bless us with a child, so that our lineage may continue and we may not leave this world in sorrow.'

Vasudeva, standing beside her, his voice firm yet filled with yearning, added, 'We ask for nothing more than a single child, O Lord—a symbol of your grace and our devotion.'

Patiently, devoutly, they continued their prayers day after day.

As the couple awaited the answer to their prayers, one day, a fierce fire swept through the jungle surrounding Mannarasala, its flames leaping high into the sky, threatening to consume everything in its path. The serpents, guardians of the sacred site, were caught in the inferno, their bodies scorched, their hoods charred. In their hour of need, it was Vasudeva and Sreedevi who rushed to their aid, their compassion unshaken by fear.

Vasudeva, his hands steady, applied soothing sandalwood paste to the burns of the serpents. Sreedevi, offering sweet honey to another serpent, spoke with tenderness, 'Your pain is ours, and we shall do everything in our power to ease it. Please, forgive us for our helplessness.'

The couple's selfless acts of love and care resonated deeply with Naagaraaja. One night, as they lay in troubled sleep, Naagaraaja appeared to them in a dream, his form radiant with divine energy.

'I have witnessed your devotion and your compassion, and I am pleased,' Naagaraaja said, his voice a soothing balm to their weary souls. 'I shall be born as your son, and I will remain here, protecting this land and its people forever.'

Tears of joy filled Sreedevi's eyes as she cried out in the dream, 'Thank you, O Lord! You have answered our prayers!'

True to his word, Sreedevi soon gave birth to two sons—one, a five-hooded serpent, the incarnation of Naagaraaja himself, and the other, a human child, destined to continue the family's lineage. The brothers grew up together, bonded by love and destiny, each fulfilling a unique role—one to carry on the family line, the other to enter deep meditation within the sacred grounds.

When the time came, Naagaraaja, now a young serpent, approached his mother with a calm but resolute voice. 'Mother,' he said, 'my time in the world of men is complete. I shall now enter Samadhi in the sacred cellar called *Nilavara*, where I will continue to bless this land for all eternity. But fear not, for I shall always be with you, guiding and protecting this family.'

Sreedevi, though her heart ached with the thought of parting, nodded in understanding. 'You have given us so much, my son. Go in peace, and know that we shall honour your presence in this home forever.'

Before he departed, Naagaraaja gave his mother a final instruction. 'From this day forward, you, and the eldest Brahmin lady of the family after you, shall offer me worship. Only on special occasions may men participate in these rituals. You are now the *Valiya Amma*, the Mother of this sacred land.'

And so, Naagaraaja entered the Nilavara, the sacred cellar where tradition holds he remains in deep, eternal meditation, his presence a constant blessing for the land and its devotees. The family and all who visit the temple hold him in the highest reverence, referring to him as 'Muthassan,' 'Appuppan' or Grandfather. The nearby jungle, Appuppan Kaavu, is revered as his sacred grove, a place where the divine and the mortal realms are believed to intertwine.

Today, pilgrims still flock to Mannarasala from across the world, drawn by this potent legacy of divine intervention and the unique tradition of the Valiya Amma. Foremost among their prayers is often the deep yearning for children, mirroring the ancient plea of Vasudeva and Sreedevi. They arrive carrying the hope that the Naagaraja, who once blessed a childless couple with a miraculous boon, will bestow his grace upon them too, filling their lives with the cherished gift of progeny.

The Journey Continues

Sitting by the tranquil groves of the Mannarasala temple, listening to the gentle rustles of the leaves and whispers of devotion, felt like reaching a significant marker on a long, winding path that perhaps began long before I consciously recognized it. My own life started near a temple in Tripunithura housing Poornathreyeesha (Lord Vishnu in Santhaanagopala form) seated upon the coils of Ananta Shesha, a deity my *naani* prayed to fervently following my complicated birth. Decades later, the documentation for *Daiva* commenced at Kudupu, dedicated to the same Anantapadmanaabha, amidst hundreds of Naaga idols gazing westward from the *Naaga Bana*. The air there, thick with the scent of wet earth and ancient serpentine essence, seemed to hum with the interconnectedness of the Naaga traditions I had only just begun to consciously explore.

Looking back, the serpent's presence seems to have coiled subtly through the years. The childhood terror upon seeing a cobra near a well in Kanjikode, the fervent prayer never to encounter one again, followed by recurring, unsettling dreams of serpents—these felt like disconnected fragments then. Later, a temple oracle's advice to seek my roots, to locate my ancestors' Daiva and Naaga, planted a seed. Even writing my first film near the Mannarasala temple in

2017, oblivious at the time to its profound serpent lore, feels like a foreshadowing in retrospect. The sighting of a Naaga at my wife's ancestral home on our engagement day, a detail noted almost in passing, gained a poignant weight later.

The true catalyst, however, emerged from profound loss. Losing our baby on a day that, with a heavy heart, I later realized marked the birthday celebrations of Poornathreyeesha—the protector of infants I was born near—created an unbearable void. In tracing the serpent's coils through ancient stories subsequently, I found not easy answers to loss, but perhaps a reflection of life's cyclical nature, a continuity that offered a different kind of solace. It was two years after this, carrying that grief, that I attended the Dakkebali in Padubidri. The encounter with the elderly priest, his simple question—'Where is your ancestral serpent grove?'—resonated deeply, transforming a vague yearning into an active quest.

That night, witnessing the ancient ritual, felt like stepping into a different stream of time. The rhythmic dakke, the flickering lamps, the entranced paatris—it ignited something. This quest led me to finally stand before my ancestral naagabana near Kateel, offering *thambila*, a connection across generations. Finishing *Daiva* felt like closing one circle, only for another to begin. The synchronicity felt undeniable—discussing *Daiva* on a podcast, hearing about Uttarakhand's Jaagar rituals and Naagadevatas from the host, only to dream vividly of Naagas myself, and then have my editor, unaware of the dream, suggest this very non-fiction exploration about serpent deities of India. It felt less like coincidence and more like the lore itself was guiding the way.

Venturing through the Puranic accounts and the diverse folktales presented in these pages has been a journey through layers of reverence, fear, ecological wisdom and profound symbolism. From the cosmic grandeur of Shesha and Vasuki to the localized guardianship of the *kaavus* and *banas*, from the fierce maternal power of the Naagayakshi to the cautionary tales warning against greed and disrespect, the serpent emerges not as a monolithic entity, but as a multifaceted symbol reflecting humanity's complex relationship with nature, divinity and the unknown. Its persistent power across cultures hints at its resonance as an archetype within the collective unconscious, embodying primal energies of life, death, transformation and hidden wisdom.

We've seen how these traditions perceive the Naaga as *pratyaksha devata*—divinity manifest—and how this reverence, intertwined with a healthy respect for their power, fostered ancient practices of conservation long before ecology became a formal science. The sacred groves stand as witnesses to this wisdom, islands of biodiversity preserved through belief.

For me, this exploration, born from personal loss and a search for roots, became intertwined with the discovery of these ancient narratives and living traditions. The two tender leaves unfurling on the forgotten money plant on my writing desk, like Naaga hoods, felt like an affirmation then, and the journey while studying the serpent-hood iconography has only deepened that feeling. While the answers sought are often elusive, shrouded in the mists of time and belief, the quest itself—tracing the serpent's path through scripture, lore and landscape—has brought its own form of understanding.

Ultimately, whether the Naagas are gods or intrinsic parts of nature's balance is a question perhaps beyond definitive answers, and it is certainly not my intention to impose a belief upon you. Every individual has the right to follow their own beliefs. What resonates deeply through this exploration, however, is that the serpent remains undeniably intertwined with sacred truths and traditions—truths perhaps not only of doctrine, but of our primal connection to the earth, the hidden energies within, the cyclical dance of existence and the enduring power of belief.

Ultimately, the Naagas remain coiled around the heart of a profound paradox—reminders of the sacred stillness between our world and the unseen, the power held in reverence, the potential pulsing within. Their stories stir across time, whether we hear them as sacred truth, cultural memory or ecological warning. They awaken something deep within our shared human consciousness. They challenge us to listen—not just to the whispers of a forgotten world, but to the subtle, slumbering energies that connect us all. The journey into the heart of the Naaga connects us, me and, I hope, you, dear reader. And perhaps, like the serpent itself, this exploration must now shed its skin. Consider this book that old skin, complete in its form, now ready to be left behind so that the new can emerge—a fresh foray, new knowledge, already flickering into focus, into the further mystical, manifold landscapes of India's ancient occult beliefs and traditions.

Glossary

Aadimoolam: (Malayalam) Primordial origin; used in the context of the Vetticode temple's founding.

Aashlesha / Aayilyam: The ninth *nakshatra* (lunar mansion) in Hindu astronomy, considered highly significant for serpent worship, especially in south India.

Abhishekam: (Sanskrit) Ritual bathing of a deity idol.

Adharma: (Sanskrit) Actions contrary to righteousness, duty or cosmic order.

Adishesha: See *Ananta Shesha*.

Agni: (Sanskrit) The Vedic god of fire; also refers to the sacrificial fire itself.

Aham: (Sanskrit) 'I' or 'Self'; representing the ego or individual consciousness.

Ahi: (Sanskrit) A term for serpent or snake, often used in Vedic texts for powerful or significant serpents like Vritra.

Ahikshetra / Ahichhatra: Ancient region and capital city ('Region of the Serpent' or 'Serpent's Umbrella') in North India (modern

Uttar Pradesh), significant in the Mahabharata and Jain tradition, linked to serpent lore.

Aithihyamala: (Malayalam) 'Garland of Legends'; a famous collection of Kerala folklore compiled by Kottarathil Sankunni.

Amrita: (Sanskrit) The nectar or elixir of immortality churned from the cosmic ocean.

Amrita Manthana: See *Samudra Manthana*.

Ananta Shesha: (Sanskrit) 'Endless Remainder'; the primordial, infinite serpent deity, often depicted with a thousand heads, who supports the universe and serves as the seat for Lord Vishnu. Also known as Adishesha or Shesha.

Annadanam: (Sanskrit) The charitable distribution of food, often performed at temples.

Aravan: Tamil name for Iravan.

Archetype: A universally understood symbol, term or pattern of behaviour; a prototype upon which others are copied, patterned or emulated. Often used in Jungian psychology.

Ashlesha Bali: A specific ritual offering performed to appease serpent deities and mitigate *naagadosha*.

Ashtanaaga: (Sanskrit) The eight great or principal Naaga kings mentioned in Hindu tradition: Ananta (Shesha), Vasuki, Takshaka, Karkotaka, Padma, Mahapadma, Shankha (Shamkha) and Kulika.

Ashwamedham: (Sanskrit) An ancient Vedic horse sacrifice ritual performed by kings to assert sovereignty.

Asura: (Sanskrit) A class of powerful beings in Hindu tradition, often depicted as rivals or enemies of the Devas (gods).

Avatar: (Sanskrit) An incarnation or earthly manifestation of a deity, particularly Vishnu.

Bana: (Tulu) A sacred grove, particularly in Karnataka, dedicated to deities, often including Naagas and Daivas. Equivalent to *Kaavu* in Malayalam.

Bhauma: (Sanskrit) Earthly, terrestrial; used to classify ordinary serpents as distinct from celestial (*Divya*) ones.

Bhogavati: The legendary, opulent capital city of the Naagas in the subterranean realm of Paataala, often ruled by Vasuki.

Bhoota / Bhuta: (Sanskrit) Ghost, spirit, elemental being; sometimes refers to spirits of the deceased invoked in rituals like Jaagar.

Bhutagana: (Sanskrit) Attendants or host of spirits/elemental beings, often associated with Lord Shiva.

Brahma: (Sanskrit) The Hindu god of creation, part of the Trimurti.

Brahmahatya: (Sanskrit) The heinous sin of killing a brahmin.

CE / BCE: Common Era / Before Common Era; used for dating years, replacing AD/BC for religious neutrality.

Chakra: (Sanskrit) 'Wheel'; refers to energy centres in the body according to yogic philosophy, associated with Kundalini.

Chakravarthi: (Sanskrit) An ideal universal ruler or emperor whose authority is undisputed, often attained after performing rituals like the Ashwamedham.

Chiranjeevi: (Sanskrit) 'Immortal being'; refers to eight (or sometimes seven) figures in Hindu tradition believed to live eternally or through vast cosmic cycles.

Collective Unconscious: A concept in Jungian psychology referring to structures of the unconscious mind shared among beings of the same species, containing archetypes.

Cosmology: A branch of metaphysics dealing with the nature of the universe; a theory or doctrine describing the natural order of the universe.

Cosmogony: A theory regarding the origin of the universe.

Daiva: (Tulu) Divine spirit or local deity venerated in Tulunadu, often through possession rituals like Kola.

Daivaaradhane: (Tulu) The worship of Daivas, the spirit deities of Tulunadu.

Dakke: (Tulu) A small handheld drum.

Dakkebali: (Tulu) A specific ritualistic serpent possession dance performed in Tulunadu, featuring the *naagapaatri* and *naagakannike*, accompanied by the *dakke* drum.

Daksha: (Sanskrit) A *Prajapati* or progenitor god; father of many daughters including Kadru and Vinata in Puranic accounts.

Daanava: (Sanskrit) A race of beings, often Asuras, descended from Danu and Kashyapa.

Deva / Devata: (Sanskrit) God, deity, celestial being.

Dharma: (Sanskrit) Cosmic law, righteousness, duty, virtue, inherent nature.

Divya: (Sanskrit) Divine, celestial; used to classify powerful, often Puranic, serpents like the Ashtanaagas.

Dosha: (Sanskrit) Affliction, fault, negative influence; *naagadosha* refers to afflictions believed to be caused by displeased serpent deities.

Garuda: (Sanskrit) The divine eagle, mount (*vaahana*) of Lord Vishnu, and the sworn enemy of the Naagas.

Guna: (Sanskrit) Quality, attribute, virtue.

Hiranyagarbha: (Sanskrit) 'Golden Womb' or 'Golden Egg'; the primordial source from which the universe manifests in Hindu cosmology.

Ichchadaari: (Hindi/Sanskrit) 'Desire-Form'; shape-shifting beings, often applied to Naagas or Naaginis in folklore who can assume human form.

Illam: (Malayalam) Traditional house or mansion of a Namboothiri brahmin family in Kerala, often associated with sacred groves (*kaavus*). See also *Mana*.

Jaagar: (Hindi) 'Awakening'; a ritualistic performance in Uttarakhand involving invocation and possession by local deities (*devatas*) or spirits (*bhutas*), often through song and music.

Jagariya: The storyteller or main performer who leads the Jaagar ritual in Uttarakhand.

Jangamam: (Sanskrit) Mobile, moving; refers to poison originating from living creatures (animals, serpents) in Ayurveda.

Japamaala: (Sanskrit) Rosary beads used for chanting mantras.

Kaal Sarpa Dosha: (Sanskrit) An astrological affliction believed to occur due to the unfavorable placement of Rahu and Ketu, often associated with serpent curses.

Kaalakoota: (Sanskrit) The deadly poison that emerged during the *Samudra Manthana*.

Kaavu: (Malayalam) A sacred grove in Kerala, often dedicated to serpent deities (*Naagas*) and other local divinities. Equivalent to *Bana* in Tulu.

Kalari: (Malayalam) Traditional martial arts training ground in Kerala.

Kalappali: A ritual sacrifice associated with Aravan in Tamil tradition, re-enacted in Therukoothu performances.

Kalpa: (Sanskrit) An immense period of time in Hindu cosmology, equivalent to a 'day of Brahma', comprising fourteen *Manvantaras*.

Karma: (Sanskrit) Action, deed; also the universal principle of cause and effect governing destiny.

Kola: (Tulu) A vibrant, elaborate possession ritual performed in Tulunadu to honour Daivas.

Kolam: (Tamil/Malayalam) Intricate geometric patterns drawn on the floor using rice powder or other coloured powders, often as a ritual or decorative practice.

Kundalini: (Sanskrit) 'Coiled one'; the primordial cosmic energy believed to lie dormant at the base of the spine, often symbolized as a coiled serpent, which can be awakened through yogic practices.

Kurma Avatar: (Sanskrit) The tortoise incarnation of Lord Vishnu, who supported Mount Mandara during the *Samudra Manthana*.

Kusha: (Sanskrit) A type of sacred grass (*Desmostachya bipinnata*), considered purifying and used in Hindu rituals; believed to have become sacred after being touched by *Amrita* and responsible for splitting serpents' tongues. Also known as *darbha* or *durva*.

Loka: (Sanskrit) World, realm, plane of existence in Hindu cosmology (e.g., Swargaloka, Naagaloka, Paataala).

Manasamangalkavya: (Bengali/Sanskrit) Auspicious poems or narrative songs dedicated to the serpent goddess Manasa, popular in Bengal.

Maarjaaram: (Sanskrit) Cat.

Mahabharata: One of the two major Sanskrit epics of ancient India, detailing the Kurukshetra War and containing vast philosophical and devotional material.

Mana: (Malayalam/Tulu) Traditional house or mansion in Kerala (*illam*) or prominent families in Tulunadu (*mane*).

Manvantara: (Sanskrit) An epoch or age of Manu in Hindu cosmology, a vast period within a *Kalpa*.

Maya: (Sanskrit) Illusion, divine power that creates the phenomenal world, an alternate dimension of simulation; also the name of an Asura architect.

Moksha: (Sanskrit) Liberation, release from the cycle of birth and death (samsara).

Moola Naagabana / Moolanaaga Sthaana: (Tulu/Sanskrit) The root or original serpent grove/place associated with a family or lineage.

Mudra: (Sanskrit) Symbolic hand gesture used in rituals, iconography, and dance.

Muhoortham: (Sanskrit/Malayalam) An auspicious time calculated for performing rituals or important events.

Muthassan / Appuppan: (Malayalam) Grandfather; terms of reverence used for the Naagaraaja at Mannarasala.

Naaga: (Sanskrit) A term referring specifically to the divine or semi-divine race of serpent beings prominent in Indian traditions, often depicted with hoods, associated with water, fertility and treasure. Also used for individual deities of this race (e.g., Vasuki Naaga). Capitalized in this text when referring to this specific group or deity.

Naagabana: (Tulu/Kannada) Sacred serpent grove in Tulunadu. See *Bana*.

Naagadevata: (Sanskrit) Serpent deity; a general term for a revered Naaga.

Naagakallu: (Malayalam/Kannada/Tamil) Carved stone idols representing serpent deities, commonly installed in sacred groves or temples in south India.

Naagakannike / Naagakanyaka: (Tulu/Sanskrit) Serpent maiden; the female performer/role in Dakkebali/Naagamandala rituals, representing the feminine aspect of the Naaga.

Naagaloka: (Sanskrit) The realm or world of the Naagas, often believed to be subterranean, located in Paataala.

Naagamani / Naagamaanikyam: (Sanskrit/Malayalam) The mythical serpent jewel, believed to form on a cobra's hood, possessing immense power and granting fortune or protection. Also known phaniratnam.

Naagamandala: (Kannada/Tulu) An elaborate ritualistic serpent possession dance performed in coastal Karnataka, involving intricate floor designs (*mandalas*) and possessed priests (*paatris*).

Naagapaasa: (Sanskrit) Serpent-noose; a mythical weapon, sometimes described as a necklace of serpents.

Naagapaatri: (Tulu/Sanskrit) The male priest, often from a specific brahmin lineage, who becomes possessed by the serpent spirit (Naagabrahma) during Dakkebali or Naagamandala rituals.

Naagapuraanam: (Sanskrit) Puranic accounts or traditional stories specifically concerning the Naagas. (Used as Part 3 title.)

Naagaraadhana: (Sanskrit/Kannada) Serpent worship; the practice of venerating Naaga deities.

Naagaraaja: (Sanskrit) King of the Naagas/serpents; a title often applied to Shesha, Vasuki or sometimes Takshaka.

Naagayaksha / Naagayakshi: (Sanskrit) Male/female nature spirits combining aspects of Naagas and Yakshas, often guardians of groves or associated with specific deities (e.g., Dharanendra and Padmavati in Jainism). Also a term for the primary female serpent deity worshipped in South Indian groves.

Naagini: (Sanskrit/Hindi) Female Naaga; often used for serpent goddesses or female figures in serpent lore, sometimes specifically referring to shape-shifters (*ichchadhari naagin*) in north Indian folklore.

Nakshatra: (Sanskrit) Lunar mansion or constellation in Hindu astrology.

Namboothiri: A brahmin community traditionally associated with priestly duties in Kerala.

Naraka: (Sanskrit) Hell or realms of suffering in Hindu cosmology, distinct from the subterranean realms of Paataala.

Navagraha: (Sanskrit) The nine celestial bodies or deities influencing destiny in Hindu astrology (Sun, Moon, Mars, Mercury, Jupiter, Venus, Saturn, Rahu, Ketu).

Nirvisha: (Sanskrit) Non-venomous; one of the categories of earthly serpents in the *Sushruta Samhita*.

Noorum-Paalum: (Malayalam) An offering made during serpent rituals in Kerala, often consisting of rice flour, milk, turmeric and tender coconut water.

Ophiolatry: The worship of serpents.

Paardana: (Tulu) Oral narrative poems or ballads recounting the stories of Daivas and heroes in Tulunadu.

Paataala: (Sanskrit) The lowest of the seven subterranean realms in Hindu cosmology, often considered the primary abode of the Naagas.

Pancha Bhoota Sthalam: (Sanskrit/Tamil) Sacred sites representing the five elements (earth, water, fire, air, ether) in Shaivite tradition.

Panchami: (Sanskrit) The fifth day of a lunar fortnight (*paksha*).

Pandal: (Hindi/Tamil) A temporary pavilion or canopy erected for festivals or rituals.

Parashu: (Sanskrit) Axe; the weapon associated with Parashuraama.

Paatri: (Tulu/Malayalam) A ritual functionary or priest who becomes possessed by a deity or spirit during ceremonies like Dakkebali.

Pitrs: (Sanskrit) Ancestral spirits; the spirits of departed forefathers who require offerings (*shraaddha*) for their well-being in the afterlife.

Prasadam: (Sanskrit) Consecrated food or substance offered to a deity and then distributed to devotees as a blessing.

Pratyaksha Devata: (Sanskrit) 'Visible deity'; a god manifest before one's eyes, a term sometimes applied to Naagas due to their tangible presence as cobras.

Puja: (Sanskrit) Ritual worship performed to honour deities.

Pulluvan / Pulluvatti: Male/female members of a traditional community in Kerala known as hereditary bards and performers of serpent rituals (*Sarpam Pattu, Sarpam Thullal*).

Pulluvan Pattu: (Malayalam) Sacred ballads sung by the Pulluvan community, narrating stories of serpent deities.

Puncha: (Tulu) Anthill or termite mound, often revered as a dwelling place of Naagas.

Pungi: (Hindi) A double-reed wind instrument, often made from a gourd, traditionally used by snake charmers in India.

Puraana: (Sanskrit) 'Ancient'; a genre of Hindu texts containing traditional lore, cosmology, genealogies, legends, and religious narratives. Used in this text with the 'aa' spelling as per author preference.

Rakshasa: (Sanskrit) A class of powerful, often malevolent, beings or demons in Hindu tradition.

Samadhi: (Sanskrit) A state of deep meditative absorption or trance; also refers to a tomb or memorial shrine of a saint or revered figure.

Samudra Manthana: (Sanskrit) The Churning of the Ocean (of Milk); a major episode in Hindu Puraanas where Devas and Asuras churned the ocean to obtain *Amrita*.

Sankarshana: (Sanskrit) An epithet of Balaraama or Ananta Shesha, representing the principle of withdrawal or dissolution.

Sapera: (Hindi) Snake charmer.

Sarpabali: (Sanskrit/Malayalam) Ritual offering to serpent deities.

Sarpakalam: (Malayalam) Intricate floor designs depicting serpents, drawn with coloured powders during rituals in Kerala.

Sarpakatha: (Sanskrit) Serpent Tales; used as the title for Part 4, covering folktales about serpents.

Sarpakaavu: (Malayalam) Sacred serpent grove in Kerala. See *Kaavu*.

Sarpam Pattu: (Malayalam) 'Song of the Serpent'; a specific, elaborate ritual performed at Mannarasala temple.

Sarpam Thullal: (Malayalam) 'Serpent Dance'; a possession ritual performed in Kerala, often by young women led by the Pulluvan community.

Sarpasatra: (Sanskrit) The great snake/serpent sacrifice performed by King Janamejaya to avenge his father Parikshit's death.

Sarpa: (Sanskrit) Serpent, snake; often used as a general term or specifically for single-headed, earthly snakes, distinct from the multi-headed, divine Naagas.

Shastra / Shastric: (Sanskrit) Sacred text, scripture, treatise / According to scripture or prescribed rules.

Shraaddha: (Sanskrit) Ritual offerings performed for the welfare of departed ancestors (*pitrs*).

Shukla Paksha: (Sanskrit) The bright fortnight (waxing moon phase) in the Hindu lunar calendar.

Siddhi: (Sanskrit) Supernatural power, accomplishment, or yogic attainment.

Sthala Purana: (Sanskrit) Traditional accounts or legends associated with a specific sacred place or temple.

Sthaavaram: (Sanskrit) Immobile, stationary; refers to poison originating from non-moving sources (plants, minerals) in Ayurveda.

Stotra: (Sanskrit) Hymn or chant of praise addressed to a deity.

Suparna: (Sanskrit) 'Well-winged'; often refers to Garuda or other divine eagle-like beings, traditional enemies of the Naagas.

Sutaka: (Sanskrit) A period of ritual impurity or abstinence observed after events like birth or death.

Svastika: (Sanskrit) An ancient symbol of good fortune, well-being, and auspiciousness found in Hinduism, Buddhism, and Jainism.

Swayambhu: (Sanskrit) 'Self-manifested' or 'self-originated'; refers to idols or deities believed to have appeared naturally, without being crafted by human hands.

Termitophile: An organism (insect, etc.) that lives symbiotically in a termite nest.

Thaan: Sacred groves in Eastern India, often sites for tree worship or veneration of goddesses like Maarai or Manasa.

Thambila: (Tulu) An offering made during serpent rituals in Tulunadu.

Thampuran: (Malayalam) Lord, king; title used for rulers in Kerala.

Therianthropic: Combining human and animal forms.

Thirtha: (Sanskrit) Sacred place, pilgrimage site, often associated with a holy body of water.

Tirthankara: (Sanskrit) The twenty-four great spiritual teachers or saviours in Jainism.

Trishula: (Sanskrit) Trident; the characteristic weapon of Lord Shiva, also associated with other deities like Janguli.

Tulaabhaaram: (Sanskrit) Ritual weighing ceremony where a person is weighed against offerings (gold, grain, etc.) donated as penance or devotion.

Tulu: A Dravidian language spoken primarily in the Tulunadu region of coastal Karnataka and parts of Kerala.

Uraga: (Sanskrit) 'Chest-goer'; a term for snakes or serpents, sometimes distinguished from Naagas as being less divine or referring to different lineages.

Urali Kamazhthal: (Malayalam) A specific ritual performed at Mannarasala temple, involving placing a vessel (*urali*) upside down, often by childless couples seeking progeny.

Vaahana: (Sanskrit) Mount or vehicle of a deity (e.g., Garuda is Vishnu's vaahana).

Vaishnavism: A major tradition within Hinduism focused on the worship of Lord Vishnu and his avatars.

Valiya Amma: (Malayalam) 'Great Mother'; the title given to the eldest Namboothiri woman who serves as the chief priestess at Mannarasala temple.

Varada Mudra: (Sanskrit) Boon-granting hand gesture in iconography.

Veda / Vedic: Ancient Hindu scriptures / Pertaining to the Vedas or the historical period when they were composed.

Visha: (Sanskrit) Poison, venom.

Vishaada: (Sanskrit) Sorrow, grief, depression, dejection.

Vishahari: (Sanskrit) 'Destroyer of Poison'; an epithet of the goddess Manasa.

Vishnu: (Sanskrit) The Hindu god of preservation, part of the Trimurti, known for his numerous avatars.

Yaksha / Yakshi / Yakshini: (Sanskrit) Male/female nature spirits, often benevolent guardians of natural treasures or places, sometimes associated with Naagas.

Yajna: (Sanskrit) Vedic sacrifice or ritual offering, typically involving fire.

Yama: (Sanskrit) The Hindu god of death and the underworld.

Yantra: (Sanskrit) Mystical diagram or geometric design used in rituals and meditation, believed to possess protective or spiritual power (e.g., Garuda yantra).

Yoga: (Sanskrit) Union; a group of physical, mental, and spiritual practices or disciplines originating in ancient India.

Yojana: (Sanskrit) An ancient Indian unit of distance, varying in interpretation but generally several miles or kilometres.

Yuga: (Sanskrit) An age or epoch within a larger cycle in Hindu cosmology (Satya, Treta, Dvapara, Kali).

Bibliography

Bhat, Dr. Paduru Gururaja. n.d. *Studies in Tuluva History & Culture*. Mangalore.

Dr. U.P. Upadhyaya, Dr. Susheela Upadhyaya. 2002. *Folk Rituals*. Udupi: Regional Resources Centre for Folk Performing Arts.

P.S. Subrahmanya Sastri, M.R. Bhat. 1946. *Brhat Samhita of Varahamihira - Vol. 1: With English Translation, Exhaustive Notes and Literary Comments*. Bengaluru: V.B Soobbiah and sons.

Iyer, N. Chidambaram. 1884. *The Brihat Samhita of Varaha Mihira*. Madurai: South Indian Press.

Thurston, Edgar. 1909. *Castes and Tribes of Southern India*. Madras: Government Press, Madras.

Muni, Bharatha. n.d. *Natyashastra*.

Museums Victoria. n.d. "8 myths about snakes and some misconceptions." *Museums Victoria*. https://museumsvictoria. com.au/article/8-myths-about-snakes/.

Madras Mail. 1906. *Madras Mail*.

Nagar, Shanti Lal. 2003. *Brahma Vaivarta Purana - English Translation - All Four Kandas*. Delhi: Parimal Publications.

Anonymous. 1886. *Ophiolatreia - An Account of the Rites and Mysteries Connected with the Origin, Rise, and Development of Serpent Worship in Various Parts of the World.* Anonymous.

Aiya, V. Nagam. 1906. *The Travancore Manual, Vol - 1.* Trivandrum: Travancore Government Press.

OnManorama. April 2023. *Travel onManorama.* https://www. onmanorama.com/travel/kerala/2023/04/10/thrissur-pambumekkattu-mana-legends-snake-worship.html.

Wheeler, J. Talboys. 1867. *The History Of India Vol. 1.* London.

Crooke, William. 1926. *Religion and folklore of Northern India.* Oxford University Press.

A.K. Coomaraswamy, Sister Nivedita. 1914. *Myths of the Hindus & Buddhists.* London: George G. Harrap and Company.

Mundkur, Balaji. 1983. *The Cult of the Serpent.* New York: State University of New York Press.

Chödrön, Gelongma Karma Migme. 2001. *Maha Prajnaparamita Sastra.*

J.L. Shastri, G.P. Bhatt, N. Gangadharan. n.d. *The Agni Purana.* Motilal Banarsidas, Delhi.

Vyas. n.d. *Agnipuran (Hindi).* Gorakhpur: Gita Press.

Bishagratna, Kaviraj Kunja Lal. 1911. *An English Translation of Sushruta Samhita, Vol - II.* Kolkata.

risk, "Poaching Puts Snakes at Risk". 2018. *Deccan Herald.* 22 January. https://www.deccanherald.com/science/poaching-puts-snakes-risk-1917471.

Goswami, Shravan Kumar. 1902. *Nagpuri Sisth Sahitya (Hindi).* Delhi: Research Publications.

Rangaswamy, M.A. Dorai. 1958. *The Religion and Philosophy of Tevaram (Thevaram).* Chennai: University of Madras.

Whitefield, Henry. 1921. *Village Gods od South India*. Madras: Association Press.

Shastri, J.L. n.d. *The Shiva Purana*. Motilal Banarsidass Delhi.

Irwing, John. 1982. "The Sacred Anthill and the Cult of the Primordial Mound." *History of Religions, Vol. 21, No. 4* 340.

Krishnan, Anusha. 2020. "Architectural secrets of termite mounds." *Mongabay*. 28 October. https://india.mongabay.com/2020/10/architectural-secrets-of-termite-mounds/#:~:text=Termite%20mounds%20are%20incredibly%20strong,nest's%20temperature%20and%20humidity%20levels.

Pascal Jouquet, Laurent Caner, Nicolas Bottinelli, Ekta Chaudhary, Sougueh Cheik, Jean Riotte. 2017. "Where do South-Indian termite mound soils come from?" *Applied Soil Ecology, Volumes 117–118*, 190-195. https://www.sciencedirect.com/science/article/abs/pii/S0929139317301993.

Shaw, Miranda. 2006. *Buddhist Goddesses of India*. New Jersey: Princeton University Press.

Rinpoche, Tsem. 2016. "Janguli." *www.tsemrinpoche.com*. 27 January. https://www.tsemrinpoche.com/tsem-tulku-rinpoche/buddhas-dharma/janguli.html.

Dr U.P. Upadhyaya, Dr Susheela Upadhyaya. 2002. *Folk Rituals*. Udupi: Regional Resources Centre for Folk Performing Arts.

Niall Stopford, Vishal Santra. n.d. "Living alongside cobras." *bbc.co.uk*. https://www.bbc.co.uk/programmes/articles/31G32ZKp5TcHS6Y5GL7rdHr/living-alongside-cobras.

Tavakar. 1971. *The Essays Throwing New Light on the Gandharvas, the Apsaras and the Kinnaras*. Bombay: Tavakar Prakashana.

Nongkynrih, Kynpham Sing. n.d. "U. Thlen: the man-eating serpent: MEGHALAYA." *India International Centre Quarterly,*

Vol. 32, No. 2/3, Where the Sun Rises When Shadows Fall: The North-east (MONSOON-WINTER 2005) 33-38.

Mishra, N.R. 2004. *Kamakhya: A Socio-Cultural Study.* New Delhi D.K. Print World Ltd.

Parpola, Asko. 1994. *Deciphering the Indus script.* New York: Cambridge University Press.

Haq, Kaiser. 2015. *The Triumph of the Goddess.* Harvard University Press Harvard.

India, The Times of. 2015. *The Times of India.* 20 August. https://timesofindia.indiatimes.com/city/kolkata/illegal-snake-shows-stopped-at-400-year-old-jhapan-fair/articleshow/48550445.cms.

n.d. *Kerala Tourism.* https://www.keralatourism.org/1000festivals//assets/uploads/pdf/1507744378-0.pdf.

Rao, T.A. Gopinatha. 1916. *Elements of Hindu Iconography Vol II.* Chennai: The Law Printing House.

Hatch, Emily Gilchiest. 1933. *Travancore : A Guide Book for the Visitor.* London: Oxford University Press.

Legge, James. 1971. *Travels of Fa-Hien.* Delhi: Oriental Publishers.

Jung, Carl. n.d. *The Collected Works of C. G. Jung, Volume 9 (Part 1): Archetypes and the Collective Unconscious.* Princeton, New Jersey University Press.

Beal, Samuel. 1884. *Si-Yu-Ki - Buddhist Records Of The Western World.* London: Trubner and Co.

Cunningham, Alexander. 1871. *Archeological Survey of India, Volume I.* Shimla: The Government Press.

Kumar, K. Hari. 2024. *Daiva - Discovering the Extraordinary World of Spirit Worship.* New Delhi: HarperCollins India.

Team, ETV Bharat Uttarakhand. 2023. *Etv Bharat.* 7 September. https://www.etvbharat.com/hindi/uttarakhand/state/tehri-garhwal/historical-famous-temple-of-lord-krishna-in-sem-mukhem-tehri-uttarakhand/uttarakhand20230907132139778778277.

J.L. Shastri, G.P. Bhatt, N.A. Deshpande. 1956. *The Padma Purana.* Motilal Banarsidass, Delhi.

Sridhar, P. 2025. "All set for Nagoba Jatara in Keslapur, the abode of serpent deity, in Telangana's tribal heartland of Indervelli mandal." *The Hindu*, 28 January.

Vyasa, Ved. 2016. *Brahma Purana.* Gorakhpur: Gita Press.

Acknowledgements

This book, though thoroughly researched, never felt like a task, for its subject lives close to my heart. Much of this journey has been a deeply personal one.

I extend my sincerest gratitude to all those who have generously shared their wisdom about serpent deities throughout my life, from cherished childhood memories to the present day. My heartfelt thanks go to my parents, my grandparents, and my wife's parents and relatives for their invaluable contributions to this knowledge.

I am also indebted to the many writers and researchers whose works I referenced, and to our ancestors for diligently preserving traditions that have enriched my understanding.

A very special thank you to Romulus Whitaker for graciously taking the time to answer my queries regarding the Indian Cobra. Your insights were immensely helpful. My gratitude also extends to Utkarsh Patel for sharing valuable materials and verifying the story of Manasa, which appears in the fourth part of this book.

A heartfelt thanks to Prerna Gill, Udayan Mitra and the entire team at HarperCollins India for their unwavering support.

Finally, and with profound reverence, I offer my sincere thanks to the Daivas and Naagas that my ancestors worshipped.

About the Author

K. Hari Kumar is an accomplished Indian author and screenwriter, known for his captivating narratives that delve deep into Indian folklore and regional mythology. With nine books to his credit, he has garnered widespread acclaim, particularly for his popular works, *Daiva* and *India's Most Haunted*. The latter was celebrated as a must-read and earned a prestigious spot in HarperCollins India's list of *Hundred Best Books by Indian Authors*.

Beyond his literary endeavours, K. Hari Kumar is also an active screenwriter and filmmaker. His novel, *The Other Side of Her*, was successfully adapted into the acclaimed Hindi language web series, *Bhram*, further showcasing his versatile storytelling prowess.

Hari is also a sought-after speaker, having been invited to prestigious events like the Bangalore Literature Festival and Times Literature Festival, and featured on popular podcasts such as *The Ranveer Show*. He hosts his own podcast on Indian occult, spirituality and sacred narratives, *The Fourth State*.

Hari's educational background includes a B.Tech in Information Technology and a B.A. in English Literature, both pursued in Gurugram. He currently resides in Pune with his wife, where he continues to dedicate himself to his creative passions.

Naaga: Discovering the Extraordinary World of Serpent Worship is his ninth book. He can be followed @theharikumar.

HarperCollins *Publishers* India

At HarperCollins India, we believe in telling the best stories and finding the widest readership for our books in every format possible. We started publishing in 1992; a great deal has changed since then, but what has remained constant is the passion with which our authors write their books, the love with which readers receive them, and the sheer joy and excitement that we as publishers feel in being a part of the publishing process.

Over the years, we've had the pleasure of publishing some of the finest writing from the subcontinent and around the world, including several award-winning titles and some of the biggest bestsellers in India's publishing history. But nothing has meant more to us than the fact that millions of people have read the books we published, and that somewhere, a book of ours might have made a difference.

As we look to the future, we go back to that one word— a word which has been a driving force for us all these years.

Read.